MIT AND THE RISE OF ENTREPRENEURIAL SCIENCE

MIT and the Rise of Entrepreneurial Science is a timely and authoritative book that analyses the transformation of the university's role in society as an expanded one involving economic and social development as well as teaching and research. The Massachusetts Institute of Technology invented the format for university–industry relations that has been copied all over America and latterly the rest of the world. This excellent book shows that these groundbreaking university–industry–government interactions have become part of the foundations of modern successful economies.

Henry Etzkowitz has written a book that will be of great interest not only to all those with a connection to MIT, but also to anyone with a more general interest in entrepreneurial universities, innovation and economic development as a whole.

Henry Etzkowitz is Director of the Science Policy Institute at State University of New York.

STUDIES IN GLOBAL COMPETITION
John Cantwell
University of Reading, UK
David Mowery
University of California, Berkeley, USA

JAPANESE FIRMS IN EUROPE
Edited by Frédérique Sachwald

TECHNOLOGICAL INNOVATION, MULTINATIONAL
CORPORATIONS AND NEW INTERNATIONAL COMPETITIVENESS
The case of intermediate countries
Edited by José Molero

GLOBAL COMPETITION AND THE LABOUR MARKET
Nigel Driffield

THE SOURCE OF CAPITAL GOODS INNOVATION
The role of user firms in Japan and Korea
Kong-Rae Lee

CLIMATES OF GLOBAL COMPETITION
Maria Bengtsson

MULTINATIONAL ENTERPRISES AND TECHNOLOGICAL
SPILLOVERS
Tommaso Perez

GOVERNANCE OF INTERNATIONAL STRATEGIC ALLIANCES
Technology and transaction costs
Joanne E. Oxley

STRATEGY IN EMERGING MARKETS
Telecommunications establishments in Europe
Anders Pehrsson

GOING MULTINATIONAL
The Korean experience of direct investment
Edited by Frédérique Sachwald

MULTINATIONAL FIRMS AND IMPACTS ON EMPLOYMENT,
TRADE AND TECHNOLOGY
New perspectives for a new century
Edited by Robert E. Lipsey and Jean-Louis Mucchielli

MULTINATIONAL FIRMS
The global–local dilemma
Edited by John H. Dunning and Jean-Louis Mucchielli

MIT AND THE RISE OF ENTREPRENEURIAL SCIENCE
Henry Etzkowitz

TECHNOLOGICAL RESOURCES AND THE LOGIC OF CORPORATE
DIVERSIFICATION
Brian Silverman

MIT AND THE RISE OF ENTREPRENEURIAL SCIENCE

Henry Etzkowitz

London and New York

First published 2002
by Routledge
2 Park Square, Milton Park, Abingdon, Oxon, OX14 4RN

Simultaneously published in the USA and Canada
by Routledge
270 Madison Ave, New York NY 10016

Routledge is an imprint of the Taylor & Francis Group

Transferred to Digital Printing 2006

© 2002 Henry Etzkowitz

Typeset in Goudy by Taylor & Francis Books Ltd

All rights reserved. No part of this book may be reprinted or
reproduced or utilised in any form or by any electronic,
mechanical, or other means, now known or hereafter
invented, including photocopying and recording, or in any
information storage or retrieval system, without permission in
writing from the publishers.

British Library Cataloguing in Publication Data
A catalogue record for this book is available from the British Library

Library of Congress Cataloging in Publication Data
A catalog record for this book has been requested

ISBN10: 0–415–28516–X (hbk)
ISBN10: 0–415–43505–6 (pbk)

ISBN13: 978–0–415–28516–2 (hbk)
ISBN13: 978–0–415–43505–5 (pbk)

CONTENTS

Acknowledgements		ix
Introduction: MIT and the rise of the entrepreneurial university		1
1	The second academic revolution	9
2	MIT: the founding of an entrepreneurial university	20
3	Controversy over consultation	31
4	The traffic among MIT, industry and the military	42
5	Knowledge as property: the debate over patenting academic science	55
6	The regulation of academic patenting	66
7	Enterprises from science: the origins of science-based regional economic development	78
8	The invention of the venture capital firm: American Research and Development (ARD)	89
9	Stanford and Silicon Valley: enhancement of the MIT model	102
10	Technology transfer universalized: the Bayh-Dole regime	113
11	The making of entrepreneurial scientists	127
12	Innovation: the endless transition	139
	Notes	152
	Index	163

ACKNOWLEDGEMENTS

I wish to express my thanks to Professor Everett Mendelsohn of the History of Science Department, Harvard University, in whose summer seminar this study originated. I also wish to express my deep appreciation to the late Edward Shils who encouraged my research on entrepreneurial science and shepherded several articles through publication in *Minerva*. My thanks also to Professors Robert K. Merton and Harriet Zuckerman for providing a venue to test my ideas in their seminar on the Sociology of Science at Columbia University.

My special thanks to the archivists at MIT and Stanford for providing access to materials, and to faculty members, students and administrators for acceding to interviews. I wish to acknowledge financial support from the National Science Foundation, the National Endowment for the Humanities and the Andrew Mellon Foundation. My special appreciation goes to Dr Rochelle Hollander of NSF for her long-term interest in this project.

New York, 14 November, 2001

INTRODUCTION

MIT and the rise of the entrepreneurial university

MIT has played a distinctive role in US academia, creating formats for interaction with industry and then diffusing them to other schools. Although the idea of science as the basis of economic development is not new, policies encouraging the university to become a driver of the science-based economy are relatively new and sometimes controversial. Logically, however, much of that controversy should dissipate in the light of how the university's engagement in this key economic role is inherent in its first mission, teaching, and manifest in its second, research. Nevertheless, just as tension has persisted between teaching and research even as it has been found to be fruitful to locate them jointly in the same institution, so may we expect a continuing friction between the university's newest mission and its older ones.

The MIT model, combining basic research and teaching with industrial innovation, is displacing Harvard as the academic exemplar. Until quite recently, pursuing the "endless frontier" of basic research was the primary ideological justification of elite US academic institutions.[1] Harvard University was the model, with numerous schools identifying themselves as the "Harvard" of their respective regions. Such claims are seldom heard anymore. With an entrepreneurial mode increasingly followed at Harvard, and at academic institutions that model themselves upon it, the prediction that MIT would eventually conform to the traditional US research university mode has been disconfirmed.

Instead, the reverse process has occurred as liberal arts research universities adopt a mission closer to the "land grant" tradition of regional economic development, MIT's founding purpose and historic forte.

The thesis of this book is that a new academic model – the entrepreneurial university – is created as universities combine teaching and research with the capitalization of knowledge. The university's assumption of an entrepreneurial role is the latest step in the evolution of a medieval institution from its original purpose of conservation of knowledge to the extension and capitalization of knowledge. As the university increasingly provides the basis for economic development through the generation of social and intellectual, as well as human, capital, it becomes a core institution in society.

INTRODUCTION

MIT and the rise of entrepreneurial science

This book analyzes the origins and development of the entrepreneurial university model at MIT, its transfer to Stanford and its subsequent spread throughout the academic world. Four individuals were central to the creation of the contemporary entrepreneurial university that combines research and teaching with regional economic development through creation of high-tech spin-off firms: William Barton Rogers, Karl Compton, Vannevar Bush and Frederick Terman.

The founder of the Massachusetts Institute of Technology (MIT) was William Barton Rogers, a geologist from the University of Virginia, with family ties in the Boston area, then (the mid-nineteenth century), as now, a technology center. Rogers originally conceived of a science-based university committed to the industrial development of its region. That vision, however, was considerably greater than the reality of the resources then available to support its realization, even with 30 percent of Massachusetts "land grant" funds committed to the new MIT. Later, Karl Compton, MIT's President in the 1930s and 1940s, specified Rogers' vision of a university role in fostering regional economic development; he pioneered the venture capital firm as a transmission-belt between academia and industry, supplying seed capital and business counsel to academic firm-founders.

Vannevar Bush: from consultation to firm formation

It wasn't until the 1920s that Rogers' conception began to take tangible shape, when Vannevar Bush, MIT professor, administrator and consultant to industry, systematically originated the university-based high-tech firm. Vannevar Bush attained renown as a World War II science policy administrator and as originator of the post-war "Science as an Endless Frontier" thesis. Earlier in his career Bush adumbrated the model of the entrepreneurial academic as consultant, patent holder and firm founder. A graduate of Tufts College, he earned one of the first MIT PhDs in electrical engineering and stayed on to teach. As a young professor, just after World War I, Bush spent his own money to get an invention patented but lost his investment when he found that no one was interested in licensing the patent. Bush learned from this experience that inventing a new device, "building a better mouse trap," was not enough. Further steps had to be taken. During the 1920s Bush worked part time in the R&D labs of local companies as a consultant. He also passed along problems to his students to work on and some of the industrial problems fed back into academic research on campus.

Bush became a firm believer in the value of the consulting relationship for bringing new issues into academic research. He also kept an eye out for research with commercial potential. In the course of work for Amrad, a firm sponsored by J.P. Morgan, Bush met an inventor of a device that the financier was not interested in. Bush, however, saw a use for the technology in the emerging radio

2

INTRODUCTION

industry. Through college acquaintances, Bush was well connected in the Boston financial community. With these financial and technical colleagues, Bush helped organize the Raytheon Corporation, an early electronics company that grew into a major firm. As with other such ventures, the fate of the company gives value to the stocks, enriching the holders, if successful. If not, it leaves them with handsomely engraved papers stored in their university desk drawers and a rueful tale to recount.

Vannevar Bush's consulting and firm formation activities provided an influential model, especially since Bush later rose in the administrative ranks to vice-president and Dean of the Engineering School. Nor was he alone in this practice. Several firms in the businesses of consulting and production of scientific instruments emerged out of MIT and Harvard in the late nineteenth and early twentieth centuries. One of these firms, the Arthur D. Little Company (ADL), founded in 1886, was located adjacent to the Institute and drew upon its teachers. Dozens of MIT faculty members, over the years, have augmented their modest academic pay by moonlighting as consultants for ADL. A few of them received annual retainers from ADL for merely agreeing not to do consulting work for anybody else. Often, in reciprocation, they would recommend to their most gifted students that after graduation they consider employment at ADL.

Bush's experience exemplified the prospect for the unity of conduct and commercialization of research, with each activity enriching the other. Given the industrial experience and close industrial connections of many teachers at the Institute, an interactive approach to consultation, research, teaching and invention was commonplace. Vannevar Bush reported that he obtained many of his research ideas from his consulting practice. He would then have his students at the Institute work on their academic implications, under his supervision. At times, new practical implications would emerge from these investigations.

The final element, closing the loop, was to place these ideas into industrial use either in existing firms or new ones formed for the purpose. Bush told the Temporary National Economic Commission that he had never directly made any money from a patent.

> But indirectly is another matter, as they well understood. I was early a professor and also a consultant to industry. It was a salutary combination; it drew me out of the ivory tower and put life into my teaching, and it greatly helped the family budget.[2]

Through his college roommate, Laurence K. Marshall, Bush made the acquaintance of a group of Boston financiers. They invested in several technical enterprises, such as the Spencer Thermostat Company, that Bush helped organize as a consultant during the post-World War I years. Through a series of mergers, the Thermostat firm eventually became part of Texas Instruments.[3]

These instances inspired MIT Treasurer Horace Ford's 1930s vision of a

3

INTRODUCTION

"research row" of technologically based firms derived from Institute research to be established between MIT and Harvard on Cambridge's Memorial Drive. Indeed, while a few technology firms such as Edwin Land's Polaroid Corporation did establish themselves on the Drive, the notion of a roadway as the string for a necklace of technology firms was realized on a larger scale after World War II on Route 128. Nevertheless, Ford's vision of MIT as the source of a technology complex began to be translated into a regional economic development strategy in the mid-1930s, during Karl T. Compton's presidency.

Compton and his colleagues in the Boston financial and academic communities originated a model for science-based regional economic development, linking a venture capital instrument to academic research groups. The venture capital firm provided a systematic method for organizing high-tech firms based upon academic research, codifying Bush and other early academic entrepreneurs' individual experiences. Georges Doriot, a professor at Harvard Business School and head of the American Research and Development Corporation (ARD), a venture capital firm established in 1946, eventually put this academic entrepreneurial model into practice, bringing together technical expertise from MIT with business expertise from Harvard.

ARD provided business advice and seed funding to potential entrepreneurs in academia. The officers of the firm would tutor them in firm formation and serve on their boards of directors. The firms were sometimes housed in under-utilized space in MIT's own buildings, which served as a proto-incubator. Harvard's Georges Doriot realized his MIT colleagues' vision for a new role for the university and helped found the venture capital industry during the early post-war era.

The practice of firm formation from academic research assisted by venture capital became widespread. MIT's entrepreneurial model was transferred to Stanford University by Frederick Terman, who had been Bush's PhD student at MIT. A professor of electrical engineering and later Stanford's Provost, he improved upon the model by systematically creating research centers, larger-scale research units, built from several related research groups, to speed the production of commercializable innovations.

Terman also found creative ways to fund Stanford's expansion, hiring additional faculty members with revenues generated by a shopping center and an industrial park constructed on the university's extensive land holdings. In doing so, he inadvertently invented the science park, as high-tech firms, including Hewlett-Packard, created from Stanford research in the 1930s, located their facilities within Stanford's industrial park in the 1950s and 1960s, in order to maintain close ties to the university.

In the late 1970s a confluence of opposition to academic technology transfer and a desire to find a way to allow government to assist industry led to the passage of the Bayh-Dole Act. This legislation amended the Patent and Trademark Act to provide that the intellectual property emanating from federally funded research at universities be turned over to them to patent and market as a condition of receipt of government funds. At one and the same time the Act

INTRODUCTION

legitimated academic technology transfer and closed the gap between academia and industry opened up by the endless frontier linear model of government funding of academic research. Before Bayh-Dole, there had been no assurance that the results from publicly funded research would be transferred to industry.

Thus, the loop in a spiral of institutional innovation, begun in the mid-nineteenth century, was completed in the mid-twentieth century. In the interim, many of the firms in the textile and metalworking industries had disappeared, but they were replaced during the post-war era by electronics and computer firms. These companies were often started in the abandoned factories of older industries, and now, in turn, they are being displaced by genetic engineering and software firms. Although the firms and technologies have changed over the decades, the vision of knowledge-based industrial development that William Barton Rogers expounded to a nineteenth-century industrial leadership in the Boston region has been realized, and has since spread widely.

Just as a research ethos was universalized throughout the academic sphere, so now is a concern with maximizing the economic uses of research that was formerly the province of a specialized academic sector – the land grant schools.[4] Still, industrial research funding and receipts from licensing of intellectual property rights are small in absolute terms in comparison to government funding sources that have become traditional, with their controversial origins forgotten by succeeding academic generations.[5] Nevertheless, a secular trend can be projected of an academic system, closely involved with industry as well as government. During the 1980s industry funding of academic research rose from 4 percent to 7 percent and, by the end of the 1990s, to 10 percent. Much of this increase was concentrated in a few fields with strongly perceived industrial relevance such as biotechnology and civil engineering. University research centers closely tied to industry increased nearly 2½ times during the 1980s. The number of patents awarded to US universities tripled between 1984 and 1994.[6] While still small in scale – if not in scope – a new academic model is emerging from its chrysalis.

As to the question of whether this is significant in terms of the future capitalization of knowledge, universities are now taking equity in these firms. If we look back just 20 years to the firms that came out of Stanford University when it was not the policy to take equity, several of these firms, such as SUN and Silicon Graphics, are now multibillion dollar firms. Within ten years, universities will hold significant equity in similar firms and the universities will be transformed from eleemosynary institutions based on receiving resources from others into at least partially self-generating institutions, generating resources not only for industry but also for themselves, and this will be the way out of the universities' funding dilemma.

Understanding the dynamics of entrepreneurial science

To examine how the university's new and old roles (economic development, research and education) interact and conflict with each other, more than 150

INTRODUCTION

in-depth interviews were conducted with academic entrepreneurs, other faculty members and administrators. A sample of eight public and private universities, at the Carnegie I and II levels, was selected to represent universities and departments with newly emerging and long-standing connections to industry. The disciplines studied included: physics, chemistry, computer science, electrical engineering and biological sciences. Following a pilot study of two disciplines (physics and biology) at two universities in the early 1980s, interviews were conducted in two waves, in the mid-1980s and mid-1990s. Documentary materials, including patent guidelines and committee minutes relating to the assumption of an economic mission, were also examined. Archival research was carried out at MIT and Stanford University.

The premise of this investigation is that the university is not merely a support structure supplying human capital to other organizations. Its daily research activities involve a continual flow of young people who are future inventors. No industrial or consulting firm has access to such a broad stream of talent. The inventions that come out of universities typically come from students rather than directly from professors. As teachers, professors provide guidance and resources, but the actual work and often the ideas come from students. The university's teaching function, therefore, cannot be divorced from its emerging "third mission" of economic development.

Economic legitimating themes are becoming as important as cultural ones as universities are increasingly viewed as drivers of economic growth. These themes are not contradictory. Although academic research in an increasing number of fields in the natural and social sciences, for example in molecular biology, artificial intelligence and risk management, is carried out in full recognition of its commercial possibilities, the traditional academic reward system – the esteem of colleagues, the ultimate accolade of a Nobel or other prestigious prize – remains a powerful incentive. Pecuniary motives have not displaced the pursuit of academic honors: rather, each incentive overlays and reinforces the other.

Chapter 1 depicts the transformation of the university through the introduction of research and then economic and social development as academic missions, the first and second academic revolutions, respectively. Chapter 2 discusses how the Massachusetts Institute of Technology was founded in 1862 to infuse Boston and environs, the United States' first industrial region, with new technology. The concept for MIT integrated three academic strands: the European Polytechnic School focused on applied research, what we today call the basic research university and the combination of research, training and outreach in an academic institution focused on agricultural innovation, which later became known as the "land grant" model. Indeed, MIT's founding was partially financed by the Massachusetts land grant.

Chapter 3 begins the discussion of the invention of various modes of university–industry relations designed to realize MIT's founding purpose. The hiring of industrial engineers as professors to introduce research at MIT

INTRODUCTION

provoked a controversy over "conflict of commitment." Its resolution through establishment of the one-fifth rule of one day per week, allowing professors to work for industry in moderation, provided a regulated framework for academic–industry relations. The rule spread throughout US academia, becoming so taken for granted that few, even at MIT, are aware of its origin.

Chapter 4 shows how formats for university–government relations were built upon those established for university–industry relations. Thus, an office created to manage a program for contracts with companies, created to resolve a post-World War I financial crisis, was utilized during World War II to manage government-funded wartime research projects at MIT. Thus originated the contemporary academic Contracts and Grants Office, with the "contract" a template for linking university and government, both financially and meta-phorically.

Chapter 5 returns to the evolution of university–industry relations, how formats were originated to patent the commercializable results of academic research, while taking into account the objections of opponents. The initial format maintained a certain distance between academia and business by utilizing an intermediary organization to assess and market intellectual property rights. Chapter 6 discusses controversies over academic patenting and how they were resolved, creating overlaps between academia and industry

Chapter 7 discusses the extension of academic consultation into the formation of new firms. Examples of firm formation at MIT in the 1920s became the basis of a regional growth strategy that was adopted by a university–industry–government coalition in New England during the 1930s. Chapter 8 shows how New England's comparative advantage, a concentration of research, was turned into new economic activity. In collaboration with Harvard Business School, MIT invented the venture capital firm and filled a gap in the New England "innovation environment" by providing business advice and seed capital to academics who might not otherwise have taken steps to found a firm.

Chapter 9 tells the story of how the entrepreneurial university model was introduced into Stanford from MIT. The post-war high-tech conurbations of Route 128 and Silicon Valley shared a common origin in university–industry relations. The unique aspect of the Stanford case was the generation of high-tech industry from a newly established "critical mass" of academic research with industrial potential in a region which largely lacked an industrial base in the early twentieth century. In both instances, post-war government funding, largely for military purposes, expanded upon an industrial–academic dynamic that had been set in motion as early as the turn of the previous century.

Chapter 10 delineates how the entrepreneurial university model was generalized throughout the US research university system as part of a response to the decline of US industry and the economic downturn in the 1970s. Deleterious economic circumstances coincided with a controversy over how to dispose of intellectual property rights emanating from federally funded research, the post-war expansion of university–government links established during World War II.

7

INTRODUCTION

The resolution of this controversy, through the passage of the Bayh-Dole Act of 1980, an amendment to the Patent and Trademark Law, merged previous formats for university–industry and university–government links into a common framework for university–industry government relations: the triple helix.

Chapter 11 returns to the implications of these developments for academic institutions and academic scientists. An entrepreneurial dynamic that was introduced in US universities as part of the introduction of research was extended into firm formation. Entrepreneurship was part of the culture of the research university even before the commercial implications of research became apparent.

Chapter 12 discusses the emergence of the entrepreneurial university as part of a triple helix dynamic. The entrepreneurial university plays an increasingly important role in society as industry becomes more knowledge-based. As the university takes a more central place in the institutional firmament as the basis of economic activity, it may, in the future, become a self-sustaining institution.

1

THE SECOND ACADEMIC REVOLUTION

As academic science is transformed into an economic as well as an intellectual endeavor, the separation between science and industry to which most universities traditionally adhered breaks down, as the university itself becomes an entrepreneur. Until quite recently only a relatively few schools, such as the Massachusetts Institute of Technology (MIT), saw it as an important part of their mission to develop a close relationship with industry or to take steps to commercialize their research. During the past two decades a broad range of universities, well beyond MIT, Stanford University and a few other schools with traditional ties to industry, have undertaken to mine their research resources for profit.

As their interest in making money from their research resources grows, universities compete in a new arena. When Columbia University announced a patent, covering both US and international rights to co-transformation, a genetic engineering technique invented by faculty member Richard Axel, the university's director of technology licensing exclaimed, "We captured both in one."[1] The implicit comparison was to the Stanford Cohen-Boyer patents, the basis for genetic engineering, which had failed to gain such a high level of protection because the two researchers had already disclosed the techniques before their university could apply for patents in Europe and Japan.

Academic institutions participate in various ways in the capitalization of knowledge and its transmutation into factors of production. The University of Colorado and Columbia University accept equity in faculty formed firms. Washington University, St Louis and MIT take the role of venture capitalist and Harvard has participated in ventures through its corporation. A university licensing administrator outlined the new academic regime: "Instead of publishing it and giving it away, you license, publish, but don't give it away."[2] For example, Rockefeller University announced the receipt of a $20 million payment for a patent license for the "obesity gene" from Amgen, a biotechnology company, "with an agreement to pay many times that amount if the protein proves useful in treating fat people."[3] The entrepreneurial university is a continuation of the development of a medieval institution for the conservation and transmission of knowledge into a multifaceted institution that also creates new knowledge and transforms it into practical uses.

9

THE SECOND ACADEMIC REVOLUTION

Precursors of entrepreneurial science

Opportunities to translate research into industrial applications were always present, yet few academics took advantage of them. The few who did were a distinct and unusual minority. In early nineteenth-century Germany, several instances have been noted of ill-paid chemistry professors initiating commercial ventures, and supervising production processes, to supplement their incomes. One entrepreneurial effort stands out from these mundane ventures, Liebig's mid-ninteenth-century use of chemical theory to develop an artificial fertilizer. Although unsuccessful, this venture represented a significant precursor of contemporary academic efforts to originate marketable products.

Universities have acquired the capabilities to engage in business activities, well beyond the traditional bursary functions such as collecting student fees and paying faculty salaries. Transcending their traditional industrial role of training persons for employment, the new entrepreneurial role of universities is based upon creating new knowledge-based firms, locally, as well as selling technology to the highest bidder among existing firms, nationally and internationally.

As technology transfer activities expand, they are often grouped within a distinctive administrative structure even as they are linked to previous academic missions through industry–university research centers and entrepreneurship training programs. A school's portfolio of industrial connections (industrial liaison programs, technology transfer offices, incubator facilities, etc.) is the organizational attribute of entrepreneurial science, much as research specialties and distinctive courses of study distinguished universities from one another in the past. A transformation of the university's mission is underway that is comparable to the academic revolution of the late nineteenth and early twentieth centuries, when research became an accepted academic task.[4]

The first academic revolution

An academic revolution would appear to be a contradiction in terms. As a medieval institution, going back more than one-thousand years to its founding in Paris and Bologna, universities appear to change at a glacial pace. Originally conceived as institutions of cultural conservation, preservation and transmission, they existed solely for that purpose for many centuries. The university has retained its original purpose even as it has expanded its purview to encompass new missions.

The continuity of the university resides in its history of development: each new task has evolved out of an effort to meet a previous goal. Research emerged, initially in philology and then in other disciplines, from a concerted effort to revive classical learning in the eighteenth century. New knowledge was inevitably created and a better understanding gained through the innovative methodological techniques invented to retrieve the meaning of Greek and Roman texts.

THE SECOND ACADEMIC REVOLUTION

The seminar, an innovative advanced teaching method also arose out of the development of philological research. The cooperative examination of texts took place though presentations by advanced students and professors, with discussion of findings among them. This led to both levels of academics becoming inquirers into new knowledge. The seminar supplemented lectures and enhanced the educational mission of universities even as it became a basic format for organizing research in the humanistic disciplines.

As research became a distinctive activity at some universities in Europe, the experimental sciences were also incorporated into the university. The invention of the teaching laboratory in chemistry at Giessen University in Germany in the mid-nineteenth century was accompanied by the development of a precise methodology in organic chemistry. A senior researcher, utilizing advanced students to conduct direct supervision, could train dozens of students at a time. This basic format persists in academic science teaching to this date.

In the United States the first academic revolution originated in the mid-nineteenth century at some of the older teaching institutions such as Harvard and Columbia, where professors, often inspired by their German doctoral mentors, sought to initiate research training programs and advanced degrees. However, the gap between academic vision and available resources was evident for virtually all US academic institutions during the mid-nineteenth century, with the notable exception of those working in agricultural research.

The attempt to establish chemical research laboratories according to the German model largely failed.[5] Harvard's Eben Horsford, for example, was able to raise the funds to build a building but not to hire assistants and buy supplies, let alone heat the laboratory. There were simply not enough funds available to realize the research ambitions of the increasing number of American scholars who returned from Europe with their PhDs.

Since research funds did not come with academic positions as was typical in Germany, individual researchers were responsible for seeking their own sources of support. The organization of doctoral research was a creative response to these financial constraints. Research expanded beyond an individual effort when academics employed as teachers obtained small amounts of money to purchase research materials and to hire students to help carry out research.

Academic research was greatly advanced later in the century by the founding of new universities such as Johns Hopkins and Chicago. These institutions adhered to a model of pure research, outlined by Johns Hopkins physicist Henry Rowland in the late nineteenth century. Early in his career Rowland had been a consultant to industry but when he took office and gave his inaugural address as President of the American Association for the Advancement of Science, he put this industrial career behind him in raising the banner of pure research.

Until the late nineteenth century, in the USA no clear distinction was made between basic and applied research. The infusion of funds into academia from the great industrial fortunes created in the late nineteenth century was accompanied by fears that donors would attempt to influence the research agenda.

11

THE SECOND ACADEMIC REVOLUTION

The creation of an ideology of basic research was part of the effort to carve out a protected, yet financially secure, space for science. The practically oriented leaders of academic science in the mid-nineteenth century, such as the Sillimans at Yale and Columbia's Chandler, well known as consulting chemists, were pushed aside by a younger generation devoted to pure science who became the academic exemplars.

The distinction held until World War II when scientists who had grown up in the basic research culture found themselves immersed in war-related engineering projects, such as radar, which also led to the development of radio astronomy and the elucidation of theoretical issues in cosmology during the post-war period. The somewhat surprising emergence of theoretical issues during their wartime service, ostensibly devoted to practical issues, closed some of the gap between pure science and engineering for these researchers. Built with foundation and industry funds early in the century, the US academic research system was greatly expanded with federal funds during and after World War II. It has brought with it an increased velocity of scientific activity and pressures to further increase funding in order to support existing research groups and form new ones. Emanating from the research base created by the first revolution, economic development is becoming an academic mission, as well.

The second academic revolution

The role of the university in society is currently undergoing a transformation comparable in scale and scope to the first academic revolution of the late nineteenth and early twentieth century when the university integrated research along with teaching into its academic mission. As the first academic revolution spread to the sciences, a second revolution was set in motion. Making findings from an academic laboratory into a marketable product requires a series of intermediate steps that follow from acquiring the intention to sell as well as to publish one's research. In these circumstances, organizations as well as individuals act as entrepreneurs.

In 1963, Clark Kerr, then Chancellor of the University of California, Berkeley, set forth a vision of the future of the university, extrapolated from the recent history of his campus.[6] He called it the multi-versity to encompass a proliferation of activities. Conventional discipline-based departments were cross-cut by interdisciplinary research centers covering newly emerging fields such as materials science and foreign area studies, giving the university a matrix-like structure. Greatly expanded divisions of continuing education offered credited and non-credited courses to the general public on an even wider variety of topics than could be found in the regular academic catalog.

Parallel to the trends that Kerr identified, and in part based upon them, another academic transformation was gathering force based upon the commercialization of academic research. For example, the Alumni Foundation of the University of Wisconsin marketed patents derived from academic research to

12

industry and financed faculty research projects with the monies made. These funds enabled Wisconsin to become a major research center in biology in the 1930s and 1940s.[7]

Transformation of the academic–industry interface

Academic scientists have a long history of working with industry, having helped establish the early industrial research laboratories in the United States.[8] Until quite recently most university–industry connections separated academic and commercial practices. Even as ongoing relationships, consulting arrangements were usually conducted apart from academic research, although based on the academic's expertise accumulated from campus-based research. Consulting relationships typically involved brief visits to industrial sites or conducting discrete projects on university premises. A consequence of this separation was that it left control of commercial opportunities of academic research in the hands of industry whereas control over the direction of research and choice of research topics was left to academic scientists. Although regular payments were made to individual consultants, the large-scale transfer of funds from industry to the university was left up to the generosity of companies.

The older forms of university–industry connections involved payment for services rendered, whether it was received directly in the form of consultation fees or indirectly as endowment gifts. Thus, the traffic between university and industry was policed so that those boundaries were maintained even as exchanges took place through consultation and philanthropy. From the early years of the research university in the late nineteenth century, university–industry relationships were largely established at the behest of industry to serve the needs of existing companies. Engineering schools reorganized themselves to serve the research needs of the growing science based electrical and chemical industries and to supply them with personnel. The linkages included cooperative programs which sent students to industry for part of their training, university professors undertaking research at the request of industry and donations of money and equipment by industrial firms to support engineering education.[9]

University–industry relationships declined in the 1930s due to the financial stringency of the depression and became relatively less important in the postwar era with the growth in government funding of science. Traditionally, academic–industry relations denoted the provision of research support from a firm to a campus-based researcher. Such funding, despite offering far fewer restrictions than government support in many cases, and thus being viewed favorably by academic research staff, has represented a very small proportion of academic research support during the post-World War II period, even though it has recently increased from a low of 2 percent to 7 percent.

Most of these funds flowed through consulting relationships with faculty members who provided advice (on campus to visitors from the company and at the industrial lab), conducted tests of materials and products in their laboratories and occasionally carried out small research projects for a company. Based upon the consulting model, some universities like MIT and Cal Tech established liaison programs to link up firms with professors. In its most developed format, a liaison program staff member would keep up with the technical interests of a group of companies who paid a fee to a member of the program and then received suggestions of faculty members to contact.

New forms of university–industry relationships involve the multiplication of resources through the university's and faculty members' participation in capital formation projects such as real estate development in science parks and formation of firms in incubator facilities. These also include academic scientists' involvement in firms, for example through membership of advisory boards or boards of directors, stockholding in exchange for consultation services, assumption of managerial responsibilities and direct involvement in the formation of firms.

During the past two decades, a broad range of US universities have taken on the tasks of economic development, at times because of external pressures including funding constriction, but also as the result of internal initiatives arising from the expansionary dynamic of scientific research. Professors' participation in the founding of firms based upon their academic research represents a new stage in the development of academic–industry relations. The objective is to multiply the value of intellectual property derived from academic research through the stock market, either directly through the formation of a new firm or indirectly through a stream of royalty income from an existing firm.

The new focus of relations with industry builds upon the development of scientific research capabilities and the creation of a series of boundary-spanning mechanisms, including technology transfer offices and spin-off firms. Incubator facilities provide a home and support services for new firms while research parks are designed to link successful firms to academic resources, in a format designed to be compatible with academic goals. Whether this goal can be achieved is a matter of considerable academic soul searching and debate.

Controversies over relations to industry

This transformation of the university brings with it a shift in values and practices as faculty and students take on entrepreneurial roles, within and outside the university. Roles such as faculty member, researcher and firm founder may be in conflict and also confluence with each other as well as with traditional academic roles. The combination of entrepreneurial activities with the university's traditional roles of education and research has created a hybrid organization in pursuit of multiple goals that simultaneously conflict with and support each other. Thus, research may cause a time conflict with teaching even as research infuses teaching with new ideas and examples. Firm formation from academic research may cause a conflict of obligation with service to the department even as it provides new resources and ideas for investigation. While conflicts of interest are often viewed negatively as potential malfeasance, they also signal transition to a new academic model. They expose assumptions about the purpose of higher learning and the legitimacy of an economic role for the university.

One axis of opposing views about the utility and propriety of academic–industry ties concerns whether it is possible for the university to contribute significantly to the economy – the practical question. The overall modest level of this activity, despite a steady increase in income earned from patents and a number of multi-million-dollar research contracts, has led some observers to conclude that relations with industry are, and will continue to be, of minor import in comparison to university ties to government. For example, it has been argued that universities are ill-advised to commit resources to the marketing of technology, especially since companies prefer that academic institutions concentrate on making information freely available.[10]

The ethical question posed is whether such participation will detract from the traditional educational and research missions of the university – the value dimension.[11] There is concern that attention to economic issues will cost the university its independence. Some of these same fears were expressed by academics opposed to federal research support in the 1930s. Critics of academic–industry relations believe that the university risks losing its independent identity and special purpose by engaging in such activities.

Controversies have erupted such as the one at Harvard in 1980, when the administration proposed that the university participate financially in a firm based on the research of one of its faculty members. The ensuing debate rapidly escalated into a struggle over the goals of the university, the purpose of science and the professional ethics of scientists. According to one observer, "What has drawn Harvard into this quagmire is the heady expectations of a genetic Eldorado."[12] In the face of widespread faculty opposition, Derek Bok, the President of Harvard University, withdrew the university from the plan to invest in a joint university/faculty-initiated biotechnology firm.

Instead, he issued a statement eschewing such projects in the name of protecting the disinterested stance of the university while reserving the right to capture the economic worth of university research through other means. In 1988, a joint venture involving the Harvard Corporation, an administrative entity, and the university's medical school was announced. Although the *New York Times* questioned whether traditional academic values were being abandoned, there were no reports of on-campus opposition as there had been eight years before.

Academic–industry relations provide a litmus test of a university's goals. Just as a litmus test partially changes color indicating degree of acidity, conflicts over relations with industry signal the stage of transition that a university is in, shifting from a feudal to a capitalist mode of production. How much has changed during the past two decades and how much has not? In the early 1980s, the *New Scientist* reported that a London University professor proudly refused to assert an economic interest in the results of his research.

THE SECOND ACADEMIC REVOLUTION

Along with the announcement from Edinburgh that Dolly Parton's namesake was a cloned sheep, was the mention that the academic institution where the research was conducted had helped found the biotechnology firm that had part funded the research. Capitalized on the London stock exchange, the present firm was the result of a merger with a US company, founded by faculty at Johns Hopkins University and Virginia Polytechnic Institute, with support from their state science agencies. The *New York Times* also reported interviews with scientists at the University of Wisconsin who asserted that the NSF would never have funded the Edinburgh research, it simply wasn't basic enough![13]

Universities try to balance their academic and business roles in the increasingly brief interval between discovery and utilization of research findings. Once academic research is redefined from a free to a marketable good and treated as intellectual property, the traditional forms of dissemination, such as publication of articles in academic journals and presentation of papers at conferences, continue but under a new set of conditions. "Limited secrecy" becomes the watchword as publication is delayed to allow time for patenting.

If universities take a strong stand for openness and do not want the time span for delay to be long, companies will usually agree. Nor, once a university has a technology transfer office ready to act quickly is there any need to take a long period of time to file an intention to patent. Having a paper published in a major journal can be advantageous to a company seeking funds to support product development or an appreciation in the price of its stock. Forces within the academic technology transfer process militate for and against the freedom of scientific information as the university creates a business from its research activities.

Causes of entrepreneurial science

One vision of the university of the future is as a generator of spin-off enterprises, creating income and employment by infusing a local regional or national economy with new sources of growth such as a cluster of science-based firms. In 1980, Congress created the virtual equivalent of a second "land grant" in the Bayh-Dole Act, turning over to the universities intangible intellectual property arising from federally supported academic research. Faculty in basic research areas, who were previously far from commercial applications, have moved closer to practical uses and some have earned considerable monies from their inventions. This is in contrast to employees of corporate labs who typically sign their intellectual property rights away as a condition of employment. What has led to the growth of the entrepreneurial university and the academic scientist as an entrepreneur?

The attention to the pecuniary value of research findings has a series of proximate and long-term causes. While short-term causes vary in different countries and academic systems, the common long-term factors driving the emergence of entrepreneurial science have to do with the increasing significance of science to economic development as well as changes in the internal structure of scientific research itself. Several hypotheses have been offered to explain the emergence of entrepreneurial science.

1. A convergence between basic and applied research that creates commercial opportunities from basic research

Although insufficient as a full explanation of entrepreneurial science, recognition of a congruence between basic research and invention vitiates the ideological separation of these spheres of activity. As a closer relationship has emerged between basic research and industrial development the time gap between the two processes has shortened, resulting in several new syntheses. Previously, there was a long-term relationship in which basic understanding of physical phenomena later resulted in practical devices utilizing earlier discoveries. For example, Marconi's patent application of 1896 for a long range radio transmitter was "the technological embodiment of Maxwell's theory of the electromagnetic field, stated thirty years earlier."[14] Thus, a major scientific advance in the understanding of a physical phenomenon was translated into a working device. Different persons, with different professional outlooks and goals, discovery and theoretical advance versus commercial and military use, conducted each phase. More recently these processes have been collapsed into each other, sometimes with the same individuals involved in each phase. For example, the first successful insertion of foreign DNA into a host microorganism in 1973 was quickly followed from 1976 by the founding of small entrepreneurial firms to make industrial applications of this new genetic technique in the production of new drugs and chemicals.[15]

2. Scientists suddenly awakened to the opportunities attendant upon the application of recent scientific discoveries

Implicit in this explanation is the notion that there were scientific discoveries in recent decades, for example molecular biology and nanotechnology, unique in that they could be quickly developed as sources of profit. This explanation is deficient in its assumption that previous scientific research did not have direct commercial potential. Opportunities to translate research into industrial applications were always present, yet few academics took advantage of them.[16] The few who did were a distinct and unusual minority. In early nineteenth-century Germany, several instances have been noted of ill-paid chemistry professors initiating commercial ventures, and supervising production processes, to supplement their incomes. Although the rewards for producing useful knowledge have grown greater, the commercial potential has manifested since the founding of modern science. What is clearly different, is the invention of more powerful incentives such as the initial public offering (IPO).[17]

THE SECOND ACADEMIC REVOLUTION

3. An underlying congruence between scientific research and entrepreneurship, especially in an academic system in which researchers are responsible for obtaining resources to support their research

The academic world has long been involved in a relatively hidden process of organizational development leading up to firm formation through the expansion of group research. Science and entrepreneurship became ever more closely associated as a consequence of scientists' need to find support for their research, before opportunities to commercialize their research became available. Academic science is an entrepreneurial venture, similar to a start-up firm, as the research group leader, who manages a collectivity of researchers at various levels, displaces the individual scientist. Such scholars interact with a few students separately, a model still commonplace in the humanities. The roles of the scientist and the entrepreneur, defined respectively in 1820s England by philosopher William Whewell as a synthesizer of knowledge claims and in 1830s France by the economist Jean Baptiste Say as an economic risk taker, appear to be distinctly different types.[18] Nevertheless, they have much in common in their inner logic even apart from the intersection of science and business. Both concepts emphasize the importance of individual ingenuity in creating new formats, whether conceptual or organizational, to bring order to an uncertain environment.

The origins of the entrepreneurial university

The idea of the university as an entrepreneur, a label of not so subtle disparagement among some academics, is becoming a positive scholastic attribute. Nevertheless, given the traditional individualistic orientation of entrepreneurship, the organizational entrepreneur has only recently been recognized as a viable concept. For example, the US Department of Agriculture, in creating an agricultural innovation system from the late nineteenth century, has been identified as a collective entrepreneur.[19] State and local governments in the USA have also played an entrepreneurial role in fostering economic development through public initiatives during the post-war era.[20] Moving beyond capturing each other's businesses, these efforts focus on creating enterprises, often relying on the human, social and intellectual capital resources of a local university. Some universities have actively sought this new role; others have had it thrust upon them. A few schools, such as MIT, were founded for this very purpose.

MIT drew for its development upon various streams of academic formats invented in or imported to the USA during the early and mid-nineteenth century, for the purpose of establishing a close relationship between the university, technology and the economy, initially in agriculture and then in industry. The contemporary entrepreneurial university is a synthesis of various academic models, including the classical teaching college, the polytechnic engineering school, the land grant university and the research university. As a science-based, technological university with strong industrial ties MIT does not easily

THE SECOND ACADEMIC REVOLUTION

fit into the existing categories of academic institutions. Whereas the research university primarily balances teaching and research, the entrepreneurial university adds the task of economic development and maintains these three academic missions in a creative tension with each other.

MIT also exemplifies a creative synthesis of academic research formats based upon contrasting models of innovation. The research university exemplifies a linear model of innovation, going from academic research to practical use, traditionally through publication of research results that have been adapted for product development by interested industrial scientists. The land grant university, on the other hand, exemplifies a reverse linear model of innovation, starting from societal needs, such as those represented by farmers' wishes to improve their agricultural practices, as the basis for formulating research projects. MIT combined both of these formats, linear and reverse linear, following a non-linear interactive model of innovation. The next chapter discusses the growth of MIT as a distinctive type of science-based university in sharp contrast to the ivory-tower mode. Founded in the mid-nineteenth century, MIT was the first entrepreneurial university.

2

MIT

The founding of an entrepreneurial university

As early as the 1840s, William Barton Rogers, a professor of geology at the University of Virginia, envisioned a school that would systematically infuse industry with science-based technology. In its early years, MIT took the form of a classical college with a specified common curriculum but largely filled it with the content of a polytechnic education. Nevertheless, MIT was also founded with the ideal of training its students in the liberal arts as well as practical disciplines to enable them to become leaders in their professions, not mere technicians. The informal objective was to ensure that MIT graduates had broad preparation for industrial leadership and thus would become top executives rather than end up working for Harvard graduates. Rogers' vision of a university that would train sophisticated industrial leaders and create major innovations, rather than narrow inventions, inspired the early prominence of liberal arts and science disciplines in the curriculum of an engineering school.

MIT integrated various academic formats, including the classical teaching college, the polytechnic engineering school, the land grant university and the research university into a unique configuration. These academic paradigms provided the inspiration for various aspects of MIT's development as a technological university with a strong science base and a special version of the liberal arts related to its purposes. During the nineteenth century, US academia divided into separate streams of "pure science"- and "technology"-based institutions, with distinct cultures and academic missions. There were also mixed forms with technology schools included within universities in a lesser status, such as the Sheffield School at Yale, but these were typically unstable, temporary coalitions. After rejecting an attempt made in the early twentieth century to place science first, MIT subsequently developed a strong research base in both science and technology. The losers in this struggle left MIT and moved west to develop their academic concept, an implicit linear model going from research in academic disciplines to eventual practical uses at the California Institute of Technology. MIT combined the research university's "linear model" with the land grant university's "reverse linear model" predicated upon deriving research goals from societal needs.

MIT forged its distinctive identity by establishing close relationships with industry, both with existing firms and with the new companies that arose from the research and consulting activities of its professors. As the unitary curriculum of the classical American college opened up, defenders of the traditional liberal arts questioned whether science and engineering should be incorporated within existing institutions of higher learning. Advocates of pure science, believing in a gap between the discovery of laws of nature and their application and use, stood for the establishment of basic research departments within the university but without necessarily including the engineering disciplines on an equal status. MIT's educational design raised technological education to the first rank in association with the arts and sciences. Nevertheless, it took several decades, after MIT's founding in 1862, to realize Rogers' nascent entrepreneurial design. From concept to funding took almost twenty years; it then took decades longer, well into the twentieth century, to fully realize the original idea. MIT then influenced the course of US academic development through transfer of the entrepreneurial university model to Stanford.

The founding of MIT: a science-based institute of technology

MIT is a unique university, with strong engineering, science and humanities specialties. The fact that MIT is strong in technology is to be expected, but the Institute's perhaps surprising broader strengths derive from the intentions of its founder. Rogers' concept for a new kind of science-based technological university, linked to industry, was intended to be broader in purpose than existing American engineering schools such as Rensselaer Polytechnic Institute and West Point, with their respective specializations in the civilian and military branches of civil engineering. In a carefully thought out charter document written in 1846, Rogers wrote that:

> there is no branch of practical industry, whether in the arts of construction, manufactures or agriculture, which is not capable of being better practiced, and even of being improved in its processes, through the knowledge of its connections with physical truths and laws and therefore we would add that there is no class of operatives to whom the teaching of science may not become of direct and substantial utility and material usefulness.[1]

Science and technology were seen as interrelated and mutually supportive activities with a common purpose – rationalization of the production processes of Boston's industries and the creation of new industries from scientific discoveries.

Realizing that his objective could not be attained in rural Charlottesville, Rogers left Virginia and moved to Boston where his brother Henry, who had established himself in business, introduced him to potential supporters for his

THE FOUNDING OF MIT

project. Then, even more so than now, Boston held primacy as the USA's industrial, technological and educational hub. With a substrate of science-related industry already in place in the region's textile and metalworking industries, the Boston area was a fertile ground for implanting the notion of a technological university. During the middle years of the nineteenth century, Rogers recruited from among the manufacturers, merchants and intelligentsia of the Boston region. In time, with their assistance, he gained access to private and state funds and a share of the federal government's land grant to the Commonwealth of Massachusetts.

Rogers found an especially receptive audience among the industrialists of the region for his new academic concept. Lowell's textile manufacturers, for example, appreciated the usefulness of science to industry and had already hired trained chemists to direct their dyeing and printing works. In a series of meetings, he outlined a plan for a school of practical science that would offer training in scientific principles and laws that could be utilized to guide engineering and manufacturing practice. Rogers found support among Bostonian industrialists because of his insight into the need to create a technical intelligentsia and thereby raise the industrial growth of the region to a new level. He discussed with them the application of the principles of science to industry by developing and introducing new machinery and production processes into manufacturing enterprises. Rogers also stressed to them the importance of scientific guidance of production processes. He was contemptuous of "blind experimenters" who cluttered up the patent office with useless devices by attempting to make technical improvements without knowledge of physical laws.

Rogers believed that scientific training was required to produce inventions of "real and permanent value" and that there was no industrial art that could not be improved upon though a systematic understanding of natural laws. Rogers' school would:

> embrace full courses of instruction in all the principles of physical truth having direct relation to the art of constructing machinery, the application of motive power, manufactures, mechanical and chemical, the art of engraving with electrotype and photography, mineral exploration and mining, chemical analysis, engineering, locomotion and agriculture.[2]

Utility was the primary but not the sole legitimating theme of applied science. Beyond mere utility Rogers provided the applied sciences with a higher purpose of their own, equal in worth to that of other forms of higher learning, but linked to the subordinate class level of its practitioners. Such study was morally uplifting,

> leading the thoughts of the practical student into those wide and elevated regions of reflection to which the study of Nature's laws never

THE FOUNDING OF MIT

fails to conduct the mind ... thus linking the daily details of his profession with the grander physical agencies around him.[3]

Rogers did not wish to debate the relative value of science and classical culture but he did wish to establish the dignity and value of the practical professions and the need for schools to serve them.[4] Two types of instruction were required: (1) the scientific basis of engineering; and (2) particular areas of technical expertise. He expected that scientists, through their understanding of physical laws, would provide the theoretical underpinning and unifying framework for the diverse specialties of the engineers. This "applied science" focus distinguished MIT from more practically oriented engineering schools, at least in intention. Nevertheless, there was always the danger that scientists and engineers would each pursue narrow disciplinary goals at the expense of the broader, interdisciplinary objective of the scientific basis of engineering.

The Boston area already had an academic institution, the Lowell Institute, focused on enhancing technological competence and on raising the intellectual level of the workforce. During the fifteen-year organizing period, MIT's founders worked out a division of labor with the Lowell Institute. The Lowell Institute would continue to educate the general public on scientific and technical matters through open lectures and extension classes on technical subjects for workers while the new Massachusetts Institute of Technology would focus upon degree programs. Sufficient private funds were raised to match a state grant and a suitable building was constructed in the new Back Bay area of Boston.

MIT was founded with assistance from a 30 percent share of Massachusetts' land grant. Federal lands were provided to each state under the Morill Act, which supported the development of institutions of higher education and whose purpose was to assist the development of agriculture, then the major US industry. In Massachusetts, where industrial development had already occurred to a considerable extent, the Act was read in such a way that the legislature gave significant funds to a non-agriculturally based school. This result can be credited to Rogers' ideas and lobbying activities which found fertile soil in a region that already had a strong technological and industrial base.

The confluence of academic streams

By the mid-nineteenth century, the two organizational formats of a research institute and a teaching college were amalgamated, first in agriculture and then in other industrial spheres. The combination of research and teaching focused on practical outcomes but was also tied to fundamental investigation. Dual functions, carried out in a single academic institution, were the basis for the agricultural innovation system that has grown up since the early nineteenth century. This model was then transmuted in some very interesting ways in its translation from agriculture to industry. Change has also occurred through synthesis with another model of higher learning, the research university that was created as an independent and even opposing format to the land grant system.

The development of the Massachusetts Institute of Technology can be seen as an interplay between the academic model produced by the international polytechnic movement and US collegiate and university formats, including the "land grant" and research university formats. Teaching colleges based upon the traditional unitary classical curriculum, such as Harvard and Columbia, expanded into general purpose universities with graduate schools in the arts and sciences and separate technical schools. New universities such as Johns Hopkins and the University of Chicago, founded to further newly defined notions of "pure" research, typically did not have technical departments. The "land grant" universities, so-called after the federal law of 1862 that provided federal lands to each state to sell in support of universities, were designed to further the agricultural and mechanical arts. The US polytechnic movement, of which MIT was a part, was influenced by the creation of a distinctive, autonomous set of technical universities in France and Germany, among other European countries.

Each of these academic models has its special purpose. For example, the teaching college trained its students in a common body of classical knowledge, qualifying its graduates for the learned professions. Harvard College, MIT's Cambridge neighbor founded in 1636, exemplifies the classical teaching college in its origins. The second stream is the so-called "land grant" university, which trained its students in agricultural science and related mechanical arts, the nations' major industry until the late nineteenth century. The land grant schools typically had experiment stations and conducted research aimed at improving the productivity of local agriculture. The third stream is the polytechnic institute, a European import, focused on training students in the engineering professions that arose in tandem with the industrial revolution. The fourth stream is the research university, based on an ideal of investigation as an end in itself, first in the humanities and then in the sciences. These various academic streams were never entirely separate. Many research universities were built upon the foundations of classical colleges and some polytechnics were affiliated with classical colleges or research universities, and are to this day. Indeed, MIT was once offered such a status as an affiliate of Harvard, but rejected it.

The origins of the land grant system

This concept for the economically involved, industrially related university was based on a model that originated in agriculture. The first agricultural experiment station was founded in the state of Connecticut in 1816, with considerable popular support. At that time agriculture was not only the leading US industry, but most people were involved in it. Among them were farmers who believed that science could be used to transform agriculture and who carried out experiments on individual test plots to improve their crops. Perhaps

THE FOUNDING OF MIT

the best known of these "scientific farmers" was President Jefferson who maintained test plots at his Monticello estate, where visitors today can examine his experimental records. Scientific farmers very soon realized that they could not produce good science individually. Research had to be done collectively and it had to be done by professionals. Therefore, the scientific farmers lobbied government to establish institutions to conduct agricultural research on their behalf. And it was done. The Connecticut experiment was eventually replicated in every state.

It was very soon realized that setting up a research institute by itself, an experiment station, was only a partial solution. It was not very efficient to do research in an isolated setting when the objective was to put that research into practice. A further innovation, in order to transmit that research, was to combine the experiment station with a college to train farmers' children. Schooled in scientific agriculture, the next generation completed the forward loop between experimentation and utilization when they returned to carry on the farm. Combining a research institute with a teaching college also completed the reverse loop between problem generation and research as a new generation of technically knowledgeable farmers was better able to pose problems to researchers.

The final link in the agricultural innovation system was the the county agent, who served as an intermediary mechanism for technology and knowledge transfer between sophisticated users and researchers. Farmers and researchers interacted directly at times, but were mainly in touch through these agents, who moved back and forth between the farms and the academic research sites. County agents also brought their own expertise to the table. They synthesized the experience of the large numbers of farmers with whom they interacted, making it available to farmers, researchers and fellow professionals.

Even before scientific research emerged as a general university practice, special universities were founded to conduct research and training in agriculture, the major US industry in the early nineteenth century. Based upon a vision of "scientific agriculture," schools such as the University of Connecticut used the results of research to improve agricultural practice. In the mid-nineteenth century this model was extended nationally. The Hatch Act of 1867 and the Smith Lever Act of 1918 built up on the Morill Act foundation, providing block research funds and then technology transfer and liason capabilities.

The land grant universities helped make US agriculture the world leader. The agricultural experiment stations at the universities, jointly funded by the federal and state governments, assisted farmers with new technology and advice. The experimental stations also supported fundamental research. For example, the genetics research of George Beadle and others in the 1930s led to hybrid corn, vastly increasing agricultural production.[5] The land grant movement invented a university that was committed to the economic and social development of its region. It created a university that took local needs and circumstances into account in developing its research and training programs.

THE FOUNDING OF MIT

The land grant academic model inspired a significant element of the development of MIT as a school committed to regional development, of the Boston area in the mid-nineteenth century and New England in the mid-twentieth century.

The rise of the polytechnic movement

In addition to the unique American "land grant" movement, a European import, the polytechnic institute, provided another building block for MIT's development. Proponents of the polytechnic ideal set forth an integrated conception of the relation of science to practice. In their view science and technology were interrelated and mutually supportive activities with a common purpose – rationalization of the production processes of existing industries and the creation of new industries from scientific discoveries. In a division of labor between scientists and engineers the task of scientists was to develop new and potentially useful physical laws and to assist engineers in using existing physical laws to systematize the conduct of industrial activities. The task of engineers was to reorganize craft practices into systematic bodies of knowledge, using relevant science.

The polytechnicians believed that a new class of academic institutions was required to realize this goal. The engineering disciplines were to be the heart of such institutions with the basic sciences playing a supporting role. The traditional liberal arts were tolerated insofar as an acquaintance with them supported the claim to gentlemanly status of the new scientifically trained engineers and gave them a common basis of culture with their managerial superiors who, if college-trained, were typically educated in the traditional liberal arts.

MIT emphasized connections to industry rather than agriculture in contrast to the typical land grant school. Perhaps the closest analogue is Georgia Tech, founded as part of the "New South" movement after the Civil War to renovate an agricultural, plantation-based economy along technological and industrial lines. Similar attempts to establish a polytechnic university took place in other industrial regions but none were on the scale of the Institute plan. For example, a parallel Philadelphia initiative was underway under the leadership of Charles E. Smith, President of the Philadelphia and Reading Railroad. In much the same way as MIT's founder William Barton Rogers, he perceived the need for a new type of scientifically trained professional in industry and in 1852 devised a plan for a technical school to be attached to the University of Pennsylvania.

The support of the local elite of a city with a growing industrial base was sought to support the introduction of a new model of higher education in which science would be used to systematize industrial processes and universities would be utilized to train "a new technical, managerial class."[6] At the time the need to train an ancillary class of technologists could be made only partially compatible with the leading colleges whose purpose was to prepare a governing elite.

There were deep status differences between classical education and the new technical subjects. When technical courses were instituted at the universities which grew out of the old classical colleges they were typically accorded inferior status and awarded lower prestige degrees. Thus, the Sheffield Scientific School at Yale and a similar department at Harvard, the Lowell Scientific School, were ancillary and isolated foundations.[7] The difficulty of gaining entrance for technical subjects into the older colleges and the desire of proponents of technical education for equality with classical liberal education led to the attempt to found new institutions. The marginalization of technical education at traditional colleges provided another impetus for creating an institution of higher education committed to technology as its main purpose. The tension between the liberal arts and technology was sufficiently strong that MIT later rejected a merger with Harvard, even though it was in an extremely difficult financial position.

The evolution of the classical college into the research university

The split of academia into "pure" and "practical" strains formerly divided higher education. In striking contrast to an earlier era, when MIT and its sister schools struggled to gain legitimacy for their educational model, universities that originated from other premises now model themselves on MIT. For example, the British government recently committed many millions of pounds to support a collaboration between Cambridge University and MIT, a relationship clearly intended to infuse the older foundation with the relative new-comer's luster. Despite Cambridge being the site of considerable high-tech firm formation activity in recent decades, the government's concern was that this was simply a side effect of the concentration of quality research and an attractive cultural and living environment, three very important impetuses to high-tech regional growth. However, the expectation was that the introduction of more formal measures could provide an additional increment of economic development. The introduction of practical topics into the curriculum also began in earnest during the early nineteenth century at colleges founded for other purposes, most notably the reproduction of a religious leadership. The eighteenth-century teaching college was based on a closed corpus of classical knowledge that could be transmitted by a relatively few teachers, each of whom was usually responsible for covering more than one discipline. This simple format made it possible for hundreds of colleges to be founded in dispersed settings as the frontier moved westwards. A multiplicity of colleges was also encouraged by divisions among Protestant religious denominations each of whom insisted on having their own local institution of higher education. Their objective was to insure doctrinal purity in the teaching of religion, a mainstay not only of the curriculum but also of daily college life through compulsory chapel attendance.

New, more practical topics were gradually and imperceptibly inserted into the curriculum in the form of a course in geology or chemistry offered by an individual faculty member. Change also occurred directly through outspoken leadership of the founder or president of a new university, espousing different ideas of what should be taught. These academic entrepreneurs often wished to legitimize new subjects through their new foundations as well as distinguish their universities from the traditional format. Thus, agricultural coursework was begun at rural Cornell and urban themes, such as commercial studies, were introduced at New York University. New England, home to the first agricultural experiment station in the USA, was also the location of the Massachusetts Institute of Technology (MIT). The region was also home to teaching colleges such as Harvard and Yale that soon experienced the first "academic revolution" through the introduction of research. The academic revolution occurred most intensively, however, in new institutions founded primarily for this purpose, such as the University of Chicago, Clark University and Johns Hopkins.

The research university

The basic or "pure" research model was propounded most notably by Henry Rowland, a physicist at Johns Hopkins University, in his Presidential address to the American Association for the Advancement of Science (AAAS) in the late nineteenth century. Rowland proposed a model of starting from curiosity-driven science, going to applied research, and eventually to long-term benefits. This became accepted as the institutional ideology of the major universities that were being founded in the late nineteenth century by the holders of great industrial fortunes. In some ways that ideology was a useful fiction, a way to protect those universities from expected and feared intervention from their funders.

With rare exceptions, mostly concerning political issues related to the social sciences, intervention in academic research programs did not occur. Most actions were in the form of pre-emptive strikes within an academic institution. For example, William Rainey Harper, President of the University of Chicago, failed to reappoint an outspoken faculty member, economist Richard Ely. Harper wished to forestall opposition and raise funds for his new university from the Chicago business community, which was averse to Ely's critique of capitalism. John D. Rockefeller, the university's major funder, kept a low profile, rarely even visiting the university. Indeed, he refused offers to have the university named after himself, though he allowed this with other organizations, such as the Rockefeller Medical Institute, that he helped found.[8]

Perhaps one reason for the lack of interference was the unfavorable reaction that it would have brought from the press at the time. Had this occurred, much of the goodwill obtained from a public with ambivalent feelings toward industrialists who had otherwise been called "malefactors of great wealth" might have been lost. If the founders had not been able to resist placing their personal stamp on the schools to which they had given their fortunes, and often their

THE FOUNDING OF MIT

names, there would likely have been an intense backlash. The concept of academic autonomy was engrained, not only in the beliefs of faculty members, but in public opinion, as well.

The development of research at MIT

The transformation of the Massachusetts Institute of Technology into a research university paralleled the development of research laboratories in the industrial corporations that it supplied with engineering graduates. Indeed, Institute professors such as Willis Whitney helped found such laboratories. From the winter of 1900, Whitney divided his time for several years between General Electric and the Massachusetts Institute of Technology. He commuted by train between the two sites, spending four days in Boston and three in Schenectady, before leaving the university and joining the company full time. Whitney drew upon his university connections to staff the new lab which, in succeeding years, became a model for other US technology-based companies to start their own corporate laboratories.[9]

But how was academic research to be supported? A report issued by the Smithsonian Institution argued the case for academic science: "Pure scientific research unlike industrial scientific research, cannot support itself by direct pecuniary returns from its discoveries."[10] But from where, then, would the money come to support professors' research efforts? One idea was for the schools to pay for it themselves, drawing upon tuition income and endowment funds to support research laboratories. Another was for professors to turn over part of their consulting income from industrial firms to support more basic investigations at the university. In this fashion, research efforts jointly supported by the Massachusetts Institute of Technology and its own faculty members began to emerge in chemistry in the early twentieth century. On the one hand there was an impetus to basic research among several alumni, such as A.A. Noyes, who had returned from graduate work in Germany to join the faculty.

In 1901, chemistry professor Alfred Noyes proposed that the Massachusetts Institute of Technology establish a chemical research laboratory jointly supported by the school and himself through $5,000 a year that he offered to pay from his consulting income. The request was turned down but in 1902 Noyes successfully asked the Carnegie Institute of Washington for $5,900 to support his work on the physical chemistry of solutions. When he next approached his school, this time together with fellow chemistry professor, Willis Whitney, the proposal was accepted. Both agreed to donate some of their consulting income if the school's executive committee would also contribute to support a laboratory for physical chemistry.[11]

In 1903 the Research Laboratory of Physical Chemistry, oriented toward pure research, was founded under his leadership. A few years later, W.H. Walker, who had taught at MIT since 1894, organized The Research Laboratory of Applied Chemistry, focused upon industrially relevant research. William

29

THE FOUNDING OF MIT

Walker was a principal of the Arthur D. Little Inc. consulting firm from 1900 to 1905. During those years, he divided his time between MIT and the company. He returned to MIT full time, becoming Director of the Laboratory of Applied Chemistry in 1908. Walker is the prototype of the contemporary entrepreneurial scientist who moves back and forth between the academic and business worlds.

The two laboratories represented different visions for the future of the Institute, either as a science-based university with a graduate school oriented toward basic research or a school of engineering and technology devoted to preparing undergraduates for work in industry. In the longer term, the development of the Massachusetts Institute of Technology encompassed both alternatives. However, at the time, the two were in conflict and chemical engineering was attracting majors at the expense of chemistry.[12] Walker ensured the continued predominance of applied work by winning a battle over the future direction of MIT against Alfred Noyes, who wished to steer the school in the direction of pure research.

Academic administrators, from the president to the head of the chemistry department, attempted to reconcile the two approaches but were unsuccessful. After World War I, Walker, the director of the applied laboratory, using a threat of resignation, forced the president of the Institute to choose between them. Noyes, the director of the theoretical laboratory, was placed in an untenable position and resigned. He went to California where he played a leading role in reorganizing the Throop Manual Training School into the California Institute of Technology according to his ideas of emphasizing fundamental research. With the departure of Noyes, the Massachusetts Institute of Technology affirmed its founding mission of concentrating on technology and developing relationships with industry.

The dispute between Walker and Noyes exemplified the conflicts between proponents of alternative research visions that appeared in state- and federally sponsored research efforts during the nineteenth century. Typically a scientist with an inclination toward broad ranging systematic investigation would be hired by government authorities interested in quick practical results. The research produced by the agency would be deemed too abstruse and, as in the case of Josiah Whitney, head of the California State Geological Survey, support would be reduced and the agency subsequently closed, with the scientist retreating to an academic position, in Whitney's case, a Harvard professorship. At MIT, despite an early commitment, close ties to industry were slow to develop. In the next chapter, we turn to the emergence of industrial ties in the late nineteenth century as part of MIT's strategy to develop its research strengths by bringing in to its faculty practicing consulting engineers to complement its primarily teaching faculty.

3

CONTROVERSY OVER CONSULTATION

The groundwork for US professors assuming multiple roles as teacher, researcher and entrepreneur was laid in the resolution of the controversy over consulting at MIT in the late nineteenth and early twentieth centuries. The rules adopted at MIT to resolve the particular controversy became a model for other universities and spread throughout US academia in the following decades. The controversy over consultation had broader implications for the definition of the professorial role. It is now taken for granted in the university that professors should do research as well as teach. However, when research was introduced in the mid- and late nineteenth century in the USA it was often controversial. There were charges of conflicts of interest. If a professor was going to do research would that not mean that they would be taking time away from their students? Therefore those professors who believed that teaching was the only appropriate role of the professor argued that research should not be allowed as a professorial role. Today, such a position would be seen as heresy, but at that time it was a matter of pointed debate.

This chapter focuses on the origins of the one-fifth or one-day-a-week rule legitimizing professors' consultation with firms. One indicator of the taken-for-granted nature of the one-fifth rule governing consulting is that its origins have largely been forgotten, even at MIT, where the rule was invented early in the twentieth century. Two groups of faculty members, with different ideas about higher education, came into conflict over whether it was appropriate to work for industry. Faculty who had known MIT as a small teaching college in the late nineteenth century opposed their new colleagues who were hired by the university to develop research, from careers as consulting engineers, around the turn of the century. The former group of professors believed that the academic enterprise should be internally focused on students and teaching, while the latter group argued that an external focus on assisting industry was appropriate as well.

The significance of controversy

The development of a controversy is often a necessary prelude to negotiating a compromise, with each side having its essential interests taken into account.

CONTROVERSY OVER CONSULTATION

Controversy thus plays a crucial role in the game of legitimation, the process of gaining acceptance for new practices. Such a resolution is most likely to occur when a dispute is brought into an arena where each side can engage the other and consider its opponents point of view as well as what is essential to its own position. The creation of a "consensus space" brings opposing views into clear focus, and opponents into dialogue, even if heated, and then perhaps negotiation and compromise. This process contrasts sharply to disputations in which opponents broadcast their views from a distance, reinforcing their own positions, without the opportunity to take opposing views into account.

A controversy is an indicator that significant positive social change may be underway as well as a sign that an old order is breaking down. The life histories of controversies are also revelatory of institutional dynamics as proponents and opponents in an agonistic struggle make their best logical and emotional case for support. Raising an issue to an explicit level through the expression of strong differences can initiate discussion and negotiation, leading to the establishment of a new norm. Controversy over the intersection of institutional spheres, such as university and industry, can also be a signal of a shift in the balance of power between and relative importance of the two spheres. On the one hand, when no way can be found to regulate a potentially controversial activity, its future may be impeded. On the other hand, the achievement of a resolution can provide the guidelines for a new institutional regime.

The resolution of a controversy may allow an otherwise divisive practice to become accepted. For example, during the 1970s a controversy arose in Cambridge, Massachusetts over the potential dangers of allowing biotechnology firms to locate themselves in the city. The resolution of a debate that played itself out in the City Council set strict safety standards for biotechnology research. In succeeding years, the existence of these standards made Cambridge an attractive place to locate such firms, in addition to its pool of academic research resources in the field.

Paradoxically, the existence of tough rules made Cambridge a preferred location because companies could count on a secure regulatory environment. On the other hand, when controversy is short circuited, the resulting reaction can be explosive, placing the entire activity at risk. The Monsanto corporation learned this lesson when its tactics of suppressing debate over genetically modified foods inthe USA backfired, creating a larger negative response than would likely have occurred if it had engaged its opponents directly. The firm has since changed course and invites discussion.

The MIT experience

Similar to the experience of other colleges, the introduction of research at MIT created conflicts with the original mission of teaching. However, the industrial context of MIT created special conflicts, whose pattern of resolution eventually led to the creation of a new academic format. MIT's path to the development of both extensive research capabilities and strong relations with industry emerged through an unexpected indirect route: implementation of a plan to strengthen its educational programs. At the turn of the century many of MIT's faculty were its own graduates. To avoid becoming ingrown and to build up its engineering departments MIT hired as faculty several leading engineers from industry to develop the school's research capabilities.

The consulting-engineer professors' previous everyday work activities had been research-based. When they became professors at MIT it was explicitly arranged that they be allowed to operate off campus consulting firms. For example, Dr Louis Duncan, formerly chief of the Third Avenue transit lines in New York City and organizer of the engineering firm of Sprague, Duncan and Hutchinson, was brought in to chair the Electrical Engineering department. He maintained a considerable consulting practice while at MIT and returned to full time consulting after leaving the Institute in 1904. His successor, Dugald Jackson, long-time chair of the Electrical Engineering department, also maintained an extensive consulting practice.[1]

These industrially oriented engineers continued to pursue aspects of their previous careers in tandem with their new task of teaching. This caused a conflict with the traditional professors who were at MIT exclusively as teachers. They criticized their new colleagues for going out of the university and consulting, taking time away from their students. The consulting engineers argued that through their consulting activities they brought back from the field to the classroom knowledge that enhanced their teaching. They believed that their courses would be enlivened by real-life examples. Rather than upholding a right to interact with industry, the consulting professors attempted to legitimate their consulting practices on the very principle on which they were being taken to task, their commitment to teaching.

The controversy brought into broad relief an emerging dimension of academia: its relationship with industry. Although this theme was a central part of the foundation of MIT, it had only been realized in a very partial and traditional manner, through the provision of trained graduates to industry. Consultation, on the other hand, involves the professor in a more direct relationship with industry, rather than taking place at one remove through students. Consultation includes individual advice, research projects or tests in exchange for payment of a fee to the provider of the service rather than to the university.

Academic consultation

Consultation is the traditional mechanism for academic–industry relations. It has been suggested that "the first step in diagnosing the health of a university–industry interface should always be a survey of consultancy arrangements" since they are a foundation on which other forms of university–industry relations can be based. Consultancy can be organized in different ways, either to maintain a barrier between institutional spheres such as academia and industry, while transferring information between them, or to create a close relationship of mutual influence. Consultancy is a private version of the public format of knowledge transfer through publication.[2]

It is an inexpensive, rapid means of transferring information effectively. It provides a two-way communication channel and is often the precursor to more intensive relationships.

Consultation divides the professorial status into an academic and a business role. As academic, the professor is committed to the development of knowledge that is freely available to all in open publications, as consultant the professor is a business person selling knowledge to a buyer who has the right to keep it secret. In practice, academic consultation involves striking a balance between these two principles. Consultation can involve use of university facilities and application of academic expertise to company problems. Through visits to enterprises and discussions with industrial researchers, professors provide an independent perspective to assist the development of company research programs. It has been suggested that "The expansion and improvement of consultancy links should be regarded as the necessary first step in the process of stimulating direct university–industry links."[3] These links pre-date the MIT experience, which represents a revival and reintegration of the practice into academia, from which it had been largely excluded as a result of the emergence of an ideal of pure research.

The origins of academic consulting

Adumbration of academic-industry relations can be identified in the mid-nineteenth century and even earlier, for example, consultation by the Sillimans (father and son) in chemistry at Yale, and firm formation by Justus Liebig, the renowned Professor of Chemistry at Giessen University in Germany. However, these remained isolated instances that did not become accepted practices locally or models for universities elsewhere. Academic consulting became commonplace early in the nineteenth century, making expertise available to government, industry and farmers. Soil testing for farmers was the first widespread consultation activity, followed by the evaluation of mineral deposits for prospective investors. Government also used consulting for an independent evaluation of the viability of potential economic activities such as a sugar-refining industry and companies for the identification of sources of technical flaws, such as the cause of a steam explosion.[4]

From the mid- to late nineteenth century, at Yale, the Sillimans, father and son, and at Columbia, Charles Frederick Chandler, maintained extensive consulting practices. Silliman senior took pride in his first paid consultantship as demonstrating evidence of his high level of professional accomplishment and did not view it merely as a pecuniary advantage of his professorship. As chemists with a knowledge of geology, the Sillimans were much in demand to test mineral deposits and assess their worth to prospective investors. On occasion they received a financial interest in companies in exchange for their assistance. Public lecture tours took them around the country and served to introduce them to new opportunities for consultation.

However, Chandler's younger colleagues at Columbia, influenced by the emerging basic research academic model, viewed his extensive consulting activities negatively. They drew back from such extensive involvement with practical matters in their own academic careers. Even Henry Rowland, the leading proponent of pure research, had engaged in consultation earlier in his career. Nevertheless, as the basic research ideal grew stronger, a new generation of academic scientists focused almost exclusively on disciplinary concerns. Growing expectations of strong boundaries between the university and industry affected even universities such as MIT, premised on close collaboration with industry.

The consulting professors at MIT

The MIT administration held an ambivalent attitude toward consultation. On the one hand it was proud of the services its faculty rendered to industry and used them as an argument against industrialists, in order to raise endowment funds. On the other hand, during the 1920s, a perception arose that outside work was interfering with the faculty's campus responsibilities. Those who viewed teaching as the major function of the faculty tended to support restrictions on consulting. They were worried that consultation drew faculty away from MIT and that Institute resources were being inappropriately used for private purposes.

The chair of the chemistry department, F.G. Keyes, exemplified the traditional internalist academic perspective. Keyes thought that:

> Much of the abuse, if such a word is appropriate, that has arisen in connection with outside work has its origin in the widely held belief among the staff that the work was the affair of the individual exclusively. The time seems ripe to modify this thesis for the Institute is an educational institution and its product scientifically educated engineers. To accomplish its objective MIT must have the entire time and attention of the best talent procurable.[5]

The administration responded to these concerns by looking into the prevalence and effects of faculty consulting activities. A report commissioned from a department chair critic reported that there were three classes of professors in the chemistry department: faculty who did not engage in outside work and were willing to subsist within their salaries; faculty who were also deeply interested in their Institute work but who felt the financial need to seek outside work; and, finally, faculty, "who balance their scientific and teaching interests against their desire for extra funds for a life on a more generous scale."[6] The latter two groups engaged in three types of consultation: advice without use of MIT facilities or absence from the Institute; research at the client's site; and research at the Institute involving the use of its equipment, facilities and space. It was not unusual for a faculty member to hire an assistant in his department's lab to carry out work for firms. Although some faculty kept accounts and regularly made payments for their use of Institute facilities and equipment in their consulting practices a perception arose that Institute resources were sometimes being misused.

These critics felt strongly that some regulation of consulting was necessary. Although they found fault with the practice they did not propose to abolish consulting. It was believed that many faculty consulted merely out of the necessity to supplement inadequate academic incomes. The report proposed to reduce, if not eliminate, consultation by lessening the financial need for faculty to seek outside work. On the one hand, the author believed that if salaries were raised the practice would decline. On the other hand he proposed to "tax" the income from consultation in those cases where a professor was either called off campus or was using Institute facilities. It was also proposed to institute charges for use of laboratory space, especially when assistants were employed.

The effect of the depression

The depression of the 1930s brought an underlying tension between academic and professional consulting engineers to the surface. The independent consulting engineers denounced university professors' consultation with industry as unfair competition, arguing that universities, in effect, subsidized their faculty members' consulting practices. The independent consulting engineers charged that professors worked out of laboratories provided by their university and did not have to pay to maintain a laboratory or reimburse the university for its private use, and inquired whether this business was carried out in the name of the university.[7] An MIT representative responded that there was little or no solicitation except when the work was pioneering in nature and that most routine requests were passed on to commercial laboratories. However, some routine work was undertaken when the university was asked to act as a referee on commercial tests.[8]

Nevertheless, the distinction between academic and professional consultant was not clear cut. The A.D. Little Company, a consulting firm that had originated from MIT in 1886, exemplified the ambivalent relationship of the independent consulting firm to its academic collaborator and competitor. The firm was located adjacent to MIT and drew upon its faculty members, many of whom, over the years, augmented their modest academic salaries by moonlighting as consultants for the company. A few received annual retainers from

CONTROVERSY OVER CONSULTATION

A.D. Little merely for agreeing not to consult for a competing firm. Often, in reciprocity, they encouraged their most gifted students to consider employment with the A.D. Little Company after graduation.[9]

There was a close, even symbiotic but nevertheless ambivalent relationship between the university and the firm. On the one hand, the Little firm regarded connections to MIT as an asset, frequently subcontracting to its professors. Thus, "It might almost seem that instead of the Institute's being a competitor of the A.D. Little Company, the proximity of the Institute was one of its greatest assets."[10] On the other hand, MIT's consulting faculty members sometimes provided unwanted competition, offering some of the same services at lower rates. The special expertise of the faculty made them in demand both by the consulting firms, for whom they acted as an intermediary between university and industry, and by industry, for whom they acted directly in contracting for the advisory services of the professorate.

Resolution of the controversy over consulting

Since the consulting engineers were among the most prestigious professors at MIT, and their activities put into practice service to industry, a founding theme of the Institute, it is not surprising that that they became the models for younger professors in succeeding years. Among their successors was a young faculty member in electrical engineering, Vannevar Bush.

During the 1920s Bush worked part-time in the R&D labs of local companies as a consultant. He also passed along problems to his students to work on. As some of the theoretical implications of company problems fed back into academic research design on campus, Bush became a firm believer in the value of the consulting relationship as a source of new issues for academic research. Following his mentors, Bush also found an educational value in consultation: it brought teaching alive by making available, to its practitioners, exciting "real life" examples to insert in their lectures. On a more practical level, consultation allowed an academic, with a practical bent, to enhance a relatively modest salary.

Restrictions on consulting were eventually instituted in the early 1930s as part of a plan to raise salaries but there were insufficient funds to fully implement it. For a few years faculty paid the university an overhead charge for use of university space and equipment. This requirement was soon abandoned due to "administrative difficulties"[11] and faculty members' objections to interference in their affairs. MIT faculty were to be left to their own discretion on using MIT resources subject to the guidance of their departmental chair. Such activities as providing advice, testing materials in university laboratories and solving problems at company sites had become so much a part of the work of academic engineering professors that it proved impossible to disentangle them from the academic role. Prominent professors felt that their connection to the industrial world through consultation was essential to their research and teaching.

CONTROVERSY OVER CONSULTATION

The academic decision-making process

Despite autocratic presidents in an earlier era and the more recent growth of academic bureaucracy, the tradition of professorial governance survives even as universities become more complex organizations. It plays an important role in academic decision making in institutions where the faculty, correctly or incorrectly, perceives itself as the center of power. The tradition of academic self-governance also forces administrators in lesser academic institutions, where academics often see themselves as being under the thumb of the administration, to take faculty views more seriously than they might otherwise have.

Academic committees, representing different points of view, play an important role in arriving at an organizational consensus. This is the case even when their decisions are not final and their advice is sometimes overruled. Committee process provides a medium for integrating different views, taking opposition concerns into account in the decision to go forward in one direction rather than another. Committees that are given a charge to formulate a course of action become the basis for legitimating a decision to the entire campus.

The committee established to resolve the controversy over consultation at MIT met on and off for approximately twenty years. By the time the committee came to a conclusion, the students of those consulting engineers, such as Vannevar Bush, were then in positions of power at MIT. Several influential teachers, including Vannevar Bush, successfully fought a rule charging for use of university space and equipment for consultation on the grounds that they were entitled to it as a part of their academic appointment. Bush had no intention of keeping a rule which he felt was contrary to the development of collaborative research with industry. After decades of debate, channeled into a committee representing both sides, a regulation was devised that accepted consultation, within limits.

Consultation was not fully accepted as a legitimate activity at MIT until the early 1930s when the committee invented what has come to be known as the one-fifth rule, that is, one day a week a professor might consult and earn what he or she could through involvement in industry, no questions asked. For the rest of the working week, their obligation was to the university. The resolution was in between what the traditional professors wanted and what the consulting engineers wished. It took several decades, however, to achieve this balance. Despite concerns about unfair competition which came to a head during the depression, and opposition to any activities which took professors away from their students, consultation with industry became an entrenched practice at MIT. Although consulting was officially limited to one day per week it was never entirely clear if this requirement should be interpreted as one day out of five or could be expanded to three out of seven. The professor who worked part time for industry and could find work for his students while they pursued their studies became the model MIT academic.

Controversies as precursors of change

The "one-fifth rule" that was invented as a compromise to resolve the dispute over consultation at MIT has become so much a taken-for-granted aspect of US academia that its origins have largely been forgotten. It has been accepted as normative at virtually every university in this country. The existence of this rule legitimated a parallel activity that could otherwise have been defined as a conflict of interest. The one-fifth rule ensured that the university–industry relations could proceed in a relatively uncontroversial way on this issue of consulting because a well-defined stringent limiting rule was in place.

It is recognized virtually everywhere in the world that there is potentially useful knowledge in the universities that could assist industry. However, in countries where academic consulting is not regulated, in places which have not had this controversy, and which have not had this issue debated, discussed and resolved, there is often confusion about what is appropriate behavior. In Portugal, for example, there is great interest among many policy makers and academic administrators in having professors become more closely involved with industry. The government says professors should go out of the university and become active in dealing with industry. However, Portuguese academics are not sure if this is something they really should do because a rule of how it should be arranged and organized has not been settled upon. Therefore, even though they are told to do it, professors are concerned that if they become involved with firms, it might be viewed negatively. They are constrained from action because there is no accepted pattern of conduct.

Although it may seem counter-intuitive, a controversy is very important to the eventual legitimization of a contested practice. Usually in the academic world, an issue becomes raised as a conflict of interest issue. A conflict of interest is an indicator that change is about to take place. There are, of course, different possible resolutions of a conflict of interest. The activity can be defined as deviant and not allowed to take place any more. Or the new activity can become the only thing that is done. What has happened in the academic world, however, is that each time there has been this conflict over the role of the university, the university has tended to take on this new role. The new role exists in coordination and in continued low-level conflict with the old role. There is still a conflict between research and teaching in the university, and over the exact weight that should be placed on each. Nevertheless, it has been found more productive to have these two activities, research and teaching, take place together.

Predictably, it will also be found more productive to have the new economic role of the university take place within the university in relation to research and teaching, without moving technology transfer outside. The overall thesis is that the university is becoming a much more important institution in society, not a less important one. It is becoming an institution on a par with industry and government, not something off to the side that we respect because it has some intelligent people seeking after knowledge and training students, but more importantly, because as we become a knowledge-based society, the institution which has the ability to create and transfer that knowledge, and form it into new firms, becomes the most important institution. That is the second academic revolution, which began early in the twentieth century and is ongoing. The founding idea of MIT in the middle of the nineteenth century was to create a university which would infuse industry, not only with new technology, but also with ideas from basic research. It was not the founding of an engineering school, but rather the founding of a much broader idea which took many decades to realize.

By incorporating consultation practices into the faculty role, industrial relations became a part of the educational program of the Massachusetts Institute of Technology and the basis of its strategy for faculty development. The Institute had developed many of its strongest academic programs through its close ties with industry, including the "unit production" model in chemical engineering and the placement of students in industry for a semester in their junior year. The teachers in the electrical engineering department who had been recruited from industry, maintaining their consulting practices and industrial connections while developing their academic careers, became the model for future generations of professors.

University–industry relations

In the early twentieth century, controversies over the introduction of research, consultation and patenting would define MIT as a special type of academic institution, the entrepreneurial university. An entrepreneur, whether individual or organizational, takes new roles and develops new relationships, often transforming traditional practices during the process. Consultation became transmuted into the first step toward firm formation when it was introduced into the academic system.

Controversies over the appropriate role of the university in relation to industry, and the compromises negotiated to resolve these disputes, defined practices that could be accepted by both proponents and opponents of technology transfer. The resolution of a series of such conflicts at MIT, in the early twentieth century, first over consulting and then over the patenting of research and firm formation, created a regulatory framework for university–industry relations. Although the limits of academic involvement in technology transfer are still an issue and new conflicts periodically reappear, the issue of whether or not academia should interact with industry was resolved in these early disputes. This premise is widely accepted even by critics who typically question the manner and extent of academic involvement with industry but not the legitimacy of the practice itself.

Two distinct modes of university–industry relations can be identified: informal and formal. The informal typically occurs through contacts between professors and their former students and may lead to consulting and joint research projects with a company, typically one with a well established R&D laboratory. These informal relations are more prevalent in Europe and Japan where formal mechanisms have only recently been established. Informal relations may be viewed as an underground economy that takes place "submersso," in Italian parlance, and they are not counted or identified typically as part of the official academic work process.

In contrast to the tunnels are the bridges, the formal structures (liaison and technology transfer offices) through which formal introductions are made in seminars for potential industrial partners, disclosure statements of inventions are collected, patents licensed and contracts negotiated. These outcomes are enumerated, with perhaps the most important difference being that the financial results are typically shared with the university. Either mode, formal or informal, can precede the other; there is no necessary order. Nevertheless, the fullest regime of academic–industry relations is one in which both modes are present, the bridges (the formal organizations) and the tunnels (the informal ties through which social and intellectual capital moves from graduating students into firms and back again into the university).

Government–university relations and university–industry relations are modeled on each other. University–government relations inthe USA were built on the base of the formal mode of university–industry relations. It was MIT's office, established in the 1920s to formalize its faculty members' informal ties to industry and channel them through an administrative structure that could collect negotiated payments, that was called upon to deal with government contracts during World War II, and it became the model for other university offices for grants and contracts during the post-war era. This mechanism was then turned back into dealing with university–industry relations when that topic became salient again. This story, beginning with the establishment of MIT's office in the 1920s, is the topic of the next chapter.

4

THE TRAFFIC AMONG MIT, INDUSTRY AND THE MILITARY

University–industry relations, developed early in the twentieth century, provided a format for the establishment of government–university relations during World War II. During the war, the federal government negotiated a format for supporting research at MIT that became a model for wartime contracts with other universities. Individual research projects rather than broad-scale institutional funding, as in the agricultural research model, became the format for post-war federal funding of academic R&D. MIT used an industrial contract format left behind from a post-World War I effort to formalize its relations with industry to interact with government in wartime.

Apart from agriculture, where a government–university R&D system focused on entire schools and broad research programs had been put in place by the "land grant" system during the nineteenth century, there was little federal funding of university research before World War II. During the depths of the depression, most academic scientists had rejected MIT President Karl Compton's proposals for such support, viewing it as illegitimate. In a manner redolent of apprehensions currently expressed about corporate support, universities feared that government funding would inevitably be accompanied by control over research. When leading academic scientists, such as Compton of MIT and President Conant of Harvard, took the lead in convincing the federal government to support advanced R&D to meet wartime needs, the traditionally distant government–university relationship was transformed.

During World War II MIT transformed itself into an R&D laboratory for radar and other militarily useful devices, performing more military R&D than any other US university. Dissatisfied with the military's use of academic science during World War I, a group of leading scientists and engineers, including Compton and Bush from MIT, wanted to establish an agency, under the control of scientists, which would liaise with the military from an independent position. This framework for equality in relationships between academic science and the military drew upon a series of innovations that MIT had developed since its founding for interaction with industry. The current system originated in a scheme to resolve an internal financial crisis at MIT during the post-World War I era.

TRAFFIC AMONG MIT, INDUSTRY AND THE MILITARY

An industrial solution to MIT's financial crisis

Loss of state funding that had originated with the founding of MIT placed the school in dire financial straits. A Massachusetts constitutional convention announced that the state could only support institutions under state control. Despite arguments by MIT that it was closely connected to the state through receipt of its charter and a land grant, the subsidy was cut off. The financial crisis deepened when a Court dissolved an agreement with Harvard whereby the Institute trained Harvard students in engineering in exchange for income from a bequest to Harvard.

MIT decided to increase its links to industry to make up for the ending of state funding by putting its relationship to industry on a business footing, exchanging services for funds. A policy of direct cooperation with industry arose out of MIT's financial needs and the feeling that the war had demonstrated the value of applying science to industrial processes. Yet "while the gap between educational institutions and the industrial interests of the country cannot be said to have been completely bridged in all instances, it was materially narrowed."[1] Thrown into financial crisis, the Institute faced a choice between accepting an offer of a merger with Harvard, becoming that university's engineering school, or finding an alternative source of support.

The Polytechnic ideal had taken root at MIT. The strength of the wish to remain independent can be seen in the negative reaction of MIT faculty and alumni to various proposals from 1870 to 1920 by Harvard University to make the Institute into its engineering school. At one point a consortium of businessmen, including Andrew Carnegie, purchased the parcel of land adjacent to Soldiers Field where the Harvard Business School was later located, as an inducement for MIT to realign itself under the aegis of Harvard.

These efforts were resisted by MIT faculty and alumni who felt that Harvard's orientation to the traditional liberal arts would inevitably lead to giving engineering subjects a second class status. The strong belief that MIT had its own distinctive mission and purpose was expressed during one of these negotiations by a speaker at the 1904 alumni reunion, quoting Nehemiah, Engineer of Jerusalem, from the Bible: "I am doing a great work and will not come down."[2] This feeling of equality of purpose led to a fundraising effort to ensure MIT's independence.

To refinance itself MIT looked beyond the Boston financial community to its alumni, many of whom were by this time strategically located in high positions in national corporations such as Eastman Kodak and Dupont. The founder of Kodak, George Eastman, was so favorably impressed with the contribution of MIT alumni to his firm that he became an important (and for a time) anonymous donor to the Institute. Eastman provided half of the eight million that had been judged as necessary to put the Institute on a firm financial footing. Donations from alumni brought in an additional part of the required amount.

To complete the sum a scheme was organized to formalize MIT's largely informal relations with companies. Individual consulting arrangements with professors were to be replaced with contracts between the university and the

43

firm in which faculty consultation would be part of a larger package of assistance. The "plan" provided that participating industrial firms paid an annual fee which allowed them special privileges in using the results of the research done by teachers at the Institute. This aspect of the plan did not turn out to be very significant since teachers whose research was of interest to firms were already being retained as consultants. Some firms felt that they were being unfairly required to pay a fee to the Institute for the same knowledge that they had already contracted for with an individual teacher.

Companies that contracted with MIT were entitled to lists of undergraduates available for employment and conferences with staff on problems pertaining to the business of the company. Advice was to be given to companies on where technical help could be obtained and "if that can best be done at MIT a member of its staff shall undertake such services for a fee to be mutually agreed upon by both parties."[3] Although there were objections that "the plan called upon industrial corporations to pay for services that they had hitherto obtained gratuitously," it was soon found that "men who had refused to give as individuals saw to it that corporations in which they held responsible positions made substantial contributions."[4]

In addition to its practical elements, the Plan also came with a covering framework to establish a more coordinated relationship between university and industry, not only regularizing existing relationships but establishing a new common ground between the two institutional spheres. The Technology Plan was based upon the premise that improvements in the efficiency of American industry required importation of scientific methods from the university. The necessity for this scientification of business was demonstrated by the World War industrial experience that exposed the inefficiency of trial and error methods.

A triadic outline of research areas was formulated including what would now be called undirected basic research, mission-oriented research and product development R&D. A proponent of the Plan held that closer university–industry relations, including making the problems of industry the basic material of some university research, "does not mean that the search for knowledge will not continue to subtend a large arc of the activities of the Institute."[5] However, when there was a spectrum of possibilities in addressing a research problem, an industrially relevant case should be chosen.

Nevertheless, there were limits. Professors should "not be withdrawn into purely industrial work by reason of the greater financial reward offered by the great corporations or the acute pleasure which many red blooded men feel in being professionally connected with great technical developments."[6] Solving problems for industry would be balanced with independent scientific investigation, in part, by creating a middle ground of research in which both goals would be simultaneously carried out. However, it was often difficult to get companies to see the need for such strategic research and company payments did not carry enough overheads to finance many staff-initiated investigations.

Financial support for MIT from the Technology Plan declined steadily after an initial first year highpoint (see Table 1). The sharpest drop was between

TRAFFIC AMONG MIT, INDUSTRY AND THE MILITARY

Table 1   Technology plan receipts

Year	Amount (US$)
1919–20	424,090
1920–1	157,007
1921–2	138,616
1922–3	170,646
1923–4	136,426
1924–5	25,350
1925–6	38,312
1926–7	27,621

Source: Leroy Foster. 1984. "Sponsored Research at MIT," unpublished manuscript, MIT Archives, p. 86.

1923–4 and 1924–5. When the initial five year commitment made in 1919–1920 came up for renewal many companies dropped out. Thus, the depression of the 1930s cannot be viewed as the primary cause of MIT's loss of financial support from industry.[7] Support had already declined in part due to overselling of the plan. Apparently some companies had viewed their membership in the plan as a special contribution to MIT to meet the matching funds requirement of George Eastman's large gift.

Others were dissatisfied with the research services provided and thought they were being double-charged in being asked to pay for research over and above the retainer fee they had contributed upon joining the plan. The greatest satisfaction expressed with the Plan was for the assistance received in recruiting MIT graduates for corporate employment. By 1939, it was accepted that the Technology Plan was a failure.

Although the "plan" soon fell into disuse, one of its consequences was the office that had been established to negotiate contracts between the institute and private firms for the conduct of research. Although industrial firms did not use this office very much, it did make enough contracts during the 1930s to justify its existence. At the outset of World War II, it served to arrange the contracts which the Massachusetts Institute of Technology made for research to be performed for the federal government.

The volume of the activity undertaken on behalf of the government far exceeded the scale of the contracts it had previously made with private firms. What had begun at MIT as a way to deal with contracts with industry, was turned into an arrangement to deal with government. Other universities that were also doing research for the federal government soon formed similar offices to deal with the government. The closeness of these arrangements was in striking contrast to the relative distance between the universities and the military during World War I.

University–military relations: World War I

During World War I, the military directly utilized the educational capabilities of the universities, but not, to any great extent, the research capabilities. Thus, World War I had relatively little effect on MIT other than the use of its facilities as an officer training school. Although President MacLaurin had expected MIT to be called upon as an institution to conduct military research, a strategy of organizing research on campus was not adopted.

Instead the military continued its policy of conducting its research in-house at its own establishments. However, some professors were invited to join these laboratories for the emergency and, at some facilities newly established to deal with new military technological problems such as tracking enemy submarines, academic scientists were a major part of the research staff. These scientists worked under military control and in accordance with research guidelines established by the military.

Some scientists found these strictures to be confining and even counterproductive. For example, at the submarine research center in New London, the Navy told scientists that their detection devices must be designed so that they would work on steel-hulled boats. This requirement created a difficult design problem. Later, it was found that using more easily available wooden-hulled boats would be sufficient.

Meeting the initial requirement caused considerable delay in readying the detection technology for use. The scientists involved had no say in setting the criteria for operational use of the technology they were developing and thus no ability to design around possible limitations of the technology. Only military considerations were taken into account in setting the criteria and in this case not consulting with the scientists allowed an irrelevant criteria to be established that delayed the use of new submarine detection equipment.[8]

Transformation of the academic role in World War II

At the onset of World War II, leading academics including the President of Harvard, James Conant, and Vannevar Bush, former Vice President and Dean of Engineering at MIT and then Head of the Carnegie Institute of Washington, advocated a different course. They convinced the government that academic science could be used to develop technology for the military and successfully lobbied the executive branch of the federal government to found an agency to support research on military problems.

Scientists were low in the organizational scheme of things in World War I. Their lack of input into policy decisions made them determined not to repeat the same experience in the event of another war. To make the best use of science in wartime, they believed that scientists should have an input into research policy. Bush and Conant thought that this goal could best be accomplished by scientists controlling their own research organization.

Their goal was not to establish a government research institute but to use federal resources to support research at universities. Universities were not the obvious choice for locating such research. At the time, industrial research groups at major corporations had greater R&D capabilities. Academics had to be drawn together from campuses across the country to establish large-scale research centers at a relatively few universities: MIT, Johns Hopkins, Berkeley, Chicago and Columbia. This resulted in a research build-up at these universities in electronics, nuclear physics and other scientific and engineering areas relevant to solving military problems.

Although the armed forces were satisfied that they could meet their own requirements for technological innovation, the government intervened to improve the technical base of military research by connecting it to the universities. The Office of Scientific Research and Development (OSRD) was placed under the direction of academics rather than government officials or industrialists.

Large-scale laboratories that could be turned most quickly to military use were mostly within industry. But industrial scientists and engineers had not taken the lead in approaching the government. Industrial scientists such as Frank Jewett, the head of Bell Labs, took part, but in a secondary role supporting the lead taken by academics such as Bush and Conant. Since the research leaders who took the lead in this initiative were from the universities, they were placed in control of the agency established to carry out their plan and thus had the responsibility to dispense the funds allocated for the task. At that time, with very few exceptions, no university had large research centers with the ability to carry on research and development of weapon systems.

The World War II model of university–government relations

During World War II, universities were chosen to manage many research projects rather than other institutions such as industrial research laboratories or non-profit institutes. At the time, industrial research laboratories at General Electric, At&T and Dupont Corporations managed research programs on a much larger scale than virtually any university research program, with the possible exception of Lawrence's cyclotron lab at Berkeley.

Nevertheless, academic scientists had taken the lead in proposing a new federal agency to undertake research for the military immediately prior to World War II. Although leading industrial scientists were involved in the committee work leading up to the establishment of the Office of Scientific Research and Development (OSRD), academic scientists and administrators such as James Conant, the chemist and President of Harvard University, and Vannevar Bush, former Vice President of MIT and Director of the Carnegie Institute of Washington, had taken the initiative.

Academic scientists preferred to remain in universities and former university professors and administrators such as Vannevar Bush occupied decision-making positions in the government, as agency heads and leading officials. Given their background and current positions of leadership; it is not surprising that major wartime research contracts were given to universities, even though these academics excused themselves from decisions affecting their present and former institutions. Laboratories that prior to the war were the extensions of a single professor were enormously expanded by drawing together academic scientists and engineers from around the country to research sites at a few selected schools.

Several major universities, including MIT, Johns Hopkins, the University of Chicago and the University of California, received contracts to administer government laboratories during the war. Such undertakings permanently altered the scale of these universities. During the post-war era, the Argonne budget, for example, was approximately equal to that of the rest of the operations of the University of Chicago.

The proximity of universities to wartime projects which employed many academic scientists habituated university administrators to collaborative research, and to the joint work on scientific projects which were to be used in technology in the shortest possible time. The academic leaders of OSRD had to draw together researchers from universities across the country to a few sites to establish these capabilities.

MIT became one of the main centers of wartime research due to its technical capacity, initiative and administrative experience. The Institute's technical capabilites made it a likely candidate for high priority projects as it was the "only institution at which the work could be done with the speed which the armed forces desired."[9] The so-called Rad Lab at MIT and a few other laboratories were established at half a dozen universities. This resulted in a concentration of research in a few institutions, against the ideologies of both government and universities. The American academic system is highly decentralized with a multiplicity of institutions competing for funds of all kinds.

Under conditions of military necessity, a few academic leaders were able to persuade their fellow academics to accept a concentrated system. Academics also agreed to accept federal research funds which they had refused during the 1930s even though the universities were starved of funds. During the depression efforts to persuade academics to ask the federal government for funds were defeated. It was against the ideologies of both government and the academy. Again it was an overriding purpose, the exigencies of war, that changed their actions.

In formulating their plan for OSRD they used MIT's industrial relations policy as the basis for their government–university relations arrangements. For example, MIT's patent policy in which the Institute assumed control of patent rights became the model for OSRD's policy. "From this precedent it was only a small step to the concept that the Chairman of NDRC (and later the Director of OSRD) convert to the government all patent rights of the private research he sponsored."[10] Bush also drew upon his consulting experience in deciding to use the cost-reimbursement contract, guaranteeing that expenses would be paid, to prevent uncertainty from impeding innovation.[11]

The MIT contract model

A post-war MIT educational planning document, the Lewis Report, recognized that government contracts had come to MIT, in part, because it was unique among American universities in the pre-war era in having an administrative office experienced in dealing with contracts.[12] Even before US entry into the conflict, MIT's administration had decided to commit the Institute's resources to defense research and, using its own funds, began work on projects before contracts were finalized or funds received. Well aware of the relevance of technology to modern warfare the administration had already sent a questionnaire to MIT graduates and compiled a database of their skills.

MIT was unique among American universities in the pre-war era in having a special office to administer research contracts: the Division of Industrial Cooperation (DIC). With twenty years experience in dealing with industry behind it, MIT was able to immediately take on government research contracts. On a Saturday morning in late October of 1940, the president of MIT, Karl Compton, walked over to the DIC office and informed its Assistant Director, Leroy Foster, that "MIT was about to undertake a contract in connection with the country's defense program which would be by far the largest research contract that we had ever had or even contemplated at the Institute."[13]

At that time the division's staff consisted of a director, assistant director, bookkeeper, secretary and a few persons handling alumni and student placement.[14] In fiscal year 1940, the division was administering slightly less than $100,000 worth of contracts, of which less than $10,000 were with the government. By 30 September of the next year, MIT had research contracts in excess of $10 million, almost entirely with the federal government.

While MIT had an administrative structure in place to handle research contracts, a new type of contract format had to be negotiated with the government. When the OSRD was established in 1940, "there was no method of giving a workable cost contract for research work."[15] On the one hand the government was concerned that public funds be accounted for in a much more stringent manner than those of industry. While MIT did not want to make money on defense contracts, neither did it wish to subsidize them.

Through negotiations with the government MIT established a new mechanism for supporting research at universities using the industrial contracts that had evolved from the Technology Plan as a starting point. The government took academic conditions into account, including only items that reflected "the increased costs of doing business due to the presence of the [military] research in the university."[16] "It was impossible to collect these excess costs [e.g. wear on facilities and administrative costs] in an educational accounting set up. You don't have monthly profit and loss statements."[17] So OSRD made an executive decision on overhead rates, setting them at 50 percent of salaries and wages for education institutions. The contract format that was worked out (providing for overheads to the university and a simple voucher procedure for accounting for expenses) satisfied both sides.

This financial instrument became the primary channel for the flow of funds from government to academia. It "set the pattern for the subsequent major contracts of the OSRD and had a very profound influence on all subsequent governmental contracts with private institutions, extending even now into peacetime."[18] The research grant and the contemporary university contracts and grants office, acting as an intermediary between government and academia, evolved from this wartime experience.

The pre-war feelings of many academics and scientists about the illegitimacy of government funding of research dissipated during this period. The wartime experience legitimated government funding of academic research and the research capacities of US universities that had been built up during the war were maintained thereafter largely with federal funds.

The growth of research teams

Although group research with significant division of labor was not unknown before the war, especially in industry, it was an unusual experience for most academic scientists. During the conflict many academic scientists who had previously worked individually or through occasional collaborations became members of large research organizations. There was some pre-war precedent for such collaborations. At MIT, engineer Vannevar Bush had worked with mathematician Norbert Wiener on a mechanical analog computer, the differential analyzer. On a somewhat larger scale, Lawrence had established an interdisciplinary team for his cyclotron project during the 1930s that he carried forward into wartime research on the Manhattan project. Bush had also translated industrial research projects into academic work and vice versa as a professor cum industrial consultant.

Nevertheless, the integration of these various elements of collaborative interdisciplinary research and development was something new. The first large-scale interdisciplinary and multifunction R&D organization set up at a university was the Radiation Laboratory (Rad Lab), established at MIT under OSRD contracts in 1940 to improve radar technology. The Rad Lab integrated research, development and production functions in a single organization. British scientists had earlier learned the value of working closely with the military personnel who would actually use the radar equipment they devised, gaining first-hand knowledge of operational problems that they could take back to the laboratory and work up into improvements.[19]

At MIT equipment received from the British was duplicated and placed on rooftops to be tested. "Most of the knowledge was gained by building something as quickly as possible and trying it out. Theoretical knowledge was generated

TRAFFIC AMONG MIT, INDUSTRY AND THE MILITARY

pari passu to be plowed back into the work at a later date."[20] Improvements were made and the apparatus was tested again.

A highly decentralized and flexible organization speeded the conduct of research. For example, parts and components were left in bins that personnel could draw from at will without paperwork and the bins were refilled as necessary. Even as the laboratory grew, "procurement and production was so completely decentralized that ... many of the Groups were, in effect, well nigh independent business concerns whose activities were coordinated through the steering committee."[21]

Its historian concluded that "At its maturity the RadLab resembled a big business concern, but it was without the visible concomitants of a big business."[22] In its internal organization the Rad Lab "reversed the established industrial order, for ... the scientists were in control and the business office was subordinate."[23] Scientists and engineers set the policy direction and administrators were available as their subordinates to help implement decisions.

Originally, the Rad Lab was to turn a working model of a piece of equipment over to a company for manufacture. Instead the Lab soon became a manufacturer, producing $25 million of equipment by the end of the war. The Research Corporation of New York was brought in to administer a "model shop," the Research Construction Corporation (RCC), building upon the relationship established in the mid-1930s when the Corporation took on the task of patenting, building prototypes and marketing the inventions of MIT professors.

RCC at first produced small numbers of developmental devices, and then larger numbers on a crash basis until production lines could be set up by industry. Working closely together with the Labs development engineers RCC was able to predict what systems would be requested by the armed forces and provide units months before production equipment was available. The Lab also sent representatives to work with companies to translate prototypes into production line products.

The role of Rad Lab in development and production as well as research came under attack from some industrial organizations who believed that "the Lab was encroaching upon the legitimate sphere of industrial enterprise and was not moreover properly constituted to be an engineering organization."[24] They wished to limit the size of the Lab and keep it confined to "fundamental research." However, the Microwave policy committee of OSRD decided that the combination of research, development and manufacturing functions within a single university-based organization was conducive to innovation and recommended further expansion, leaving only quantity production to industry. The model for a university-originated spin-off firm had met the test of wartime exigency.

The impact of World War II on MIT

The conduct of military research during World War II, integrating theorists and engineers from diverse disciplines to accomplish common tasks, transformed the organizational structure and educational policy of MIT during the post-war era. This traffic among university, industry and the military reshaped the role and function of the university and as a consequence academic institutions became a major institutional sector of American society.

The wartime experience of teachers and administrators led to a fundamental change in organizational structure and educational philosophy at MIT. Interdisciplinary research centers, some of them continuations of war time labs, became as important to the life of the Institute as traditional academic departments, and interdisciplinary cross-fertilization was institutionalized as a fundamental value.

Wartime research greatly expanded the Institute and the technical base of the Boston region. The number of researchers on campus grew significantly and some who had been drawn from universities around the country stayed at MIT after the war. The Rad Lab, which was expected to consist of 50 persons at its inception in 1940 ended the war with 3,897 personnel, 1,189 of whom were scientists and engineers.

Although the Rad Lab as an operating entity was rapidly disbanded at the close of the war, its theoretical division became The Research Laboratory for Electronics (RLE). RLE included faculty and students with a departmental base as well as researchers solely associated with the research center.

Table 2   Size of MIT

	Students	*Staff*	*Departments*
Pre-war (1939)	3,100	680	17
Wartime (August 1945)	6,200	1,165	18
Post-war (1947)	5,172	1,244	20

Sources: J. Burchard. 1948. *MIT in World War II*. New York: Tech Press/Wiley; MIT Presidents' Reports, MIT Archives.

The post-war era

After the war universities' administrations attempted to keep the war time laboratories in place. Robert Hutchins, the Chancellor of the University of Chicago, went so far as to obtain a special act of Congress to subsidize the continued operation of the atomic research facilities at Chicago, the so-called "Metallurgical Laboratories." Chicago thereby hoped to retain as many as possible of the first-rate scientists who had come to the university on wartime assignments.

The Office of Naval Research, and other military funding sources, as well as the National Institutes of Health expanded research programs. Soon the National Science Foundation provided more regularized sources of funding for large-scale research projects.

TRAFFIC AMONG MIT, INDUSTRY AND THE MILITARY

The growth of government funds for research in the post-war era, and their spread from the physical to the health-related sciences and then to the social sciences, provided the opportunity for an increasing number of professors to expand their research. This took place first by supporting graduate students and then by adding post-doctorates, technicians, secretaries and research associates to their staffs.

Some faculty were dissatisfied with the conditions set by their universities for administering research projects, such as the amount of "overhead" retained by the institution. They could complain to each other at the faculty club or attempt to overcome such restraints by establishing an independent institute adjacent to the university, using the university's library and faculty club as ancillary resources.

The institute or research unit, whether formally inside or nominally outside of the university, provided employment for graduate students and underemployed academics. A generation of academics learned salesmanship and grantsmanship skills, bringing in the steady stream of contracts and grants necessary to maintain their research operations.

Government–university relations

The onset of World War II led to the creation of a new set of ties between the federal government and MIT, and universities more generally. The impact of a negative experience in World War I military research, under the aegis of the military, shaped the course of this emerging relationship. Past experience led MIT academics to formulate an independent status with respect to the military, sanctioned by the federal government and modeled upon some of MIT's mechanisms for relating to industry that had been developed just after World War I.

Although MIT's charter as a "land grant" school was based on the presumption of a close relationship to government and industry, ironically it was the revocation of this status that led MIT to consider establishing a closer, more formal set of relationships with industry.

As MIT became involved in military research, it did so from a standpoint of having shaped the development of a contractual relationship with government in which universities retained their independent status even as huge amounts of funds flowed into campus to support research projects.

Actual contracts for research, negotiated and signed by representatives of the federal government and the university, became the model for a symbolic contract between government and academia that took form during the post-war era. MIT's industry and government connections might only have been of parochial interest were it not for the fact that other universities later followed the Institute in establishing their own external relations offices.

Their World War II experience fundamentally altered the scale and scope of many scientists' expectations for collaborative research projects. The experience of running large organizations, acting as advisors at the highest levels, and working in teams with responsibility for research, development and implementation, gave many scientists a new vision of what they could accomplish both in and beyond the laboratory. The experience of combining theoretical elucidation with development and production, supported by virtually unlimited funding, gave them a taste of power and status.

Scientists' participation in interdisciplinary research attuned them to the practical implications of their work and left many with engineering skills. Their interaction with military officers, industrial managers and political leaders created new networks. All of these experiences combined laid the groundwork for the movement of many scientists out of the laboratory and into positions of organizational responsibility in government, academia and business during the post-war era.

The relationship between the federal government and the research university was also transformed. The request for support was placed on a competitive basis to be decided by evaluation of scientific quality rather than meeting local economic needs, as in the land grant model. Government funded academic research thus took the form of a bi-coastal concentration with a few midwestern peaks.

Academics who matured during the post-war era came to see government–university relations as a permanent part of the landscape. This new mode of university–government relations was tied to the training of graduate students through research grants to individual professors. It went beyond the land grant pattern of start-up funding followed by continuing support for research institutes tied to specific practical purposes.

The close connection between research and utilization that was forged during the war was transmuted into longer-term expectations of utility in the post-war period, based on the "Endless Frontier" thesis. Nevertheless, Cold War competition ensured military funding of technological development, as well. The Institute's distinctive pattern of collaboration with industry had, under pressure of wartime exigencies, evolved into sponsored research from the federal government. The following chapter examines how patenting practices, as outlined in the US Constitution, to ensure rewards to inventors, on the one hand, and societal technological and economic advance, on the other, were integrated into the university.

5

KNOWLEDGE AS PROPERTY
The debate over patenting academic science

A patent is a compromise that balances private and public interests. Obtaining a patent is conditional on publicizing proprietary knowledge in exchange for a governmentally enforced right to prevent its unauthorized appropriation. Because secrecy is the intellectual property protection alternative to patenting, the patent system serves an important public interest – access to knowledge – by providing databases for discoveries and publishing them on the Internet.

The private right conferred by a patent to exclude others from utilizing an invention except through agreement with the originator/owner, usually for monetary consideration, further serves the public interest through the capitalization of knowledge. By allowing an inventor a temporary monopoly, patenting encourages investment in technological innovations and contributes to economic development because it reduces the risk that others will take free advantage; conversely, lack of such assurance discourages initial investment. Those outcomes have been illustrated in recent years by biotechnology firms, which have been able to obtain long-term investments in part due to their secure patent rights, and by software firms (where patenting is not the norm), which have had to rely on short-term capital.

Once inventions were emerging regularly from academic research, the question arose of how they were to be dealt with. Should inventions be treated in the same way as discoveries in pure science, and be made freely available only through publication? Was there a necessary distinction between discovery and invention? Should universities treat practically applicable discoveries made under their auspices as sources of financial benefit to themselves? Must the university address unintended negative consequences of not assuming responsibility for the commercialization of inventions made on campus? These questions arose in the early twentieth century and some are still being debated today. MIT's experience, along with that of the University of Wisconsin and the Research Corporation, played a key role in defining the relationship between patents, professors, universities and firms. This chapter focuses on the debate over the university taking patents and commercializing research.

KNOWLEDGE AS PROPERTY

The origins of patents and their role in economic development

There is nothing new about the patent system fostering knowledge capitalization; indeed it has been documented that patents originated as industrial policy.[1] Patents originated in early Renaissance Europe from governmental practices extending ownership of tracts of land to individuals, granting monopolies for the manufacture of certain goods to guilds, and enabling miners to protect their operations from disruption by competitors. The right to protect a discovery of natural substances was expanded into a right to protect inventions of machines, processes and products.

Exclusive use rights were granted to promote the economic growth of a locality. Craft knowledge as a form of intangible property was recognized in municipal regulation of the Venetian glass industry as early as the thirteenth century. By the fifteenth century, cities regularly granted limited monopolies to develop newly introduced crafts or new inventions. Physicians were similarly allowed monopoly rights over new drugs on the condition that ingredients of high quality were used in their manufacture. Rather than serving solely as rewards for individual discoveries, these monopolies were granted in the expectation that they would contribute to economic and social life. Thus, even in their earliest form, patents recognized, and indeed articulated, a balance between individual and communal interests in a new technology's introduction into use.

Technology and the legal framework to promote its growth developed hand in hand. In 1474 the Venetian Senate expanded individual grants of exclusive use rights and monopoly into a general patent law, creating by public authority a limited private monopoly in new inventions. The granting of patents to promote economic growth based on new technology soon spread. Mechanisms for the local protection of the rights of inventors grew into tactics used in the economic competition between cities as they competed to attract skilled crafts persons who could train local talent and build new industries. Later, the principles of patent law accompanied the transition from the city-state to the nation-state. Following these precedents and their model in English common law, the US Constitution established the limited right to patent protection for the sake of social progress: "The Congress shall have the power to ... promote the progress of science and useful arts by securing for limited times to authors and inventors the exclusive rights to their respective writings and discoveries."[2]

Science, patents and the flow of knowledge

The scientific discoveries of the late nineteenth century that gave rise to the major industrial sectors generated an exponential increase in patenting activity. However, scientists employed by firms in these industries were soon subject to employment contracts that assigned patent rights from their discoveries to their employer. The establishment of corporate laboratories contravened some of the original purpose of the patent system that was intended to guarantee inventors the fruits of their labor. During the legislative debate over the passage of the

56

Bayh-Dole Act, which requires universities to share proceeds from innovations with inventors – faculty, staff and students – lobbyists for large firms opposed the bill, fearing that it might set a precedent for their employees to claim a share of the intellectual property that they themselves had generated. Moreover, the patent system assumes that an individual, or small group of persons, can be identified as the inventor. When a succession of scientists, both collaborators and competitors, work to develop scientific principles into a viable technology, invention as a discrete event and the notion of the individual inventor become problematic.

In the debate over whether technological advance is promoted or impeded by the patent system, opponents hold that patents restrict access to the pool of knowledge that is the basis of future innovation and that just as scientific knowledge advances through the free flow of information so also does its application as technological innovation. Since the alternative to patent protection is secrecy, however, proponents can readily counter that patenting serves as a spur to innovation. Patents are an information system, a disclosure process, since the invention and its means of achievement become publicly available upon issuance.

The tension between patenting science and following the ethic of research, which abjures secrecy, may be less than commonly believed. Patent procedures allow sufficient time after the announcement of a discovery, typically one year, to allow for timely publication. Nevertheless, an overlay of competition for intellectual property rights, onto competition for scientific priority, increases an existing tension. Both patent publication and scientific journal article alike may disclose sufficient information for replication, though it is also possible to give just enough information to satisfy the patent examiner or editor yet leave out some specific details. In this regard, both space limitations and strategic omissions are useful for maintaining the lead in scientific competition.

By its nature any particular intellectual property is transient; it is always in principle and practice replaceable by new knowledge. Thus, property in knowledge with potential economic value must be exploited promptly, and constantly renewed and updated, in order to secure maximum profit. Thus, marketing and licensing are essential to patents; they promote the use of knowledge under the constraint of cognitive obsolescence.

Patents are a "co-opetitive" knowledge format (i.e., one that combines cooperation with competition), which integrates free access and privatization. Since patents publicize as well as protect intellectual property they do not pose a threat to dissemination of scientific research findings. Rather, it is the failure to patent that inhibits the broadest dissemination of useful knowledge by excluding it from the patent database.

Academic patenting

How do universities factor into the debate over patenting's effect on the flow of knowledge? In some respects they provide a microcosm illustrating the issue in

KNOWLEDGE AS PROPERTY

sharp relief; recent trends in academia, however, add new dimensions to the question of private intellectual property protection versus free public access.

Most universities patent their intellectual property only when they can be reasonably sure of finding a market for it. However, every technology transfer officer is on the lookout for a "big fish" and is keenly aware of the transient and inherently obsolescent nature of invention. Indeed, the impetus to establishing an intellectual property regime has often been the cautionary story of "the one that got away," either because the inventor was unaware of its potential or because the university had not yet established a technology transfer office.

But is the task worth the effort? Some observers predict an impending "shake-out" of university patent offices, left unable to meet their costs.[3] This prediction is partly based on a misplaced analogy with the rise and relative decline of the Research Corporation as a major actor on the university intellectual property scene. The shift of the Research Corporation from a focus on patenting to a focus on venture capital was spurred by the decentralization of patent offices across the academic research system.[4]

There is a shift in focus underway, from an emphasis on licensing to one on incubation, venture capital and firm-formation, reflected in the development of university accelerators. Sometimes, the only asset a start-up has to support its ability to raise capital is its protected intellectual property. Without an exclusive license, the start-up process as an engine of innovation and economic growth will be inhibited.

Some large corporations increasingly view the rise of academic patenting and licensing to start-ups rather than to major companies as a threat. Likewise, many such firms currently oppose exclusive licenses, joining with the "ivory tower" critics of university patenting. Unlike those critics, however, these companies' real concern is that if a university grants an exclusive license to a start-up, then they might have to pay more for innovative university-originated technology.

Since a patent is the prerequisite force behind the exclusive license as an incentive to economic growth, we come full circle back to issue of private versus public knowledge, hopefully exposed above as an inherently false dichotomy. With academic patenting, however, public and private interests are even more intensely intertwined, and, given the academic–industry conflicts over exclusive licenses, one might even say inverted, since the "private" interest here protecting its intellectual property is the university, pre-eminent among institutions serving the public interest, whether land grant or Ivy League, while the entities clamoring for freer access are corporations, the very paradigm of private interest.

Until quite recently relatively few universities maintained offices for taking out and licensing patents. A 1940 survey of sixteen universities reported 380 patents taken out of which 114 were in active use. The study also found that: "Only five educational institutions report income from patents."[5] In 1999 a survey of 190 US universities and related institutions reported that 3,661 US patents were taken out and over 3,900 license and option agreements were made from these and earlier patents.[6] It has been estimated that in 1992 the volume of industrial sales based upon academic patents totaled $7.4 billion.[7] In 1999 it was reported that $40.9 billion of economic activity was attributable to academic licensing.[8] What is the basis for this remarkable transformation of academic knowledge and technology into commercial profit and economic development?

Realization of the commercial value of research

Given its industrial mission and academic focus, there was a strong awareness of the potential commercial value of research at MIT well before the 1920s. There was concern expressed that outsiders could tap into research results and patent them on their own behalf. Until the early 1930s, the Massachusetts Institute of Technology followed a *laissez-faire* policy with respect to patents. Sometimes members of the academic staff assigned the rights to take out patents to the Institute; other times they retained the rights themselves. Given its positive orientation to the potentially commercializable results of results, MIT began to explore an institutional role in protection of intellectual property earlier than most universities.

Thus, intellectual property considerations as well as disciplinary contributions were taken into account in faculty hiring. In 1931, when Robert J. Van de Graaff was appointed to the department of physics from the same department at Princeton University, MIT's administrators were well aware of the potential commercial implications of his research on high voltage. MIT viewed the purchase of his electrostatic research equipment from Princeton not only as a contribution to the continuity of his research but also as a way of restricting the participation of Princeton University in future patent rights. Nevertheless, since the decision to file an application for the patent was left to the inventor, the Institute had no institutional claim upon intellectual property created by members of its academic staff.

This is still the case today in many European countries and Japan where ownership of intellectual property arising from academic research resides with the professor. Nevertheless, actually taking out a patent, especially across national boundaries, can be an expensive proposition. As efforts to commercialize academic research get underway in Europe and Japan, offers to pay for the taking out of a patent, in exchange for part of the rights, have resulted in a division between the university and the individual professor. Under these conditions, individual negotiations are soon superseded by precedent as the basis for a division of proceeds between the individual, the research unit or department and the university.

As precedent takes hold a one-third rule is elaborated internationally. This division occurs along much the same lines as in the USA where ownership of the intellectual property rights deriving from federally funded research have

KNOWLEDGE AS PROPERTY

resided by law with the university since 1980. One of the conditions of the law is that the inventor must also receive a significant share of the proceeds. The relatively autonomous position of the professor in the university, in comparison to the scientist as an employee of a corporation, is the fundamental basis for this shared intellectual property regime. Whether accelerated by law, or developed more slowly through precedent, the outcome is basically the same; so are the issues that must be resolved.

The debate over academic patenting at MIT

Should publication of research results take place as rapidly as possible or should publication be delayed until patents are taken out? Should universities try to earn income from the discoveries of their academic staff to help support the institution? Will universities endanger their public support if they take a pecuniary interest in inventions rather than remaining institutions committed to the disinterested pursuit of knowledge?[9] These issues, still current, were central to a debate at MIT, early in the century, over relations with industry and whether the university was becoming a business itself. Prior to the World War II, few academic scientists and engineers thought of it as part of their task to generate commercially profitable results and to file a patent. This was thought to be a task for their counterparts in industry. Many academic scientists and engineers still hold to a traditional view of the academic role even as a significant number of their colleagues have become interested in patenting their research and capturing financial rewards from it.

As with consulting, a controversy over patenting at MIT resulted in a compromise that became an influential model. MIT wished to avoid conflict with private firms over patent rights. The Institute wished to enter into business-like relations with industry but it by no means wished to leave behind its tradition of open publication and of disinterested research. MIT was unwilling to press private firms, or its own staff, too hard in order to establish the general principle of ownership of patents by the university. After more than a decade of discussion the decision was taken in the early 1930s to utilize the patent system to structure relations with industry and to earn profits from the knowledge created on campus. This transition has been repeated in the academic world many times since and is currently underway on various campuses. Typically, the issues discussed, the model followed and the practices instituted replicate the dynamic in the controversy over consultation.

MIT's goal, in becoming involved with the patent system, was to reconcile a new academic mission of capitalizing knowledge generated on campus with existing academic missions. Even an industrially oriented academic institution did not find patenting free of problems. The Institute was aware of the negative reaction to the University of Wisconsin's policy in dealing with patents. An MIT report found that: "One educational Institution, which has derived a very considerable income from one group of patents, has been severely criticized in

60

KNOWLEDGE AS PROPERTY

scientific circles for its patent policy due to its method in handling the subject rather than to the mere fact that income is derived."[10] MIT attempted to reconcile its 1861 charter, which gave it a special responsibility to assist private industry, with traditional academic goals of education, research and dissemination of knowledge.

The MIT administration wanted to gain money from licensing the rights to industrial firms to use the significant inventions of its academic staff. MIT concluded that the problems of the University of Wisconsin did not result from its interest in making money from patents but rather from its attempt to exercise power over industry that the control of patents had made possible. By narrowly construing its interest in patent management, the Institute believed that it could avoid the pitfalls that Wisconsin had fallen into by using its patents to further the interests of a local industry at the expense of a competitor. MIT also wished to find a formula to engage in patenting that would satisfy both proponents and opponents of the commercialization of research.

For this purpose, President Compton appointed a sub-committee in late 1931 to formulate a patent policy for MIT. The committee included both proponents and opponents of academic patenting. Compton charged the committee:

1   To ensure that ambiguity in regard to questions of title shall be clarified within a reasonable period.
2   To ensure that the Institute is placed in a position to profit from its own developments in any case in which it may choose to do so, and thereby ensure a prompt realization to the public of the benefits of any such developments.
3   To sustain the interest and enthusiasm of the friends of the Institute where ever they may be placed.[11]

The charge itself presumed acceptance of an academic patent right. Nevertheless, interest in patenting was modified by a desire not to offend by exercising this right.

Karl Compton's favorable disposition towards patents on academic achievements in research was part of his larger aspiration for a role for the university in economic development. Compton's objectives were twofold. He wanted to develop MIT into a scientific technological university, with great academic distinction.[12] However, this academic objective was only a first and necessary basis for his ultimate goal. Compton and his associates in the MIT administration sought academic distinction, of a high and special kind combining fundamental inquiry with practical utility. Nevertheless, investigation was not an end in itself for these academic visionaries. They also wished to establish a direct role for the university in the creation of science-based industry through the founding of high-tech firms, as these enterprises have since been labeled.

KNOWLEDGE AS PROPERTY

The debate over patents at MIT

In the debate over patent policy during the 1930s, the proponents of the assumption of an entrepreneurial role by MIT in its relations with industry clashed with those who wanted the Institute to adhere to the traditions of financially disinterested research. The MIT administration's program to promote an economic role for the Institute met with internal resistance. The Institute's announcement of its intention to acquire patents on the discoveries made by its academic staff led some of the latter to ask whether, even if patents could profitably be licensed, that would not impugn academic claims to objectivity and disinterestedness.

The issue at MIT was not directly over whether the Institute should be closely involved with industry. That issue was settled in its charter which mandated a close connection. The debate at MIT was over whether the taking out of patents by MIT would promote or detract from the Institute's relations with industry. Would taking out patents make MIT a competitor with industry rather than a collaborator? Would the university become a business itself rather than an entity based on different and distinct principles from business, even as it attempted to assist industry?

The issue of the necessity for functional differentiation between university and industry, or whether the two institutional spheres should overlap in their functions, is a fundamental issue of university–industry relations. On the one hand, proponents of differentiation argue that the university can best fulfill its industrial role as a producer of knowledge, leaving the utilization of such knowledge to industry. On the other hand, proponents of integration hold that a gap opens up between the creation of knowledge and its use if the university does not engage in steps to see that knowledge is transferred.

There is a misconception inherent in this debate if it is assumed that the university by taking on some of the appurtenances of a business becomes wholly transformed into one. This is the "one bite of the apple" thesis. The alternative possibility is that the university takes on some of the aspects of a business while retaining essential traditional academic functions such as student intake and training. In this model, assuming a movement from both sides, the roles of university and business shade into and overlap each other.

The relative merits of two strategies: mutual interdependence versus "taking the role of the other" were strongly debated. Two faculty members, John Bunker and Vannevar Bush exemplified the contrasting positions on academic patenting at MIT: Bush, through establishing a model of behavior as an entrepreneurial scientist; Bunker, through his critique of this emergent model. An opponent of academic patenting, John Bunker, a professor of engineering at the Institute and member of the committee on patents, argued that the most important reason for the avoidance of seeking to take out patents was that it would disturb the relations between the university and private industry. Bunker said:

KNOWLEDGE AS PROPERTY

> I have talked with a representative of the largest Chemical manufacturing House in the U.S. and his reaction is one of surprise that MIT should even consider placing itself in a situation that he described as "equivocal".
>
> The vice-president of a testing laboratory headed by a tech alumnus stated with some heat: "If Tech is going into competition with Industry, perhaps Industry will not be interested to continue its financial support." The head of research of a chemical house explained to me that he regarded Tech as a scientific Institution free from the onus (I think he meant odium) that attaches to other educational institutions which are regarded as making a business of exploiting patents.[13]

Beyond the issue of desirability was the question of feasibility. Could academics undertake the tasks and practices commonplace in industrial laboratories that were necessary to establish patent rights? Bunker took the view that: "To the average professor, patents are distasteful. The average professor probably does not fully comprehend what is involved when a patent is taken: nor does he understand the value of systematic records, of dates etc."[14] Bunker held patenting to be more appropriate to a bureaucratic research institution such as existed in the laboratories of large industrial corporations rather than to the university, where research was a more informal, individual activity.

Nevertheless, the transformation of academic research from an individual to a group activity was already well underway. There was the attendant necessity to keep records for a variety of purposes, both fiscal and experimental. The academic scale-up was not to the level of a corporate lab but rather to that of a small group. Nevertheless, the tradition of academic research as a series of faculty student dyads was already shifting to a more complex model in which lateral ties among a group of students were becoming as important as the teacher/student relationship.

Bunker's skepticism of the ability of academic scientists to do research which was practically applicable was augmented by his conviction that academics were ill-equipped to protect their intellectual property. Patenting was a difficult topic: "the subject is essentially new to many of our colleagues."[15] He also cautioned against the danger of obtaining income from patents; he thought that "the tax exempt status of the Institute" might be jeopardized by the taking of patents.

The argument that professors could not adapt themselves to the requirements of the patent system was undermined by the fact that MIT faculty members were already taking out patents on their own behalf. Indeed, the patenting activities of teachers were among the reasons for the organization of the patent committee. Moreover, even in the early twentieth century, the research activities of the staff at the Institute were well administered and detailed administrative records were kept.

Bunker also questioned the need for formulation of a patent policy for the Institute on the grounds that it was unlikely that a large enough number of patents would be taken to justify the expenditure of time and money that would be required. He held that:

KNOWLEDGE AS PROPERTY

The members of the staff who can exercise ingenuity in investigation and at the same time keep a weather eye on the practical application and obtain gainful patents can not be many. I wonder if it is worth while to run the risk of creating a disturbance by promulgating a formal policy applying to all, for the sake of assuring hypothetical gain from a few.[16]

Bunker summed up his objections in a memorandum to his colleague Dean Vannevar Bush, chairman of the patent committee of the Institute in a series of rueful parenthetical observations to an article in a national magazine that was highly critical of academic patenting.[17]

Perhaps the laboratory is pressed with economic necessity (how did he know about my situation? J.B. [John Bunker]) – but is that a warrant for changing its charter? Possibly it can support itself handsomely (cf Chem Engineering at MIT formerly, J.B.) and independently – but can it survive the shiftings of bases and readjustments of outlook which commercialization entails? (Here he puts his finger on the potential sore. J.B.) One of its greatest glories is its intellectual integrity and independence – but can this reputation (n.b. "reputation" JB) continue unsullied in the clash of competitive mass campaigns of patented commodities, infringement suits and other contentions of the market-place in which financial interest of the research institution is on one side of the dispute?[18]

There is no record of a written response from Dean Bush. He could have pointed out that the MIT charter was significantly different from that of an ordinary university. It had a unique obligation as a "land grant" institution to assist industry to improve its technology even as other land grant colleges were contributing to the scientific basis of agricultural practice. Not too many years earlier, despite being in severe financial straits, the Institute had rejected overtures for it to become the engineering college of Harvard on the grounds that such association would divert it from its special purpose.

It is likely significant for the outcome of the debate over patenting that Bush not only rose to a high place in the MIT administration but was also a distinguished researcher. His colleague in the MIT administration, President Compton, wrote of him:

No picture of the Institute would be complete without tribute to the dynamic genius and able leadership of its Vice President and dean of the School of Engineering, Vannevar Bush. He introduced operational calculus into modern electrical engineering, has invented various devices now in commercial and domestic use, and is the originator of a series of highly useful machines for performing difficult engineering

KNOWLEDGE AS PROPERTY

computations ... most important of all, no man comes to Dean Bush with a problem who does not leave with a keen criticism and a constructive suggestion.[19]

Bush continually extrapolated theoretical and practical implications from any technology that he came across: in his service on the Institute's patent committee he occasionally recommended improvements or extensions of particular inventions which came before it. During a discussion of the significance of a new method of making replicas of ruled gratings, Bush suggested as an extension that "precise scales might be made in a similar way."[20] This incident, in which a new idea arose out of the workings of a patent management scheme, adumbrated current efforts to revive national patent systems as information resources to stimulate, as well as register, inventive activity.[21]

The next chapter discusses the resolution of the controversy at MIT, which provided a framework for academic patenting during the pre-war era.

6

THE REGULATION OF ACADEMIC PATENTING

Much of the division on academic patenting arises from differing conceptions of the role of the university in society. If the university is seen as having an explicit economic and social role, the transfer of technology and utility of patenting becomes an issue of means, how best to organize this activity in relation to the other missions of the university. If the role of the university is believed to be limited to the production and dissemination of knowledge, then the issue of patenting research becomes a matter of principle and is fought on the ground of whether the university should play an explicit economic and social role in society and whether such a mission adds to or detracts from its other missions.[1] Nevertheless, irrespective of ideological positions the research mission of the university inevitably brings with it the potential for technology development, with economic and social implications that must be taken into account. Even if a university wishes to maintain a hands-off position, it may be forced to become involved in issues of patent management.

Such was the case at the University of Toronto Medical School, where as the result of Frederick Banting and Charles Best's discovery of insulin in 1921–2, a classic shift in stance toward academic patenting occurred.[2] Large profits, public health and the reputation of the university were at stake. The Toronto case also raised a series of issues between university administrators and teachers and business firms; these issues included the distribution of the money earned and the propriety of ceding of patent rights to a single firm. Putting contrary policy aside, the University of Toronto decided to acquire a patent on insulin, a much demanded drug in extremely short supply. University administrators believed that by licensing the university's patent to a single reputable pharmaceutical firm, the Eli Lilly Company, quality control could be assured and revenue gained to support future research. The ethical rules, to which the university was committed, precluded personal gain from the patent. The university's alliance with the Lilly firm enabled its researchers to translate findings into clinical practice quickly, ensuring credit for their discovery against other claimants.[3]

The University of Wisconsin, on the other hand, learned to its displeasure the consequences of not properly protecting the inventions produced by its faculty members. When Professor Babcock invented a device for testing the

66

quality of milk, several unscrupulous manufacturers marketed faulty equipment to farmers under the auspices of the Babcock invention. Without patent protection, the university had no means of protecting itself and the public from the makers of these devices. While the University of Toronto patented to protect the quality of insulin production, the University of Wisconsin suffered the downside of not having control over an invention made on campus. In 1925 the University of Wisconsin set up a patent management organization, The Wisconsin Alumni Research Foundation, to directly manage the intellectual property rights generated on campus for the financial benefit of the university and the economic benefit of the state, as well as to ensure quality control. MIT initially took a position in-between Toronto and Wisconsin. While MIT was interested in profiting from discoveries, it preferred to have a non-MIT organization, the Research Corporation, act as an intermediary with industry.

MIT's patent policy

In a series of disputes over the propriety of academic–industry relations in the early twentieth century, proponents of close industrial ties deferred somewhat to their colleagues with traditional academic values. Opponents of more intense industrial ties had greater effect on Institute policy than their political strength within MIT might justify. In addition to their own views on academic propriety, they were concerned that the public might view MIT in an unfavorable light if its industrial ties were too strong. In this context, industrial relations were regulated, rather than prohibited as at some universities, or allowed to remain unfettered as might have been expected at MIT. Issues of consulting and patenting were debated and resolved, allowing the activity to proceed in such a way that it would be carried out with due regard for traditional academic sensibilities. As with consulting, the controversy over patenting resulted in a compromise.

MIT attempted to shape a patent policy that would allow it to reap financial benefits while maintaining due regard for concerns that academic life would be adversely affected. Despite Professor Bunker's objections, patenting by the Institute was accepted in a policy adopted by the faculty in April 1932.[4] The benefits to be obtained from the commercial application of the results of research were strongly appreciated at MIT. Nevertheless, there were fears that relations with private industrial firms could become excessively demanding so that attention was diverted from teaching and research. Apprehension about possible conflicts of interest arose earlier and more pressingly than it had done at other universities, since it was expected that the type and scale of research done at the Institute was more likely to result in significant discoveries and inventions even when the research was done without practical intention.

The next task of the committee on patents was to clarify ambiguities with regard to title to inventions made by members of the academic staff. In the deliberations of the committee, two alternatives were recognized: the university

THE REGULATION OF ACADEMIC PATENTING

could claim ownership of all intellectual property or it could claim none, except when it was necessary to patent medical discoveries in order to exercise quality control over their production. The committee on patents made its decisions bearing in mind the concerns of the interested parties and constituencies including teachers who supported the taking of patents and those who opposed it, companies that wished to deal directly with the individual academic who made discoveries, and the general public, who, it was believed, might consider the taking of patents to be a departure from the tradition of a higher educational institution. The committee decided that while it intended to proceed with the taking of patents, they would only be undertaken in instances where it seemed likely that there was a discovery or invention of substantial promise to be pursued. For inventions judged to be minor, it would be left up to the inventor to decide whether or not to patent. The inventor would receive a 7 percent share of the gross returns from the invention. In setting this figure, considerations of fairness to the inventor were balanced against anxiety that inventions might be stressed at the expense of research.

In all of its arrangements for disposition of intellectual property, there would be an effort made to avoid distracting the staff from research by undue emphasis on invention:

> Since the objectives of the inventor are not completely compatible with orderly progress in academic research, it is highly desirable that our own investigators not become unduly 'patent conscious.' The Patent committee realizes that the use of this letter may encourage undue attention to patentable invention, but we believe that the hazard involved is the lesser evil, and if the letter should prevent misunderstanding, its use may enable us to avoid the greater evil of being required to straighten out disputed equities after invention has arisen from participation of a student in staff research.

Thus, while invention was favorably viewed, "such participation [in its rewards] should be arranged so that staff should not be stimulated to invention."[5] To prevent the prospect of financial gains becoming a primary reason for conducting research, it was hoped that invention could be given equal status with other legitimate academic activities such as as research and teaching. Special accomplishments would be recognized, in the same manner as in all properly academic activities, by granting of promotion and rises in salary.

A set of principles and procedures were established to regulate the taking of patents on the results of academic research. An academic committee was created to recommend the appropriate division of rights when the respective rights of individuals and the Institute were unclear. The Institute was determined to make studious efforts to resolve disputes over conflicting claims to patent rights without resorting to litigation. Rights to grant licenses on patents were not to be accumulated by the Insitute as an end in itself; if commercial use

THE REGULATION OF ACADEMIC PATENTING

could not be arranged within two years, the rights to the patents would be assigned to the inventor. The procedures for seeking patents would be organized so as "to proceed with such promptitude that no undue restrictions of freedom of publication will be necessary."[6] This principle demonstrated an early awareness that academic and intellectual property needs could be reconciled through the development of administrative procedures to speed up the filing of applications for patents and thereby reduce the urgency of delay in publication.

MIT's new patent policy was a compromise between the financial interests of the faculty and the Institute, giving due recognition to the contributions of each. The committee formulated a policy whereby the Institute laid claim to patent rights when it had supported the research financially. Where the Institute contributed nothing substantial, any patent that was obtained became the property of the individual. Students were treated differently; they were allowed to retain all rights to inventions. When a project was jointly financed with an external sponsor, rights to benefits from the patent would be split between the sponsor, the Institute and the academic discoverer or inventor.[7] The Institute would not attempt the exploitation of commercial patents on its own. It would turn over its rights to others to exploit in exchange for reasonable financial returns.

The management of patents

A patent committee system was set up to receive information from staff members about inventions. To carry out the policies expeditiously, responsibility was divided between two committees, the committee on patents and the committee on management of patents, to handle the different stages of the commercial exploitation of academic knowledge. The committee on patents would deal with questions of determining inventorship, allocate equities among the qualified parties, render an opinion on the originality of a discovery or the scientific novelty of an invention, and set the rate at which inventors would share in the financial returns. These duties primarily drew upon the engineering and scientific expertise of the academic staff. A committee for the management of patents was also established to unify policy on the business management of all patents taken by the Institute. This committee advised the administration on the adequacy of patent provisions in research contracts undertaken by teachers and research groups. The committee was responsible for advising the administration on the administrative and legal implications of patent matters and for reviewing issues of patent policy which might affect the relations of the Institute with the public.

The first committtee was largely composed of members of the academic staff; the second commitee consisted of academics and administrators.[8] A typical discussion within a committee would be about the question of whether a piece of research fell within or outside the terms of reference of the committee. For example, the committee found that Harold Edgerton, professor of electrical engineering,

THE REGULATION OF ACADEMIC PATENTING

has a rather informal arrangement concerning his stroboscopic work which has worked out excellently. Institute facilities are indeed used in connection with the commercial relationships on this affair. On the other hand the equipment developed and used by reason of commercial contacts has proved to be of great service in research work throughout the Institute. The relationship, while informal, has been mutually beneficial.[9]

In this instance academic and commercial work were inextricably intertwined, and the committee concluded that the result was, on balance, favorable to the purposes of the Institute.[10] Within a decade the scope of Professor Edgerton's external activities had expanded to such a scale that when the Atomic Energy Commission offered him contracts to monitor the early post-war tests of the atomic bomb in the Pacific ocean, the Institute encouraged him to form a firm to deal with the matter.

An informal pre-war consulting partnership with two of his former students evolved into Edgerton, Grier and Germeshausen (EGG), a diversified electronics firm that is now among the five hundred largest companies in the United States. Remaining at the Institute, Edgerton maintained a similar informal relationship with EGG, bringing back equipment from the firm for use in his academic laboratory.[11] In the mid-1970s, EGG donated funds to the Institute for an academic building in recognition of Edgerton's contribution to the firm. This corporate philanthropy derived from academic research that had been successfully commercialized.

Vannevar Bush's inventive activities became the subject of his own committee's deliberations more than once. At a meeting in 1935 President Compton took over the chair from Bush, on an occasion in which the topic was a lubricant for railways invented by Bush. It was reported that the invention was made partly with funds from the United Water Cooler Service Company and that no Institute funds were used. Since that was the case, the committee decided to turn all rights over to Bush. Bush, in turn, offered all of the rights to the Institute. The committee accepted his offer with the provision that: "encouragement of a cooperative attitude on the part of the staff in respect to patent rights, and in the general development of its patent policy, would be best served if Dean Bush should retain a substantial equity in the invention."[12] Bush accepted the principle but refused to take more than a one-quarter share in the returns on his invention.

Academic intellectual property

The emergence of the new patent policy at the Massachussetts Institute of Technology opened a discussion regarding the proper function of the universities. Decisions to take out patents on some of the inventions of its academic staff did not end the debate. Such decisions led to discussion of what the university should do with the intellectual property it was accumulating. By taking control of the inventions by its teachers, the Institute was compelled to

THE REGULATION OF ACADEMIC PATENTING

participate more directly in the management of patents. The patent system made the holders of patents responsible for the promotion of their use. The discovery of an appropriate role for the Institute in the commercial application of the results of research became an important topic of discussion.

During the mid-1930s, Vannevar Bush, by this time vice-president of the Massachussetts Institute of Technology, explored the idea of establishing an office to handle the patenting and licensing of discoveries and inventions made at the Institute. An assistant to the president and a young patent attorney were to be put in charge. According to Bush this arrangement would allow the functions of the patent committee to "be considerably reduced, much to its relief."[13] Bush's proposal for the commercial exploitation of the Institute's patents met with resistance from some of the same members of the academic staff who questioned the desirability of a policy for the Institute to deal with patents.

Concern was expressed that such an intimate participation in private business such as was suggested in the proposal for the Institute to manage its own patents would jeopardize the status of the Institute as an educational institution. In response to a statement that the proposal would not endanger the Institute's status as an institution enjoying exemption from taxes and legally able to receive gifts which would be free of taxation, a critic of the plan responded skeptically to the statement that "We do not think such a corporation would endanger the tax exempt status of any other property … I would submit that we can't afford to merely think; we ought to be sure."[14] This teacher viewed the proposal as a transparent ruse under which the university would establish a business. To me, the setting up of an ostensibly non-Tech corporation in which the entire funding and ownership of stock is by MIT is an obvious legal evasion of tax liability.[15] It was also asked whether the game was worth the candle: could patents be expected to bring in significant income? "[W]hy place ourselves in any kind of jeopardy, especially when the stake is not large on the return side of the proposition?"[16]

Critics also suggested that instead of managing its patents itself, the Institute should engage an external firm for that activity in order to shield the university from charges of impropriety. "I don't fully understand why we can't continue to do business with Research Corporation and continue to keep our skirts clear. The personal grief involved in patents is not justification for taking a course that the Institute status or reputation be placed in jeopardy." Finally, there was the spectre of the University of Wisconsin model which Bush's plan clearly emulated. "Public opinion is pretty important as shown by the Wisconsin Foundation situation and its University and the bad light of professional public opinion."[17]

Difficulties in gaining acceptance for the sale of the right to use intellectual property as a proper activity of a university can be seen in the discussion of arrangements to separate MIT from the conduct of sales. To answer objections that it endangered the Institute's not-for-profit status, Bush and Caroll L. Wilson, another administrator at the Institute, discussed setting up a body registered as a corporation in Massachussetts, or possibly Delaware, "without

THE REGULATION OF ACADEMIC PATENTING

attempting to make it tax exempt." To avoid negative appearances, "the name should suggest patent management and should not suggest the Institute."[18] Nevertheless, even proponents of this scheme were concerned about possibly negative repercussions of the Institute being associated with an arrangement for the management of patents. A question scrawled in the margin of the letter asked about the liability of the Institute in the event of a lawsuit against the nominally independent organization.

Throughout the discussions the goal was to balance the acquisition of income against a possible taint of impropriety through the taking out of patents for financial reasons. On the one hand, there was the desire to extend research programs so that they would be closer to the point of industrial application. It was pointed out that: "universities have recently studied all possible sources of income."[19] One member of the academic staff cautioned that: "Patents are dangerous. It is well to remember this and be frequently reminded."[20] The limited acceptance of patents for academic discoveries and inventions in the 1930s did not include the direct sale of patent rights. Bush's proposal failed largely because it was feared that the Institute might endanger its academic reputation and its tax-free status by realizing financial gain from the sale of the results of its research. Instead, a substitute proposal was accepted in which an outside organization was retained to patent and market MIT inventions.

The Research Corporation

In 1936, the patent committee of the Institute put forward the view that:

> There is recognized to be danger in deriving any income whatever from inventions, first because of possible influence upon our tax exempt status, and second because of possible criticism of our methods leading to ill will among those upon whom we must depend for support. The first difficulty seems to be avoided if the actual handling of our affairs is delegated to some other organization.[21]

In June 1937, the Massachussetts Institute of Technology announced that it had concluded an agreement with the Research Corporation of New York, "whereby this organization will handle all legal and commercial aspects of inventions assigned to Institute Inventors."[22] As a result of this agreement the Research Corporation opened a branch office in Boston headed by a graduate of the Institute to deal with inventions emerging from research at MIT. Given the quality of the Institute's activities, it was expected that "important inventions" would be forthcoming.

The Research Corporation had itself been founded in 1912 to exploit commercially an academic discovery and return its proceeds to support new research. Utilizing a discovery of the British physicist Oliver Lodge, Frederick

72

G. Cottrell, a professor of physical chemistry at the University of California, invented the electrostatic precipitator – a device for control of smoke and other emissions. After futile attempts to persuade existing institutions to undertake commercial development of the precipitator, Cottrell organized the Research Corporation with the support of leading industrialists who served as members of the Board of Directors of the Corporation. After the precipitator was success-fully developed and marketed, the Research Corporation placed it under a special firm, Research-Cottrell. The sale of Research-Cottrell stock provided an endowment for the Research Corporation to employ a staff and devote itself to the twin tasks of supporting research in the physical sciences and promoting the transfer of the results of research which had profit-making potential from universities to industry. From 1927, when the first grant was made, to 1948, $1.25 million from the earnings from patents was distributed to fifty-two univer-sities to support research.[23] The agreement with the Research Corporation was the culmination of five years of discussion following the establishment of a patent policy by the Massachusetts Institute of Technology.[24]

Once the initial decision had been taken to declare an interest in the intel-lectual property generated at the Institute, the question became how to carry out responsibilities of putting inventions to profitable use. The committee thought that the application for, and the licensing of, patents would have to be done judiciously and would have to consider the criticisms which would be made of it. Whatever procedure was followed, the committee was well aware of the antipathy of private businessmen to the charges that would be made for a previously free good. The Institute planned to forestall litigation by fixing royalty rates at very reasonable levels. It believed that academic and business criticism could be stilled by restraint in the granting of exclusive licenses. It was believed that these policies could place the Institute "in a position to profit from its own developments,"[25] without injurious controversies as long as only a modest level of income was sought. The arrangement of having an intermediate organization would, it was hoped, provide a buffer between the academic world and world of private business.

Expansion of academic patents

The external support of research created new problems for patent policy. For one thing it greatly increased the number of patentable discoveries and inven-tions. It increased disproportionately discoveries and inventions which seemed to be ready for commerical exploitation.

The expansion of research at the Massachusetts Institute of Technology during World War II speeded up the rate of invention. The patent management committee of the Institute noted that:

> Before the war, a majority of our patents arose from normal Institute research and research contracts were a minor part of the picture.

THE REGULATION OF ACADEMIC PATENTING

Under these conditions the Patent Committee of the Faculty could and did handle all patent matters since they had to do mainly with questions of inventorship and conception and equity on the part of MIT staff members making inventions. Under war conditions, by far the greater part of our patent business has to do with government and industrial contracts which involve questions of business and legal arrangements and of policy affecting the Institute. Only incidentally do these contracts involve matters of staff equities.[26]

Research organization expanded in scale at the Radiation Laboratory and other wartime research projects. Under peacetime conditions of small-scale, largely internally supported research, patents were sought largely because of the interest of the discoverer or inventor or of the Institute. The change in the scale of applications for patents was explained thus: "The large number of research contracts at present in effect at the Institute, most of which involve patent agreements, has created the need for a special administrative organization for patent management at the insitute and for handling the details of contractural arrangements involving patents."[27] Whereas, previously patents were an issue internal to the university, they now introduced the government as a factor. And private industrial firms entered more tangibly into the problem.

The Institute lacked the administrative capacity to deal with this increased volume and with the more complex pattern of relationships. "MIT has no organizational setup for handling the business of patent prosecution, licensing, and carrying out a contract with the inventor for inventor participation."[28] Research activity at the Institute had been transformed by the introduction of large governmental contracts. The hitherto existing arrangements with the Research Corporation became inappropriate to the new situation. Neverthelsss, the arrrangement between Research and the Institute continued until the 1960s when the two bodies came into direct conflict over a dispute regarding patent rights with the International Business Machines Company .

The issue of exclusive licenses

The issue of granting rights to a single company for the use of a patent owned by a university became very pressing after the end of World War II. The Institute had played a leading role in founding the American Research and Development Corporation (ARD), the first public venture capital firm. President Compton declared: "My objective is to point out that a formula must be found which recognizes the special position of educational institutions if any satisfactory working arrangements are to become general between corporations such as American Research and institutions such as MIT."[29] However, the Institute soon found that its objectives in founding the venture capital firm were in conflict with its previously stated principles on the management of patents on academic discoveries.

74

THE REGULATION OF ACADEMIC PATENTING

ARD wanted assurances that if it invested its capital in starting a new company with patents owned by the Institute it would not be subject to immediate competition. Its investment would be placed in jeopardy, if the Institute licensed other firms to use the same discoveries or inventions. Although the Institute was reluctant to grant exclusive rights, it decided to do so in order to ensure the establishment of a firm which would use the Van de Graaff patents. In an internal memorandum, MIT asked itself:

> Can exclusive licenses be avoided? If not, can an escape clause be found which will be acceptable? Has consideration been given to non exclusive [licenses] for a period of time in which no other will be given. What will be the effect of MIT buying into Trump Co. [High Voltage Inc.].[30]

The Institute had originally licensed the patents to the General Electric Company, but when a certain time had passed without any use having being made of them, MIT resumed the rights. When ARD determined to make one of its first investments in High Voltage Inc. and wished to license the rights exclusively, the Institute was concerned about becoming too closely tied to a single firm. The independence of the university and the public interest might be compromised by too close an association with a private interest.

> On the other hand, the responsible officers of the Institute have had long contact and experience with the problem and realize the requirements for protection of venture capital and for the establishment of a new industrial enterprise. Their sympathy with this particular enterprise and their understanding of the requirements of the situation can be counted on.[31]

The Institute satisfied ARD and its conscience by offering an exclusive license limited to ten years.

In addition to exclusive licenses for the existing patent rights, the founders of High Voltage Inc. also wanted assurances that they would receive the rights to future advances made by Institute inventors in the firm's field of technology. MIT assured ARD that High Voltage could have exclusive licenses for patents on improvements. The Institute recognized that if academic patents were to be profitably applied the concerns of industrial firms would have to be accommodated. The statement "the limits on licenses given always being directed toward protecting the Institute's responsibilities as an eleemosynary instituition serving the public, while at the same time recognizing the essential business requirements for bringing an invention into use by the public"[32] was in practice interpreted to meet the latter requirement. To achieve its goal of regional economic development, the Institute broke with academic tradition and accepted the patent practices of private business firms which required exclusive licenses.

THE REGULATION OF ACADEMIC PATENTING

Balancing patents with other relations to industry

MIT was forced to seek an appropriate balance between the traditional relationships between universities and private industry, which combined philanthropic support by the latter with training and occasional consultation by the former, and the new relationship which entailed the sale to private firms of industrial technology in the form of licenses to use patents. The issue came to a head when the Research Corporation, as holder of MIT's patent rights, and the Institute became aware that they had different objectives. The Institute decided that it was

> not in a position to ask for the full value of the patent. ... [With respect to the Research Corporation] ... our interests are not the same. The price for which we would settle is therefore not the same, but we must get a fair price. ... We must establish a record of having done everything possible to avoid litigation and to have gone ahead in a serious way to do the right thing insofar as MIT–industry relations are concerned.[33]

The Research Corporation's only relationship to companies was through the licensing of the use of patents; the Institute had a much more complex set of relationships with private firms. The Institute and the Research Corporation disagreed over how vigorously to press the International Business Machines Corporation to pay for the patent rights for use of magnetic core memory in its computers. The Institute held that Jay Forrester had made the invention on its campus, but did not want to engage in a fight to the bitter end with International Business Machines on the general grounds that it wished to maintain amicable relations with industry and on the particular grounds that, despite the company's unwillingness to pay for its use of patents, it was a significant patron of computer research at the Institute. The Institute's position was that:

> IBM is indebted to us for a great deal apart from the Forrester patent, but it is also a fact that IBM as a company has been generous in the establishment of a computation center, in providing funds for a building to house that center, and is currently funding our work in this field at the rate of 1½ million a year. ... [Moreover], there has been for a long time a mutually profitable relationship between our faculty and their engineers.[34]

The Research Corporation, on the other hand, took a purely business view of the matter and was determined to pursue International Business Machines to the full extent of the law.

For its part, International Business Machines viewed the Institute's contribution to magnetic core memory as one among several components in the invention which included contributions made by the Radio Corporation of

THE REGULATION OF ACADEMIC PATENTING

America, an independent inventor and several of its own employees. Since International Business Machines had purchased the Radio Corporation and the independent inventor's rights, it viewed itself as the major holder of patent rights to magnetic core memory. In addition, there was "the further complication that Mr Watson [President, International Business Machines] believes … that universities should not own patents."[35]

The very arrangement which was supposed to protect the Insitute from conflict with private firms was in fact exacerbating a dispute with one particular firm. The Institute's attorney advised that:

> the initial concept of our relations with the R.C. [Research Corporation] was that they should act as an insulator between MIT and industry in patent matters. However, in this particular case, the magnitude is so great and the difference of opinion between R.C. and industry has reached such a point that MIT cannot ignore the problems and if RC's actions are contrary to MIT's interests we must become concerned.[36]

Usually, the interests of the Institute and the Research Corporation were in accord. However, "There are cases, such as this one, where interests become opposed, and the situation may reach the point where the only remedy is the one provided in the contract, namely, cancellation."[37] As a result of its irreconcilable differences with the Research Corporation, the Institute severed its relationship and took over the management of its patents itself. The claim against IBM was settled for a relatively modest sum.

The dispute with IBM was complicated by the fact that the patent rights claimed by the Institute arose from research paid for by the federal government. The Institute realized that if the dispute had gone to court the underlying issue would affect the entire US patent system, especially patent ownership resulting from government sponsored research. Beyond transferring intellectual property generated on campus, the role of the university in economic development has taken a more fundamental step: the creation of new firms. The story of how this strategy originated is the subject of the next chapter.

7

ENTERPRISES FROM SCIENCE

The origins of science-based regional economic development

Boston's post-war technology corridor, which is often assumed to have been a spontaneous development, is the result of specific initiatives taken earlier in the century. An innovative strategy for knowledge-based economic development led to the creation of the Route 128 complex during the early post-war era. In this new model, universities, traditionally knowledge producers and transmitters, have also become factors of production. During the 1930s depression, MIT President Karl Compton hypothesized that New England's research-intensive universities could substitute for the natural resources that the region largely lacked. He extrapolated instances of firm formation by MIT professors into a model of university-based economic development which built upon the comparative advantage of New England, its concentration of research resources in its colleges and universities

A strategy of assisting firm formation based upon academic research originated early in the twentieth century as part of a new thesis of science-based regional economic development set forth in the 1930s by a group of MIT administrators. Much of this model was derived from the activities of Vannevar Bush, who had been involved in entrepreneurial activities during the 1920s. In his own experience with technology transfer, Bush went well beyond capturing ownership of intellectual property rights. He was a prototypical entrepreneurial academic, combining in a very effective manner both intellectual and commercial interests in the course of his career. Through his own experience with the patents system as a young academic, Bush had learned that a patent merely secured legal rights to intellectual property; it was no guarantee that anything profitable would come of it.[1] He determined that if existing firms were not ready to take up an innovation that it was necessary to found a new one.

This chapter focuses upon how the New England Council, an association representing academia, industry and government, provided a venue to analyze regional weaknesses and strengths and to design measures to remedy deficits. Instances of firm formation from academic research were generalized into a model of regional economic development for New England. During the 1930s, a cooperative program linking university and industry was a significant departure from traditional competitive modes of developing regional economies by attracting firms from elsewhere. This initiative was also a response to the long-term economic decline of Massachusetts that pre-dated the depression of the 1930s and the failure of traditional regional development strategies.

New England's regional economic dilemma

Although President Compton has been widely recognized for raising MIT to a new level of intellectual distinction during the difficult times of the 1930s depression, his efforts to apply science, and MIT's experience, to problems of economic and social development are less well known. The thesis of science- and technology-based economic development represented a striking change in regional strategy of response to economic decline. In New England, during the early twentieth century, it took a long time to realize the need to find a new basis for the region's economy. From the early twentieth century, as economic conditions worsened with the decline of New England's traditional industrial base, the problem was defined as the adverse conditions under which New Englanders had to compete with other parts of the country due to higher transportation and wage costs.

Attempted solutions were at first largely developed within a narrow framework, focused on finding natural resources and reviving existing industries. Committee work, review of old studies and commissioning of new ones, and discussions with prospective partners were part of a process of transcending received models. The struggle to break out of an outmoded conceptual framework which had become an intellectual straightjacket made it possible to develop an alternative model, based upon research, and then build new industries whose greatest resources were intellectual property and highly skilled human capital. It is perhaps ironic that this new model was closely related to an earlier one with similar characteristics. The paradigm shift, in this case, was a paradigm return.

Only a few decades before, New England had been the strongest technological economy in the United States. Its metalworking industry, in support of its textile industry, had been a mid-century inspiration for MIT's foundation. In the late nineteenth century, New England's machine tool industry provided the basis for an emerging electrical industry, drawing inventor-entrepreneurs such as Thomas Edison to Boston, for a time, to pursue their projects.[2] Nevertheless, there were already incipient signs of decline in the failure to take advantage of opportunities to develop new industries.

The financial industry's interest in applying his telegraphic devices to solve their operational problems and the greater ease of obtaining investment capital were among the reasons for Edison's departure to New York. The failure to retain an emerging industry based on a new technology was not noticed at the time amidst the prosperity engendered by the textile and shoe industries that had not yet moved closer to their sources of raw materials. Whether to focus on retaining an existing industry or to concentrate on building a new one is a debate that continues to this day.

During this period the Boston business community was divided over whether it should take a long-term view as opposed to protecting the immediate financial interests of existing firms. Prior to 1885, the main concern of the Boston business community and similar groups around the country was the infrastructure for the conduct of business, and they promoted improved roads and port facilities.[3] In 1885 a group of twelve reform-minded businessmen successfully sought the merger of existing business organizations (the Boston Commercial Exchange and the Boston Produce Exchange) and provided the funds to organize the Boston Chamber of Commerce to involve business in projects for community improvement, such as upgrading public education. Through this leadership the business community accepted measures for social improvement such as the minimum wage, which were contrary to the immediate financial interests of some member firms. During this period, the business community was amenable to use of government to solve social problems that could not be solved through private actions.

However, as economic conditions worsened with the decline of New England's traditional industrial base of textiles and shoes, from the early twentieth century onwards, there was a shift to concern with immediate profit interests and to resisting government controls over business. It was believed that the region's economic decline had been caused by government regulation and that the solution was to lower the cost of doing business by reducing taxes and government expenditures.[4] This approach failed in New England sooner than in other parts of the country. Other regions, such as the south, were able to pursue this course of action for a longer time until countries with still lower costs began to siphon off their factories in the 1970s.

The New England Council

The New England Council currently serves as the Washington lobbying group on behalf of the New England States: Massachusetts, New Hampshire, Vermont, Connecticut and Rhode Island. At the start of the twenty-first century these states encompass a mix of high-tech industries and older industrial and rural economies. They include a mix of older and newer, urban and rural, small town and suburban regions and resort areas, both coastal and mountain. The region is also host to some of the most prestigious educational and research institutions in the United States. This special feature of the region has its origins in the founding of Harvard College in 1636 for the purpose of reproducing a religious leadership for an isolated population.

The academic institutions of the region expanded in scale and scope, taking on functions in agricultural training and research and then in technological and industrially related research through the extension of old foundations and the establishment of new ones such as MIT in 1864. The manufacturing industry

ENTERPRISES FROM SCIENCE

that had grown up in the region in new industrial towns, such as Lowell, Massachusetts, established for that purpose, was based on technology imported from abroad and then developed locally. These developments made New England the technology center of the United States in the early nineteenth century.

However, leading industries such as textiles and shoes began to move closer to sources of raw materials later in the century, creating an economic crisis that called forth various responses. These responses can be broadly categorized as efforts to revive existing industries or to develop new ones. The New England Council, which in the course of several post-war moves lost most of its archives and old files, and thus the memory of its original purpose, was at the cusp of this debate from its founding in the mid-1920s. The Council was a precursor of contemporary regional knowledge-based economic development organizations, such as Joint Venture Silicon Valley and the Knowledge Circle of Amsterdam, that bring interested parties together. These organizations provide a venue for debate and brainstorming of new ideas as well as sponsoring research on regional issues. They may also provide a forum for negotiation of alliances among industry, government and universities to sponsor new projects.

There was a need for a broader, more intensive effort in response to long-term economic decline from the turn of the century. In 1925, a group of business and political leaders, including elected officials from the six New England states and representatives from major local industries and subsidiaries of national corporations, organized the New England Council to "improve economic conditions for New England."[5] In addition to pursuing traditional strategies of improving the "business climate" for existing firms in the region or persuading firms elsewhere to relocate, the Council supported the formulation of alternative approaches, such as an emphasis on research.

The Council wanted to emphasize the positive attributes of the region in the competition with other parts of the country to attract industry, and recognized that New England's concentration of academic and industrial research laboratories was a special asset. A research committee formed in 1926 attempted to persuade New England industrialists of the importance of research by holding an annual "Research Day" conference, "where new products are displayed and consulting experts are available."[6] The goal was to encourage small firms to conduct research and development programs themselves or contract with consulting firms and universities for assistance. This was the beginning of a second stage in university–industry relations: the support of smaller regional firms, following an initial strategy of solidifying ties with large national corporations. This eventually led to a third stage, implementation of an explicit strategy of science-based economic development based on new firm formation in 1946, two decades later.

Large corporations with their own research labs and scientists could easily relate to their counterparts at MIT. Smaller firms lacking such facilities and personnel typically did not have an appropriate interlocutor to relate to MIT nor a place to turn to at the Institute to meet their needs. But could this deficit be remedied by addressing only the academic side of the equation? In 1930, MIT proposed to organize a laboratory, modeled on the Mellon Institute in Pittsburgh, with its own staff devoted to industrial research.[7] The objective of the new lab was to extend the benefits of a relationship with MIT, such as the Technology Plan offered to large corporations, to small firms.

It was expected that firms without their own research facilities would be interested in the new plan. The lab would operate on a cost plus basis, "provided a group of industries or individuals will underwrite for ten years the annual loss in revenue which would be sustained by the Institute"[8] in the event that the laboratory was not used enough to pay for itself. Nevertheless, President Compton was wary about the project warning that:

> the conditional conservatism of New England may make such a project less successful here than elsewhere, but if that is the case, it would appear to me to be the equivalent to saying that the industries in New England are in danger of losing out in competition with those in the rest of the country.[9]

Compton's concerns were realistic but the problem with the proposal may have had little to do with any special cultural features of New England, or the size of the firm.

Rather, a firm would have to have its own technical capabilities, to be able to interact with university professors, or even special laboratories designed to deal with their problems. At the very least, a translation and interface mechanism, such as the county agent system for farmers interacting with university-based "experiment stations," would be required to make the project work. Nevertheless, the Council assured Compton that the proposal would be supported, "for we are more convinced than ever of the increasing importance and value of research to New England industries."[10] Although a modicum of interest was expressed, the proposal was not enacted at the time. A sufficiently developed analysis to support a regional strategy of science-based economic development did not yet exist.

Diagnosing New England's economic problems

Before appropriate organizational steps could be taken, a sufficiently analytical framework had to be developed. Old ideas had to be found wanting and new ones created and disseminated. Later in the decade, Compton participated in a series of forums and committees, together with the leadership of the New England business and political communities, to find a cure for the region's economic ills. At these meetings, Compton articulated the thesis that academic research could be a driving force of New England's economy. He analyzed the region's strengths and weaknesses, recognizing that its economic problems preceded the great depression.

New England had suffered a long-term decline due to the loss of much of its industry, which began in the early twentieth century. New England lacked most of the raw materials used by contemporary US manufacturing industry, explaining some of their unwillingness to locate branch plants in the region. Traditional tactics such as reducing taxes and wages to attract industry had failed. Nevertheless, New England still retained significant strengths. The region's financial institutions controlled significant capital based on earlier industrial and mercantile successes. New England had also developed a unique concentration of universities and research institutes. From these elements, Compton devised a strategy for science-based regional economic development.

In 1939, the New England Council organized a "New Products" committee, responding to a suggestion by Compton, a member of the Council. The purpose of the committee was to:

> foster the development of new products for New England industries; to determine whether there are resources in the area of whatever nature that may be more profitably exploited; to mobilize the scientific resources of New England, and especially to assist the smaller manufacturers to utilize our industrial research facilities.[11]

The charge still rested on the assumption of dealing with existing firms but entered into uncharted territory with the notion of exploiting new resources.

The New Products Committee's most important contribution was its diagnosis of the source of New England's economic decline and its proposal for a solution based on the special assets of the region: educational and research institutions. These human resources were seen as New England's comparative advantage over other regions, making up for its deficit in natural resources. Compton ascribed New England's industrial decline to unwillingness to put "a sufficient portion of their earnings back into improvements of plants and of techniques and into development of new and improved products."[12] Thus, in New England the "original technologist-promotor gave place to financial control more interested in receiving the year's dividends."[13] The rigidification of industrial enterprise was intensified as "much of New England capital took the form of trust capital funds not properly available for use as venture capital."[14] The implicit diagnosis was a decline of entrepreneurship and the prescription for change was its renewal.

Chaired by Compton, the committee drew its membership from manufacturing, finance, public utilities, the research departments of firms and the industrial cooperation departments of universities. Three of the eight members from Massachusetts were academics. Richard Cross, an MIT graduate with a business background, was appointed as secretary of the committee. The committee's thinking evolved through three stages, each new one more far-reaching than the previous, as flaws in a strategy were detected. The initial idea was to assist existing firms by improving their access to academic research to help them generate new products. Next it was planned to use academic experts to identify raw materials for national corporations to process in new factories in New England. Finally, a concept was developed to form new technical firms from university-based research.

Prospects for industrial renewal

The committee initially focused upon reviving New England's small industrial firms. Tied to traditional products and production processes, these firms had often lost business in their old product lines and were unable to start new lines of business before their decline was too far advanced for measures to revive them to take hold. According to the committee's executive secretary:

> the problem of the typical New England small manufacturing plant goes deeper than that of assistance in diversifying its business through the development of new products. In many cases production methods and equipment are obsolete and hence expensive. Often there is little idea of production costs.[15]

Unable to exercise much control over the production process, management may be reluctant to reveal its difficulties or may not even realize it has any until its "position has become so desperate that there is little hope of improvement without first providing additional working capital."[16]

Publicity about the committee led the head of one such company to write for assistance. He outlined the condition and prospects of the firm:

> The company was organized in 1878. Until very recently it had been a family owned concern and even now a large majority of the stock is family owned. The company originally manufactured articles of Bone, such as Knife Handles, Buttons, Rings, Crochet Hooks, etc. and the Bone Scrap went into Fertilizer. I believe that this Company was offered the right to take on Bakelite by its inventor when it first came out but like so many other Manufacturers, the management could not grasp the significance of this new product. The following years bone for manufacturing purposes became higher in price and soon moulded products were coming into the market at lower prices than bone products.[17]

The firm's old businesses had declined in the face of new technology. Forced out of the bone business due to competition from plastics, management decided to specialize in fertilizers, formerly a derivative product of the main business. A new generation of management of this family firm soon found that the seasonal

ENTERPRISES FROM SCIENCE

fertilizer business which operated for only six months of the year was inadequate to support the firm's overheads, and sought the advice of the New Products Committee. The letter concluded that "we have a certain amount of capital available for expansion. What we need is to find something to supplement this business."[18] Neither the supplicant nor the respondent had a clue as to what that new product might be at this point.

The inability of existing small business to meet technological change was believed to be a general phenomenon. The secretary of the New Products Committee responded that he was:

> sure your case is typical of countless long established family-owned New England concerns that have enjoyed a protracted period of prosperity under formerly existing industrial and social conditions. The record of the neglected opportunities to adopt new products and processes or to exploit new markets is a tragic one.[19]

Since the committee lacked the capability to offer assistance, Cross referred the inquirer to several industrial consulting firms to aid in a search for "the new product that may be adapted to your facilities."[20] Although availability of capital was not an issue in this instance Cross remarked that too often, "by the time a manufacturer recognizes the necessity for a new product his working capital has been dissipated in supporting unprofitable operations."[21] From this and similar instances, the committee concluded that the prospects for revival of local small industrial firms were discouraging.

Attracting branch plants

If local small firms were an inadequate base for industrial renewal, the next possibility to be considered was large national corporations. Could these manufacturing companies be convinced to locate some of their operations in New England? The committee then explored the possibility of attracting branch plants of these firms to New England. It was expected that they could utilize the region's natural resources, once they had been identified. A series of studies were undertaken to implement this strategy. First, existing reports and data on the economic resources of New England (geological, agricultural and forest, power, labor and transportation) were reviewed.[22] The focus was primarily on the natural resources of the region and secondarily on the financial resources that would be required to tap them, once they were identified.

Sub-committees were set up to determine the local availability of factors of production, including sources of new industrial products, new product development procedures and sources of venture capital and untapped mineral resources. It was hoped that untapped resources could be found or new uses identified for old resources "in the light of present industrial uses and modern recovery methods."[23] As the sub-committees organized themselves, they drew upon the

ENTERPRISES FROM SCIENCE

region's industrial, financial and academic communities for their membership. For example, the mineral resources committee was made up almost entirely of geologists from New England universities. The "Sources of New Products" committee was chaired by the President of the Arthur D. Little consulting firm and included the director of MIT's Division of Industrial Research and Cooperation.

The "Development Procedures and Venture Capital" committee counted among its members Dr Georges Doriot, a professor of Industrial Management at the Harvard Business School. An additional sub-committee on the "Problems of Company Management" was also contemplated but Compton was advised to wait until he could consult with Ralph Flanders, head of the Jones and Lamson Machine Tool Company in Vermont and a member of the New England Council's Industrial Committee. In the early post-war period, Doriot and Flanders became key figures in the invention of the venture capital firm, a project that resulted from these earlier exploratory efforts in regional development.

A case study of a failed effort to develop a new product locally identified the lack of venture capital as the prime difficulty in locating a new plant in New England. A Massachusetts firm conducting research on developing synthetic textile fibers from casein, a milk product, "was not able in the beginning to obtain the necessary financial support in New England and was obliged to look further afield ... [with the result that] ... control of this particular industry has passed out of the area ... [to the National Dairy Products Company of New York]."[24] The raw materials were available nationally and therefore the company that provided the capital to develop this invention decided to locate production in an under-utilized plant elsewhere. The failure to obtain a source of capital tied to the region allowed the location decision to be made on other grounds.

Would special local raw materials be sufficient to attract investment? In 1940 it was still hoped that national corporations would establish plants to process raw materials such as hardwood pulp for manufacture of rayon to feed the local textile industry. The mineral resources sub-committee reported that "certain minerals, chiefly the nonmetallics, are today susceptible of profitable exploitation."[25] Even expert opinion on natural resources found this too narrow a base to build upon. Beginning to move beyond its starting assumption of identifying natural resources for others to use, the sub-committee suggested that, if national corporations would not or could not use these resources, the special assets that New England would have to rely upon for its economic revival were its skilled labor, a tradition of manufacturing and "those facilities for research and technical development which are the modern equivalent of Yankee inventive genius."[26] Today, we would call this its human and intellectual capital.

The prospects for firm formation

By the conclusion of this study exercise, the New Products Committee had revised its focus from assisting existing companies to establishing new enter-

ENTERPRISES FROM SCIENCE

prises and from identification of natural resources to utilization of institutional resources such as research facilities. Reports in hand, Compton appointed a special committee to analyze the various sub-committee findings. This group proposed that a privately financed quasi-public corporation or foundation be established to "appraise opportunities for specific enterprises in the New England area." The organization would not undertake research and engineering projects itself but would encourage the utilization of existing facilities. The committee held that: "The availability of such outlets and facilities is not exceeded in any other section of the country and constitutes a New England asset of the first magnitude. The basic principle is to capitalize this New England resource."[27]

The foundation would study potential areas of expansion for New England's industries but its mission would not include providing venture capital or managerial services for individual companies.[28] Later cited in Vannevar Bush's 1945 "Endless Frontier" report at the close of World War II as an example of how research could be utilized to support industrial development, the Foundation barely got off the ground. Its operating authority was given to a President and a Board of seven trustees while the public character of the organization was symbolized by a group of founders "drawn from the fields of education, engineering research, the sciences, industry and finance and representatives of the six New England states."[29]

The foundation was a precursor of what might now be called a regional "High Tech Council," an organization which provides a focal point to attract attention to emerging industries and a meeting place for members of firms in these industries to discuss common problems and network with each other. Such organizations, often partly funded by government and membership fees, provide a clearing house for information for potential investors, the media and the public as well as a forum to develop new ideas and projects to promote the new industries. The executive director of such an organization typically becomes a public spokesperson for the new industry as well as a point of contact between the new industry and old ones as well as with governments and educational institutions in the region.

Although only approximately half of the projected $100,000 minimum operating budget for the first two years was raised the New England Industrial Foundation went into business on 1 January 1942.[30] Wartime disrupted the original plan and the foundation was redirected to "the search for strategic minerals"[31] and helping New England companies become involved in the war effort. Foundation staff were retained by companies to attune them to "needs and opportunities in emergency war production."[32] However, the foundation's finances soon gave out and it became inactive.[33]

Nevertheless, Compton looked forward to pursuing knowledge-based regional economic development initiatives after the war. He viewed war orders as a temporary stimulant to an economy that would require research inputs in peacetime to maintain its momentum. Compton suggested that companies

ENTERPRISES FROM SCIENCE

should prepare for peace by devoting 2 percent of their gross income to originate new products and processes for the time "when the government ceases to order large quantities of armaments."[34]

During World War II, Karl Compton refined his general ideas to build a new economic base from the potentially commercializable research of academic scientists and engineers into a plan to create a specific organizational mechanism to solve the problems of economic loss that traditional strategies had failed to resolve earlier in the century. The next chapter discusses the invention of the venture capital firm in the early post-war era to make two key elements, money and business expertise, more available to new technology firms.

8

THE INVENTION OF THE VENTURE CAPITAL FIRM
American Research and Development (ARD)

After years of discussions with the business and financial communities, Compton and his colleagues were ready to translate the academic wealth emanating from New England's first industrial revolution into a new wave of economic development. When World War II ended, President Compton renewed the effort to promote the economic renewal of New England through the founding of new technology-based firms. He had concluded that one blockage to the creation of science-based industry was a lack of financing. New England's capital was concentrated in life insurance and investment trusts and then invested in large companies in other parts of the country. Compton now wanted to foster economic growth by establishing a vehicle to put local wealth to work as venture capital to fund new companies in the New England region.

Previously, the technical and financial worlds had tended to operate separately, coming together on opposite sides of the negotiation over the financing of a technically based firm. Now financial, business and technical expertise would be brought together in a common organization with sources of capital that had often previously been excluded from investment in risky new ventures. MIT's role in the invention of the venture capital firm was not well-known at the Institute even though some of the firm's capital came from the school's endowment and several leading professors were advisors to the firm. Compton largely played out his role quietly behind the scenes, devoting perhaps 5 percent of his time to ARD. Nevertheless, Compton served on the board of directors of at least one ARD-sponsored company and ARD board meetings were scheduled to accommodate his availability.

The invention of the venture capital firm filled a gap in the process of translating academic research into firms with new products and jobs. The plan for a firm oriented to the development of new technical companies included leadership by an individual who bridged the business and academic communities and had credibility in both. This program was enhanced by wartime experiences involving responsibilities for management of research and development, shared by many of the participants in this new venture. A regional pattern of science- and technology-based economic growth was created that has become the subject of world-wide emulation.

THE INVENTION OF THE VENTURE CAPITAL FIRM

Precursors to the venture capital firm

Just before the war Compton had concluded that although venture capital was potentially available there was a need "for organization and technique to appraise opportunities for specific enterprises."[1] In addition to the availability of funds, the ability to analyze the commercial potential of a new technology in order to reassure investors that they may "proceed with a reasonable degree of knowledge and assurance" was required.[2] A professional venture capital organization was needed to reduce the risk of investing in inherently risky new ventures. Compton felt that relatively informal groups of friends' or family funds were inadequate for this task.

Nevertheless, some elements were identified in existing venture organizations. For example, "New Enterprises," a membership group, provided an intelligence service to identify potential investments for its individual members.[3] New Enterprises was basically a group of rich people who had formed an investment club. Nevertheless, its research focus adumbrated an important aspect of the venture capital firm. Additional elements were found in the Massachusetts Investment Trust mutual fund, such as an advisory board "comprised of distinguished leaders in the Boston financial community," and a research department devoted to the analysis of investments.[4] The wealthy family groups (Rockefeller, Whitney, Trask) were another model, especially when the families formalized their venture capital activities after the war, establishing firms with professional staffs.[5]

Securities laws had originally been designed to prevent insider collusion but they also precluded spreading the risk of investing in new ventures among several different sources of capital. Before an investment could be made by insurance companies, the regulations in several key states had to be changed and a waiver granted by the Securities and Exchange Commission. For example, ARD's founders persuaded the Connecticut legislature to amend its statutes to allow life insurance companies to invest up to 5 percent of their assets in more risky enterprises. Four other states also changed their rules to allow investment of a small percentage of investment company funds in new ventures. Finally the Securities and Exchange Commission established a new precedent by determining that it was proper for investment companies to join together with institutional and individual investors to jointly invest in new companies as ARD had contemplated.

The founding of American Research and Development (ARD)

ARD was formed out of a coalition between two academic institutions, Harvard Business School and MIT, bringing in administrators, teachers and graduates of both schools as its personnel and advisors. The Business School provided graduates with managerial expertise who could advise, evaluate and, when necessary,

THE INVENTION OF THE VENTURE CAPITAL FIRM

replace the firm founders that ARD financed. New company presidents were typically people with a technical, not a business background. MIT provided people with a technical background who could seek out the technologies on which new companies would be built. MIT also provided much of the technology, many of the potential firm founders, and the expertise to evaluate the technical feasibility of proposals. Harvard Business School contributed organizational and financial expertise and credibility in the business world.

The project also had the support of Boston's financial community, concerned with the future of the region in the post-war era.[6] Compton persuaded the members of an elite New England business, political and educational network to take on the task of organizing a venture capital firm. The group included Merrill Griswold, head of the Massachusetts Investment Trust and a leader of the Boston financial community, Donald David, Dean of the Harvard Business School, and Ralph Flanders, President of the Jones and Laughlin Machine Tool Company in Vermont, who had also served as head of the Federal Reserve Bank in Boston, to form the American Research and Development Corporation (ARD) to supply risk capital to new technical companies. Dean David had introduced his friend Ralph Flanders to Griswold, who he said was "worried about the same thing [lack of risk capital for new enterprises]."[7] The issue was not simply lack of funds but rather lack of funds and expertise that could be dedicated to founding new enterprises.

The founders had a variety of motives, some genuinely believing in the practicality of the project while others saw it largely as a public relations device. Flanders viewed the venture capital firm as a model for future economic growth, arguing that: "The post-war prosperity of America depends in large measure on finding financial support for that comparatively small percentage of new ideas and developments which give promise of expanded production and employment and an increased standard of living for the American people."[8] Griswold initially viewed the business prospects of ARD skeptically and mainly saw it as good publicity for the Boston financial community, but later, through service on its Board, developed a personal interest in the formation of technical firms.[9]

The founding of ARD was widely publicized in the business press and noted in general media such as *Time Magazine*.

> The sponsors of American research got together because they felt that standard investment companies and individuals were too thoroughly hobbled by Government restrictions and taxes to put up the risk capital industry needs. What was needed, they decided, was an organization that could combine a pool of venture capital with the know-how to put the money into the right investments.[10]

An optimistic Californian observer noted that "While it may be several years before its investments, as such, show a profitable return, the company's

THE INVENTION OF THE VENTURE CAPITAL FIRM

eventual success, both from a humanitarian and a financial standpoint is more or less a foregone certainty."[11] The early internal view was not quite so sanguine.

Although the original plan to raise $5 million for American Research and Development's initial capitalization was not fulfilled, the firm was begun after $3 million had been raised.[12] A purchase by the Morgan Guaranty Trust department helped legitimate American Research and Development to other financial houses and investors in New York. Financing was aided by a post-war shift of trust funds, pension funds and institutional endowments from preferred stocks and bonds into common stocks.[13] Lehman Brothers and Harriman, Ripley were among the firms that supported the distribution of ARD stock to investors but they were limited in what they could do for ARD by a relative lack of investor interest.[14] The 1947 Treasurer's report noted MIT's investment in ARD. Compton also persuaded his colleagues at other technologically oriented universities such as the Rice Institute in Houston to invest in ARD.

Flanders and Griswold took responsibility for the organizing phase of Compton's "pro bono publico" business.[15] After a brief period under Flanders, General Georges Doriot (a professor of industrial management at the Harvard Business School who had just completed a term of wartime service in the research and development branch of the US Army's Quartermaster Corps and had been a member of the pre-war New Products Committee) was made President of ARD. Doriot had come from France to Harvard after World War I, initially as a student, and then remaining as a professor. He had run a Pennsylvanian steel company, Mckeesport Plate, for a time during the 1930s and had also served on various boards of directors. In his wartime service in the research branch of the Quartermaster Corps he had attained the rank of Brigadier General and henceforth was known in public life as General Doriot.

General Doriot's interest in creating high-tech start-up firms was relatively unusual for a Harvard Business School professor in the early post-war era. Harvard Business School, through the consulting activities of its faculty and the placement of its graduates, was connected primarily to large corporations at the time. Doriot's course on "manufacturing" at Harvard Business School involved his students in carrying out studies of the potential of new industrial areas and was as much aimed at encouraging the development of entrepreneurial character as transmitting any specific analytical skills. For Doriot, heading up a venture capital firm translated what had been classroom exercises into actual businesses. Like some of the professors who were assisted in forming firms by ARD and other venture capital firms, Doriot maintained his professorship at Harvard and ran the venture capital firm at the same time, often keeping evening office hours and holding Saturday staff meetings.[16]

Legitimizing the venture capital concept

The triad of Harvard Business School, MIT and the financial community legitimized the concept of venture capital to state governments and federal regulators. The financial community and its legal representatives provided the bulk of the funds as well as legitimacy in the business world, and also used their political connections to gain necessary changes in regulation and law to make the concept feasible. An observer commented: "Had not the investment bankers associated with this new company been willing to do a great deal more than ordinarily is expected of them, the new venture might well have died aborning."[17] They gained legal approval for financial institutions required by law to invest their funds conservatively to participate in the financing of a firm designed to act as an intermediary to transfer these funds to one of the riskiest of all business propositions: the start-up of a new firm.

Legal barriers designed to protect the assets of small investors precluded large financial institutions from investing any of their funds in a new firm based on a novel concept. The thesis was that by distributing the funds among a number of new firms the financial risk would be reduced to an acceptable level, even if only a few of these ventures were eventually successful. The original venture capital concept included: a mechanism for amassing capital from a variety of sources through the sale of equity (stock) in the firm; a technical advisory board to provide leads and assess proposals; and a staff with the expertise to offer business advice and take the necessary organizational steps to assist in the formation of a firm.

Creating a role for venture capital

Beyond the question of financing ARD, there was the issue of its mode of operation and the development of a format for the creation of new firms that could successfully balance business and technical criteria. As its president defined the issue: "The Company is not a form of bank. It is a builder of new enterprises. Money, skill, knowledge and men are the tools it will use in a program requiring careful planning and long-range thinking."[18] Extensive publicity resulted in hundreds of proposals to ARD from independent inventors but innovative devices by themselves were not sufficient to attract serious interest. To create companies with innovative technologies that were competently run, technical people had to be given business advice and business people found to run the companies.

ARD's objective was to identify a technically superior product with commercial potential and find people who could bring it into production and to market. The guidelines for making an investment were as follows:

- Research and development carried on to date indicate that the enterprise will be commercially practicable.

THE INVENTION OF THE VENTURE CAPITAL FIRM

- Satisfactory profit potentialities exist.
- The competitive position is initially protected through patents of specialized knowledge and techniques.[19]

The internal structure of ARD was designed to achieve these objectives through a small staff, supported by technical and business advisors. In addition to President Compton, the technical advisory board included two leading MIT professors, Gilliland from chemical engineering and Hunsaker from aeronautics. Both were well-connected to and respected by the projected source of technology, the faculty and students of the school. The board of directors of ARD, consisting of members with financial and legal expertise and experience in a range of technically based businesses including chemicals and machine tools, as well as having final authority on investments also functioned as a business advisory group on the viability of projected firms.

In taking equity in a company in exchange for its investment ARD expected a long-term relationship.

> When we do invest in a growth company, after careful investigation, we usually have representation on the company's board and arrange for one of our men to spend time counseling the firm's management. And after a company is on its financial feet, we begin to think of recovering at least part of our investment so these funds can be re-invested in a new growth situation.[20]

This relationship included the willingness to take a longer-term perspective on return from investment than the conventional three years, placing members of the firm on the board of the company invested in and intervening in the affairs of a company when necessary.

ARD orchestrated changes in leadership when it felt that a firm was beyond a founder's ability to manage and a "head man was needed right away."[21] The company president, an individual with a technical background, was unhappy with his growing responsibilities as manager. "He has been in my office many times explaining to me that the company was too big for him, that he did not like it and wanted to quit. He has stated that he was much happier when the company had only twelve or fifteen men."[22] More typically, technically oriented CEOs refuse to recognize that personnel and commercial dealings have gotten beyond their abilities and interests.

When ARD believed that a company it had invested in had been naive in its dealings with another company, General Doriot wrote to its president:

> I would suggest that you call a Board Meeting of High Voltage whenever Dr. Compton can be there. ... You have wasted a good deal of time. You have trained A.D. Little to be "the world's greatest experts on the use of high voltage," you have given them many of your ideas,

THE INVENTION OF THE VENTURE CAPITAL FIRM

techniques and secrets so that they can get good fees peddling your information. I think we should quit.[23]

An informed observer commented on the ongoing relationship between the head of ARD and the company:

The General keeps popping in and out throughout the company's early history. He let Robinson run the company, but he is there one day telling Robinson that his sales organization is inadequate. He is there a few years later urging Robinson to take advantage of the Common Market and put up a manufacturing plant in Europe.[24]

The role of the venture capitalist was gradually defined.

It was thrashing around. Nobody had ever done that kind of work they were doing. [They were] seeking a sense of direction, trying to decide what kind of things to do and how to do them. In the post war hustle and bustle, there were so many men and women who had felt bottled up for the past 5–6–7 years. We had been in militarily oriented jobs and been given duties and responsibilities that in truth were beyond our normal capacities, our normal talents, just because somebody had to do it and you did the best you could. There was a great pent-up demand to … get going. "Let's reshape the world; let's change its ills and shortcomings". So American Research and Development had a very high tone and intent and integrity over and beyond making money.[25]

Interaction between ARD staff and advisors was mainly through informal discussions rather than formal meetings of the advisory board. However, the advisors occasionally participated in the quarterly board of directors meetings where funding decisions were made. A variety of approaches were used to build up a network of contacts and to learn about emerging technical areas. To obtain leads to people with ideas that could be turned into companies, staff members attended electronics trade shows, scanned trade journals and kept in touch with ARD's advisors at MIT. To emphasize the importance of visiting universities General Doriot once ceremoniously handed out Massachusetts Transit Authority tokens at the close of a staff meeting.

ARD "very aggressively worked MIT."[26] A staff member typically dropped by the office of a faculty member who was an ARD advisor and in the course of a conversation, "These gentlemen would alert us, tip us off, help us. 'There is a young graduate student down the hall working on something. We think it is interesting; you have to decide if it has commercial possibilities.'"[27] Since MIT's role in the founding of ARD was largely an administrative initiative that did not create controversy, most faculty and graduate students were not aware of

THE INVENTION OF THE VENTURE CAPITAL FIRM

the existence of ARD or of the Institute's role in the founding of the firm. Therefore ARD staff members often introduced themselves to professors and students by mentioning such connections and President Compton's founding and continuing advisory role.

ARD's role in the formation of new firms based on research at MIT is exemplified by the High Voltage Corporation and Digital Equipment Corporation. High Voltage shows the gradual progression of an academic research project toward commercialization while the formation of Digital Equipment illustrates the creation of networks between the university and the emerging venture capital world.

The High Voltage Engineering Corporation

In the course of twenty years the development of the Van de Graaff generator utilized virtually all the patterns of university–industry relations from assignment of patent rights to an existing firm to formation of a new firm. Van de Graaff's interest in high voltage was stimulated during employment in the summer of 1921 on the maintenance gang of the Alabama Power Company. This experience gave him a practical appreciation of the engineering difficulties encountered in working with high voltage. In 1926–7 it occurred to him that "the generation of high voltage in a vacuum would afford a means of accelerating ions and electrons to enormous energies and that these high speed particles would afford a powerful means for the investigation of the atomic nucleus and other fundamental problems."[28]

At Oxford University in the 1920s, in the course of doctoral research on another topic, Van de Graaff outlined methods of beginning this project but did not actually initiate it until 1929 when he received a National Research Council fellowship to Princeton University. The fellowship was officially awarded to carry forward his PhD research but upon arrival at Princeton Van de Graaff persuaded his sponsor Compton to allow him to drop this line of work and pursue the application of electrostatics to nuclear research. When Compton became President of MIT he encouraged the appointment of Van de Graaff.

The commercial potential of Van de Graaff's research was viewed as sufficiently promising for MIT to draft a document to specify the rights of the different parties involved in the research. The parties listed were MIT (Van de Graaff's current base) the National Research Council (which had provided fellowship support), Princeton University (which had provided an initial research site and equipment), the Research Corporation (which had provided funding for the construction of apparatus) and Van de Graaff (the inventor and leader of the research team).

MIT would control disposition of patent rights and take responsibility for development up to the point of manufacture while the various parties would hold different shares in the potential commercial outcomes of the research. Princeton's share, for example, was proposed to be quite limited as it had

THE INVENTION OF THE VENTURE CAPITAL FIRM

already been reimbursed for the cost of research equipment moved to MIT. The agreement also protected scholarly access to aspects of the research involving fundamental science and attempted to balance concerns for broad utilization of the medical treatment and power transmission applications of the research with the attainment of reasonable profits.

During World War II several high voltage generators were built at MIT with support from the Office of Scientific Research and Development (OSRD). At the suggestion of OSRD, the Westinghouse Corporation was licensed to produce generators but had "apparently done nothing" with the patents by 1946. In March 1946 Van de Graaff and his associate Professor Trump went to see John Bunker, the Acting Chairman of MIT's Patent Management Committee and proposed that Westinghouse's license be cancelled and that a new company "would perhaps be in order."[29] Compton recommended that ARD back the formation of a firm and in December 1946 the High Voltage Engineering Corporation was formed to manufacture and sell electrostatic generators for use in cancer treatment, industrial metal inspection and nuclear physics research. The high voltage generators built at MIT during World War II served as prototypes for the company's product line. Dr Dennis Robinson, a dielectric and radar expert with administrative experience as coordinator of the Anglo-American program at the Radiation Laboratory, became president of the company. ARD staff provided High Voltage with financial and business advice and by 1955 it was a reasonably successful company.

The Digital Equipment Corporation

The formation of the Digital Equipment Corporation was also based on government-funded research at MIT. Project Whirlwind originated at MIT during World War II to build a simulated flight training device to assist in the training of pilots and make it a less labor intensive task, since skilled pilots who had performed in combat were in short supply. The construction of the simulator was based on the development of electronic devices that were essentially computers. When the war ended before the project was completed, the Naval Office of Scientific Research and Development temporarily continued to fund the project but its fate was in doubt. The requirements of the Air Force for a means of coordinating the tracking of aircraft across a network of radar stations for the Distant Early Warning line in the early 1950s gave a new life and purpose to the Whirlwind project. The technology in the process of development was redesigned from a special purpose computation device to drive flight simulators into a general purpose computer to calculate, store and retrieve continually changing information about a multitude of aircraft flights occurring simultaneously. The Air Force took over responsibility for the project from the Navy, expanding its funding and scope.[30]

In the early 1950s ARD focused on computers as an area of possible commercialization. The few existing small companies such as Eckert-Mauchly in

THE INVENTION OF THE VENTURE CAPITAL FIRM

Philadelphia were visited but no deals were made. After a discussion of this foray at an American Research and Development board meeting, Horace Ford (treasurer of American Research and Development and former treasurer of MIT) took staff member William Congleton aside and told him that at a recent meeting of the board of MIT's Lincoln Laboratory, of which he was a member, he had heard about some interesting work on computers. He was a "number plumber" himself and didn't know anything about computers but suggested that Congleton contact Professor Jay Forrester, an assistant director of the project. Forrester suggested that Congleton talk to two graduate students, Kenneth Olsen and Harlan Anderson, who were working at Lincoln Laboratory. As members of a team that had lost a competition to design an airborne military computer to another group at the lab they still believed that they had come up with the best design. There had been desultory lunch conversations about going into business but no concrete steps had been taken.

After a series of conversations with ARD staff members in which "They would tell us about computers and we would tell them about the problems of starting a business ... it began to shape up into a little program to see if we could commercialize this computer concept."[31] However, since a market survey suggested that commercialization of computers was premature a cautious approach was taken. Digital Equipment Corporation would begin by making circuit boards and sell them to research labs and industrial organizations that weren't yet ready for a computer but wanted to take a first step and experiment. ARD committed $300,000: $100,000 as equity capital and $200,000 to be available as loans if the company was proceeding satisfactorily. Within a relatively few years Digital Equipment had become so successful as a maker of mini-computers, and American Research and Development's modest investment worth so much ($400 million), that a moderate success or failure on any other project had virtually no impact on ARD's financial status.

ARD's investment in Digital Equipment was distributed to the venture capital firm's shareholders so that American Research could function again in a meaningful way. The huge value of the Digital Equipment stock in ARD's portfolio meant that the relatively modest profits and losses on most new ventures would have virtually no effect on the venture capital firm's worth. Thus the payout to early investors. Ironically, MIT was not among those who gained financially from the success of Digital Equipment or ARD, having sold its stock in the early years of the firm before any increase in value had accrued. The administration's interest in the venture firm did not postdate the Compton era, despite the significance of this intiative which resulted in the foundation of the contemporary venture capital industry. MIT returned for a time to a *laissez-faire* institutional posture with respect to industry, with increasing numbers of its faculty individually participating in the formation of new firms assisted by ARD and other firms descended from it in the emerging venture capital industry but MIT did not take a new administrative initiative in technology transfer until the 1970s.

THE INVENTION OF THE VENTURE CAPITAL FIRM

The beginnings of the venture capital industry

During the initial decade observers often viewed ARD's prospects as dim but the firm's investment record began to look respectable fifteen years after it had been formed, even apart from the remarkable success of Digital Equipment. By the early 1960s, ARD was the oldest and largest publicly owned venture capital firm and an observer noted that: "For this reason, its record is conspicuously and frequently quoted."[32] By 1961, 3,300 prospects had been investigated and sixty-six invested in (about 2 percent of those worthy of initial study). Of the sixty-six, twenty-nine had been sold for a gain of $3 million on twenty, with losses of $850,000 on the other nine. The thirty-seven remaining firms in the portfolio had expanded investments totalling $11.1 million to a value of $30 million. ARD had invested in eighty-four companies in total by 1961. The forty-two still held comprised ARD's then current assets of nearly $39 million.[33]

Goverment policy expanded the nascent venture capital industry during the 1950s, capitalizing firms through its small business development programs. The example of ARD and other venture capital firms encouraged Congress to authorize an additional venture capital instrument, the Small Business Investment Corporation through the Small Business Investment Act of 1958. The purpose of the Small Business Investment Corporation was to provide loans to new companies that banks would not normally lend to. The public purpose justifying the establishment of this government agency is the creation of jobs. Despite a high failure rate such small companies have been recognized as the greatest source of US employment growth.

Almost twenty-five years after its founding it was reported that ARD had done so well "that it is beginning to spawn some imitators, both in the United States and Europe."[34] "The inspiration for most European venturers has been American Research and Development."[35] A series of venture capital firms were founded modeled on ARD, for example, the Value Line Development Corporation and Diebold Technology Ventures. Among the firms founded by ARD alumni were Greylock (Elfers) and Palmer Associates (Congleton). By 1979 there were 250 venture capital firms,[36] including those that were direct spin-offs and others that had been stimulated by ARD's example.[37] In 1997, this source listed more than 1,000 venture capital firms in the USA and abroad.

The trajectory of venture capital

The nature and definition of the venture capital firm has changed significantly since the success of ARD and perhaps because of the great potential for financial rewards generated by this mechanism for financing new businesses. Since ARD's founding, partnerships have become the norm in the venture capital industry. This organizational form, in contrast to a corporation, allows members of firm to have direct control over earnings. Acceptance of the partnership model reflects a perception that the venture capital firm is a less risky business proposition than originally conceived. On the other hand, most contemporary firms in the industry concentrate on financing the middle and later stages of new company development. It has been estimated that fewer than twenty firms are in the business of funding the early stages of development of new technical companies.[38]

The shift from corporate ownership and the increase in size of venture capital funds both had significant effects in changing the structure of the venture capital industry from the early days of ARD and its immediate offspring, who focused upon what would now be called "seed" capital investment in high-tech firms, with considerable involvement in the management of these firms, to the present era in which most venture capital investment is made at the later stages of firm formation and often to non-technically oriented firms.

Indeed, it is sometimes seen as a misrepresentation to refer to venture capital as relevant to the initial stages of firm formation, so strongly has the approach of the industry changed; so has its very definition. The larger blocks of funds involved drive investments downstream since it takes virtually the same due diligence and investment of effort to seek out an early stage candidate as a later stage one. Moreover, since the employees are making their bets with income tied closely to the firm's returns, this may have a conservatizing influence on selection of investment in contrast to the early situation when investment decisions were virtually de-coupled from personal economic interest, short of failure of the firm.

In the course of the late 1990s e-commerce bubble, intense competition for investments led venture capital firms to search at the earliest stages of firm formation again. Some formed incubator facilities to create firms themselves rather than waiting for business plans to be presented to them. Many of these firms, however, were e-commerce ventures that duplicated similar business models. Many were also variations on existing firms in what was soon realized to be an already crowded market. Nor were most of these firms based on technological innovation. As the private venture capital industry engaged in triage, shutting down some firms and putting more capital into others in a rescue effort, an alternative venture capital industry emerged in its wake.

Almost as a reprise of the original founding of ARD, universities and other investors have been establishing "seed" venture capital funds to build new businesses from technologies developed on campus. A number of schools, including Northwestern University, New York University, the University of California at Los Angeles and Columbia University, have established such funds. In addition, several new venture firms, with names such as StartEmUp, University Angels and ITU Ventures, have been set up that explicitly target next-generation, university-originated technologies as the basis for firm-formation.[39]

It can be expected that universities will increasingly use a small part of their endowments to capitalize such funds, much as MIT and Rice funded ARD in the 1940s. This time the investment vehicles will likely be maintained as part of a continuing effort to capitalize intellectual property and move to realize the vision of a self-generating academic enterprise. It can also be predicted that this

THE INVENTION OF THE VENTURE CAPITAL FIRM

trend will be broad-based as both research-intensive universities and less research-intensive universities and regions with ambitions to build knowledge-based industry foster these developments.

In the 1930s Karl Compton and his colleagues at MIT recognized that New England possessed research activities to a greater degree than the rest of the nation and sought to capitalize on this regional resource. If existing companies, whether national or local, were not interested in or capable of commercializing emerging technologies, then new companies would have to be formed. Through their role in the formation of ARD, MIT and the Harvard Business School, the Boston financial community helped create the venture capital industry. The next chapter will examine how this model for science-based regional economic development, based upon university–industry connections, was transferred from MIT to Stanford.

9

STANFORD AND SILICON VALLEY
Enhancement of the MIT model

Stanford University and Silicon Valley developed as a virtual joint venture. The metamorphosis of the region and the university was a cooperative and collaborative effort in which the evolution of the Valley was inextricably intertwined with the transformation of the university. Stanford played a significant role in creating the vision and implementing the strategy that produced the world's leading complex of high-technology firms. The rise of these firms in turn fed back into the growth of the university by providing it with a pathway for its students, a market for its technologies and partners for building new research collaborations. By assisting the economic development of its region, Stanford transformed itself into a leading research university.

Ultimately, Stanford's initiatives provided the base for the development of a high-tech region in northern California, a model for liberal arts/research universities interested in transforming themselves along similar lines and an interactive concept of innovation, transcending previous linear and reverse linear modes. This academic/industrial development project began in the early twentieth century and had made sufficient strides during the depression such that Stanford University was the source of technology firms even before World War II. The development of firms from academic research became the basis of a so-called "science push" linear model of innovation, starting from investigation and resulting in practical uses. This was in contrast to a "market pull" reverse linear model, exemplified by Thomas Alva Edison's solutions to communications problems for New York City's financial industry.

Stanford's goal became the creation of an industrial support structure for academic research. A technological industrial infrastructure was also necessary if graduates were to be retained in the area. Accordingly, Stanford appropriated the MIT entrepreneurial university model and adapted it to the contexts of a liberal arts academic setting and a developing region. Stanford then expanded upon both the entrepreneurial model and the "ivory tower" model of basic research-oriented universities by giving equal weight to the liberal arts and sciences, the engineering school and the medical school. Most universities were built upon one or two of these legs whereas Stanford had three.

STANFORD AND SILICON VALLEY

The origins of Silicon Valley

Not too many years ago, the area now known as Silicon Valley was a "greenfield site" of fruit and nut orchards. San Francisco anchored the emerging technological complex to the north, with Stanford University affixed at its southern edge. By the mid-1970s, the growing complex of San Francisco Bay-area technology firms, venture capitalists, entrepreneurial scientists and engineers, had been dubbed "Silicon Valley."

Silicon Valley had its origins in a university development strategy even as that university achieved its distinction based upon a unique approach to regional development. Stanford looked to MIT as a model for its industrial development strategy although there were clear differences between the two schools and their situations. MIT had been built upon an existing base of technological industry in the Boston area, which provided support for its founding and development. Stanford, on the other hand, was located on a pristine site surrounded by thousands of acres of scrub ranchland where valley turned to hills, and consequently had to take a proactive role in creating industry to support its growth, unlike early MIT, where the school's original purpose had been to enhance the technological capacity of local industry by infusing it with new ideas.

Founded in the late nineteenth century by a railroad tycoon in memory of a deceased son, Leland Stanford Jr University soon acquired more of a reputation as a party school for children of the rich than as a center of intellect. Pre-war Stanford held elite social status but was not yet considered a leading university; however, the groundwork was being laid for its eventual transformation into one of the top research schools in the country.

When Stanford was founded, San Francisco was a shipping, trading and financial center, with few technological and industrial attributes. Shortly thereafter, however, the beginnings of an electrical industry appeared, much of it developed by Stanford graduates, who installed and maintained technology imported from the eastern United States and soon supplemented it with their own inventions and products. Firms such as Heintz and Kaufmann and Federal originated the contemporary "western electronics industry."[1] By the 1930s, the regional electronics industry was flourishing, led by local electric firms, along with electronics programs at Stanford. Industry and university grew in tandem.

How did industrial and academic development strategies converge? Northern California was originally dependent on the east for its electrical equipment and other modern technologies, and even after the engineering school at Stanford had trained engineers who could configure and operate these technologies, the region still lacked its own technological industries. The founders of the Stanford Engineering School held that they could never have a leading school unless it was associated with local industry that had the capability for technological innovation, not merely replication of imported technology. Since that industry did not exist, it would have to be created. The available base on which it could be built was the Engineering School itself. The Stanford strategy of

103

STANFORD AND SILICON VALLEY

academic-based industrial development thus preceded Frederick Terman, whose name is synonymous with Stanford's emergence as an engine of regional economic development, and who accordingly is often referred to as "the father of Silicon Valley."

Stanford's academic development strategy

Frederick Terman had been a student of Stanford's engineering faculty members, who played a key role in creating regional business from technologies innovated in their labs. After receiving his bachelor's and master's degrees from Stanford, he obtained a PhD in electrical engineering from MIT. He returned to Stanford in 1925 and joined the engineering faculty. He soon became head of the electrical engineering department, with the ambition of making it a leader in the field. Like Vannevar Bush, his mentor and PhD advisor at MIT, Frederick Terman never became president of his university. Nevertheless, he was more influential than most presidents in shaping a new academic model. Also like Bush, Terman was active as a consultant to industry and participated, through his students, in forming new firms from technology developed at the university.

Terman's academic development strategy in the 1930s had three key elements: (1) making close connections between science and engineering departments; (2) linking academic departments and local science-based firms; and (3) concentrating resources on a few key research areas with both theoretical and practical potential. Terman included in the training of electrical engineering students visits to area firms such as HK, Eitel-McCullough, and Litton Engineering, where they learned about the commercial potential of electronic devices. Under Terman's guidance, engineering students also became multidisciplinary, joining with other departments to work on research projects. Thus, the flow of electrical engineering students went in both directions – toward industry and toward basic research disciplines, notably physics.

An important part of Terman's strategy was to create an industrial context around the department, making it possible for graduates to remain in the region. In 1939 he encouraged his students William Hewlett and David Packard to form a firm based on their invention of a resistance-tuned oscillator. In a precursor of the center mode of cooperative investigation, the six members of the physics department banded together to conduct a joint research project to build a 3-million-volt x-ray tube to explore atomic and nuclear phenomena. The Stanford electronics researchers, competing with the Berkeley cyclotron, sought to accelerate particles at a low cost and with a relatively simple device. The financial exigencies of the depression meant that professors often had to undertake the mechanical and design tasks of building equipment, which gave them a familiarity with practical engineering problems that they might not have obtained under more affluent conditions.

As department chair and later as Stanford University's Engineering Dean and then provost, Terman focused on a few key fields. He argued that by developing a coherent strategy and by concentrating new resources on a few selected fields an emerging university could move past heretofore more distinguished universities. The son of Lewis Terman, the noted psychologist and long-term faculty member at Stanford, Frederick Terman is said to have been influenced by his father's psychological research on gifted children. This background may have led him to focus on a few areas of distinction, or as Terman liked to call them "steeples of excellence," rather than to try to upgrade academic quality across the board.

Concentration of resources is contrary to traditional academic practice, which favors equality in distribution of resources in theory, if not always in practice. Terman believed that research should take first prominence in the hiring decision. He also held that several faculty members could be hired in the same research field, contrary to the usual departmental practice of spreading faculty across the discipline. Terman based this strategy on the assumption that a faculty member could teach more broadly than their research area. Thus, gaps in the curriculum that had to be filled for educational purposes did not necessarily have to influence the hiring decision. Since most schools hired on a case by case basis, keeping a variety of departmental and disciplinary needs in mind, a school with a single-minded determination to develop excellence in a few research fields could create a critical mass within an academic generation and become a world leader.

Concentrating on a relatively few existing and emerging fields, sometimes labeled towers or centers of excellence, is currently becoming a widespread strategy. Schools such as Ohio State University, that realize they cannot afford to support all disciplines equally and still attain distinction, have recently taken up Terman's academic development strategy. The other part of Terman's strategy, developing a collaborative relationship with technology firms emanating from the university, is also becoming more widespread. The State University of New York at Stony Brook, for example, was instrumental in creating a local biotechnology industry from on-campus research, which then fed back into the academic environment. A related strategy, exemplified by the Centennial Campus of North Carolina State University, is to bring existing companies with technological capabilities within the academic orbit as potential collaborators. At Stanford, university–industry collaboration also helped create a tradition of inter-firm collaboration, formal and informal, that became the hallmark of Silicon Valley.

University–industry relations: a seamless web

The Silicon Valley model of individual technologists and firms interacting and networking with each other developed early on. A "technology pool" was created that firms and academic researchers could both draw upon. In essence, universities operated within a seamless web to further their overall regional development objectives, initiating a series of firms while raising the level of academic research. Industry and academia mutually inspired each other. Although "Not a few men in the semi-conductor industry see the academic reputation of Berkeley and Stanford as a product of industrial progress and not vice versa,"[2] Terman viewed the relationship as reciprocal.

The university served as a neutral ground, creating links among firms. Those cooperative arrangements foreshadowed contemporary efforts to share pre-competitive research among a related group of firms and to have early reports cross freely between a university researcher and a firm, typically one that had emerged from academic research. Stanford professors and their former students, located in nearby start-up firms, made a series of electronics inventions in the late 1930s that took the local electronics industry to a new level. Professors collaborated with former students who had formed firms nearby the university. For example, in 1939 the Varian brothers, who had formed Halcyon, and Prof. W.W. Hansen invented the Klystron tube, a new type of amplifier and oscillator of electrons.[3] Hansen had previously invented another electronics device, the rhumbatron in 1936. In the pre-war era, both the electrical engineering department and local electronics firms lacked critical mass. To encourage the development of the university and industry, several companies released their patents on electronics devices for use with related intellectual property held by Stanford.

The inventors turned over their patent rights to the university. Even Litton, a close associate of the early Stanford electronics researchers but located in industry, assigned his patent for the generation of high frequency oscillations in multigrid tubes to Stanford. The rights to all of these electronics devices went into a common pool controlled by Stanford. Stanford's repository of intellectual property was made available to all firms in the pool, allowing each company a broader base for product development. This arrangement placed the objective of building the electronics industry for the region ahead of the individual competitive advantage. In payment for its intermediary services, the university received licensing income, which it used to enhance its academic programs.

The electronics inventions made at Stanford, and the firms that emanated from the university, fed both into wartime radar research and post-war basic research in physics. The Varian brothers gave up their early firm and moved back to the university to be able to work more closely with faculty members in developing the military implications of these discoveries. Stanford academics and firm founders shared a common perception of the dual implications of these discoveries during the 1930s, a conclusion that academics at MIT's Rad Lab drew during the war. After the war, the brothers revived their firm, under their own name, providing equipment for university research instruments as well as to industry.

Market pull: the New York model

The linear model of practical implications drawn from academic research has its complement in a reverse linear model, moving in the opposite direction.

Silicon Alley, like Silicon Valley, is a metaphor for high-tech entrepreneurship. Generally speaking, the New York model developed from a business concept in which new firms are created to use technology for solving the problems of existing businesses. This market pull perspective is exemplified in the saying "Wall Street loves a firm that has good management," and it represents an alternative to the technology push model pioneered on Route 128 and Silicon Valley.

The New York model originated in the late nineteenth century, with Thomas Alva Edison's innovations in telegraphy meeting the needs of the financial industry for secure communications. He then expanded upon this approach of enhancing existing businesses and industries by utilizing technology to meet broader needs, such as for improved lighting. He then envisioned future needs and inventions to satisfy them, in the process creating new communications industries. Edison systematically looked at needs in society and then invented products to meet those needs. He was able to find the financing in New York to accomplish his goals.[4]

At that time, New York City became one of the three leading world high-tech centers, along with Berlin and Paris. With the movement of technology firms from the city by the mid-twentieth century, however, and the failure to develop a leading technological university, New York lost its status as a center of high technology. Nevertheless, in recent years the New York model of starting from business concepts and the financial industry has been revived in the form of Silicon Alley. Newspaper editors have come up with new business ideas based around the Internet, and software firms have enhanced the productivity of traditional New York industries, including some of the same ones that Edison serviced, such as finance, and the now-traditional media industries, many of which grew out of his inventions.

Technology push

A technology push model was meanwhile developed in Boston and Northern California in contrast to New York's market pull approach. Despite some differences, Silicon Valley and Route 128 share a common origin that can be discerned in the work of MIT's Vannevar Bush and Stanford's Frederick Terman, who had been, respectively, teacher and student at MIT. In their conception, innovations can reach the market through university research assisted by venture capital. Moreover, Vannevar Bush's participation in the founding of the Raytheon Corporation in the 1920s had become an inspiration to his fellow MIT administrators who envisioned a "research row" along Memorial Drive during the 1930s.

The model of science-based economic development from academia through the mechanism of the venture capital firm was transplanted from MIT to Stanford in the early post-war period as a result of Terman having been around MIT during the war. As director of the Radar Counter-Measures Lab at

Harvard, he had the opportunity to observe MIT's mode of operation at close hand. One sign of Terman's early intention is a letter he wrote in 1943 to Stanford's treasurer proposing an even more intensive replication of the MIT model for Northern California. Terman advised the treasurer that the way MIT operated in connection with industry is what had to be done at Stanford as soon as the war was over – form research centers, establish firms and make this a central thrust if Stanford was to become a major university.

The effect of World War II

The electronics devices developed at pre-war Stanford had long-term implications for the development of the university as a center of electronics research and of the region as a center for the electronics industry. The devices had theoretical as well as practical implications as they were utilized both for development of radar systems and for building devices to study the behavior of electrons. The immediate military applications were realized elsewhere since Stanford was not chosen as a site for a major laboratory. Immediately after the war, Terman brought back to Stanford the expanded collaborative research models that he had observed at MIT.

Terman viewed the years after the war as critical for Stanford, determining whether it would become the Harvard of the west or persist on a level of national influence comparable to that of Dartmouth, "a well thought of institution having about 2 per cent as much influence on national life as Harvard."[5] Terman believed that "Stanford can be a dominating factor in the West, but it will take many years of continuous good planning to achieve this."[6] He argued that older universities gave too much prominence to the pure sciences "and this has prevented the applied science groups from having a free hand to develop in their own way."[7]

Terman advocated concentration of resources, long-term planning, balancing regional interests and attention to student demands. He proposed that Stanford concentrate its resources in selected fields according to two criteria: whether a field was of interest to large numbers of students or was relevant to regionally significant industries such as oil. Since electronic engineering and radio attract the best students, he believed that Stanford should be strong in these fields, even though an industrial base was largely lacking. Student interest in a cutting edge field thus became part of a strategy for creating future industrial growth.

Expanding upon pre-war practices, Terman proposed a twenty-year development program, linking the physical sciences with electrical engineering. A small strategically chosen number of engineering fields would be developed in coordination with relevant related fields in the physical sciences, as was done at MIT during the 1930s. He argued that:

> By determining the proper fields on which to concentrate, and then really laying it on those selected spots we can go places without

STANFORD AND SILICON VALLEY

> needing large amounts of extra money. With twenty years, a suitable
> administrative basis, and reasonable backing from the President, it
> would be a pushover to do something really big.[8]

In Terman's view, universities typically lacked the ability to plan: "Their detailed administrative operations such as new appointments, allocation of funds for new equipment. etc., are decided largely on the basis of this year's and next year's needs."[9] If Stanford could allocate resources strategically, as part of a long-term program, it could move ahead of its competitors.

When Terman returned to Stanford after the war he began a program of organizing centers modeled on MIT's Rad Lab. The obvious first choice for center development was the pre-war electronics research pioneered by Stanford but largely pursued elsewhere, including at the Rad Lab, during the war. Stanford University had not been selected as one of the sites for major government military research laboratories during the war, as had such schools as MIT, Chicago and Johns Hopkins. After the war, MIT retained the basic research component of the Radiation Laboratory for radar. Stanford established a similar center based on several of its faculty who had returned to campus from other schools' wartime laboratories.

Informal arrangements at pre-war Stanford, bringing together scientists and engineers, academics and business firms, to accomplish a research goal, became formally organized after the war through the establishment of research centers. The Microwave Lab began as a division of the physics department in 1945. The new center built upon Stanford's pre-war work in electronics but instead of sparsely funded projects, federal research funds supported permanent research positions. Depression-era professors, who could formerly be found painting their own laboratory floors, were now released from all but essential teaching duties in the post-war period in order to concentrate on the development of centers.[10]

Industrial research practices were introduced to extend basic research into applied areas, while maintaining advanced investigation. To extend the reach of a limited number of faculty, some of their duties were assigned to others. For example, key faculty were assigned full-time assistants to help manage their research teams. As funding allowed, faculty were relieved of committee responsibilities to enable them to further expand their research programs. Adding more support staff also expanded research capacity. Mechanics, tube-makers, and radio technicians were hired to translate ideas into physical devices more rapidly. In a further imitation of industrial research practice, notebooks were maintained by researchers on a daily basis and regularly countersigned by colleagues.

Faculty members were soon transformed into virtually full-time research team leaders, functioning in much the same fashion as industrial research managers. The centers modified old academic roles such as that of the teacher, transforming faculty members into virtually full-time research team leaders, and brought industrial roles such as the full-time researcher into the university. In the center, the professor functioned more as an industrial research manager organizing a group of subordinate researchers to achieve a common end than as an academic advisor guiding a series of graduate students on an individual basis.

Despite his initial belief that financing would not be a problem if development was limited to a relatively few carefully selected fields, considerable financial support was required to realize this vision. Terman initiated a three-pronged financial strategy that included: conducting defense-related research for agencies such as the Office of Naval Research; offering industry preferred access to research results; and developing some of the university's land as an industrial park and shopping center to service the area surrounding the university. As rental and lease receipts came in from the university's real estate ventures, Terman calculated the additional number of professors that he could afford to hire from the shopping center's net income of $750,000, which at the time was equivalent to 12.5 percent of faculty costs in 1965–6, not counting the medical school.[11]

The financial base for Stanford's post-war ascendance also included the attainment of $6 million in federal-sponsored research in electronics in 1976, in contrast to a pre-war funding level in the thousands. Within just a few years of establishing the goal of building up Stanford's engineering and science departments to have a critical mass of technologists to interact with industry, Terman felt confident enough of progress to claim that: "Stanford is now the most important center of electronics among American universities. Although we cannot match MIT in size, we concede nothing to them in quality and in productiveness in proportion to money expended by sponsoring agencies."[12] Attempting to be competitive with MIT, Terman clearly viewed it as Stanford's model. Terman had earlier spoken of making Stanford the Harvard of the west in its national reputation. He had actually helped make it the MIT of the west in its institutional purpose.

New firm formation from academic research projects became a defining characteristic of both regions and their universities. Perhaps the process of firm formation has become more routinized at Stanford, where it has been integrated into the curriculum of the business school. However, in recent years Harvard Business School has not been far behind in developing a broader focus on entrepreneurship. The Cambridge area has the largest concentration of biotechnology activity in the United States, demonstrating that the region's early success with high-tech innovation in minicomputers was not a one-off phenomenon. The biotech firms in the Boston area and the San Francisco Bay area have a common quasi-academic mode of operation. Advertisements for post-doctoral fellows come from firms in both regions.

Conceived well before World War II in both regions, the same strategy for science-based economic development that was initially realized in Boston after the war, was then expanded upon in Silicon Valley. The vision that Bush and others at MIT were working from goes back to the ideas of William Barton Rogers, the founder of MIT. MIT's character as an academic institution, however, was cemented during the 1930s with President Compton's recruitment of basic researchers, particularly a subset of physicists who had an interest not only in scientific research but also in the utilization of results, and concrete applications. Thus, when Van de Graaff, the inventor of the electrostatic generator, was recruited from Princeton, MIT also arranged to have his patent rights transferred MIT. His research became the basis of one of the early firms, High Voltage, funded by ARD in the early post-war period.

A divergent model?

Annalee Saxenian has emphasized discontinuities of organizational style between the two leading high-tech regions.[13] She has noted significant differences between highly networked technical persons in Silicon Valley firms and more isolated individuals in Route 128 companies. Saxenian has also suggested differences between the two coasts in the level of formality or informality in clothing styles – suits and ties in New York but open-necked shirts in California – and in interpersonal relations, structured in the east, more gregarious in the west. But even that is changing. In the multimedia industry in New York today, the so-called Silicon Alley, located in the East Village and elsewhere in lower Manhattan, there is a fairly informal scene in which many people look like they just came off the casting call of *Rent*.

Of broader significance is the issue of whether the two regions represent unique historical instances or essentially replicable phenomena. The issue is structure versus network, vertical organization versus lack of hierarchy, and openness versus secretive operation. Tracy Kidder's volume about Data General is a story of a freewheeling alternative development group in an old-line minicomputer firm.[14] Saxenian's depiction of Route 128 fits the later years of ossification at Digital Equipment Corporation and the recent past at Hewlett Packard in Palo Alto, a hierarchical "buttoned-down" operation before its recent renascence. As another observer noted, "Resource allocation (a focus on traditional bureaucratic procedures rather than unconventional ways of unleashing new ideas) is just as likely to hobble creativity in large and vibrant Silicon Valley companies as it is in boring old industrial age companies."[15] Moreover, high-tech firm concentration in connection with physical artifacts such as the Science Park at Stanford or the ring road around Boston are after-the-fact superficial characteristics, rather than an underlying cause of high-tech economic development.

High-tech regions: born or made?

If Silicon Valley and Route 128 arose from unique circumstances and cannot be duplicated, policy measures are fruitless. The question is, which policy measures are appropriate for individual regional circumstances? Merely to take a mechanism that has been highly successful in one area and assume that it is the way to

STANFORD AND SILICON VALLEY

recreate the phenomenon elsewhere may not work. Nevertheless, a typical response is to mimic an existing format without undertaking an analysis of the local strengths and weaknesses of conditions for innovation. Thus, the response in many regions has been, after a visit to the Stanford Research Park, to build a science park first, as a set of buildings, and to expect the firms to magically appear, rather than to create an infrastructure for firm formation. This is the equivalent of performing Melanesian Cargo Cult rituals, ceremonies conducted after World War II in expectation of a cornucopia of goods to be off-loaded by US forces in the South Pacific just as they were during the war.

A more appropriate approach is to make an analysis of the strengths and gaps in a region and then design new networks and organizations to bridge those gaps. That is what was done in New England in the early post-war period when the venture capital firm was initiated in response to an analysis of that region's problems and opportunities during the 1930s depression. In the New York region at present, the missing links are a major technological university, the relative lack of networks among universities, industry and government, and the leadership required to bring the institutional spheres central to technological innovation and regional development together around common projects. Of course, there can be a confluence of the two models.

An interactive innovation model can be abstracted from different starting points, bringing the technology push and market pull approaches together. Such a model could then be used as a template to identify regional gaps. By the early 1990s recession Silicon Valley had moved toward the more market-oriented model, by focusing on computer networks and the commercialization of the Internet. The economic crisis encouraged a revival of academic–industry collaboration among firms that were now often several generations from their academic origin. The newly founded Center for Integrated Systems, for example, provided a neutral meeting ground for inter-firm collaboration in the semiconductor industry as well as with academic experts in the field. The loss of institutional memory of previous academic–industry collaborations meant that lost traditions had continually to be revived as the founders of later generations of firms came to believe that the industrial complex from which they emanated was self-generated.

In some instances, however, institutionalization occurs through normative or legal change. The following chapter analyzes the passage of an amendment to US patent law, the so-called Bayh-Dole Act, and its effects, in legitimizing academic technology transfer by establishing "clear title" to university-originated intellectual property, developed with federal government support.

10

TECHNOLOGY TRANSFER UNIVERSALIZED

The Bayh-Dole Regime[1]

The Bayh-Dole Act of 1980 turned over ownership of intellectual property rights, emanating from federal government-sponsored research at universities, to the university in which the discovery was made. The premise of the law was that the results from billions of dollars of research funds contained significant unrealized potential for technology development. Certainly, government was not going to develop technology itself in potential competition with industry. Prior to the passage of the Act, government had left it up to each agency to dispose of intellectual property rights as it saw fit. Some agencies actively made an effort to see that these rights were put to use; others did not.

Companies typically felt that if they arranged to use government-owned intellectual property, and were successful in developing a marketable product, a competitor would likely want to develop a similar product. The expectation was that a claim would be made that since government had supported the invention of the underlying technology, with the public's tax monies, then the second company should be granted access to the technology as well. Making this analysis in advance, the first company would then typically decide not to get involved – a classic free-rider effect. The Bayh-Dole Act resolved this dilemma by granting universities, other non-profit organizations and small firms, a clear title.

As a condition of receiving government funds, universities were required to make an effort to transfer technology, in addition to traditional dissemination of knowledge through publication and presentations at conferences. Starting from practices developed early in the twentieth century at MIT, university technology transfer has become a significant input into industrial development. William Barton Roger's mid-nineteenth-century vision of a university that would infuse industry with new technology has become universalized from a single school to the entire US academic research system. Greatly expanded with federal research funding, the US academic enterprise has become a key element of an indirect US industrial policy, involving university, industry and government. The origins and effects of the Bayh-Dole Act are a significant chapter in the spread of the MIT model and the rise of entrepreneurial science.

A framework for technology transfer

Industry's view of academia as a source of intellectual property, prior to Bayh-Dole, was exemplified in a 1980 survey in which 56 firms were asked why they funded research at universities.[2] Multiple answers were possible. The reasons cited are shown in Table 3. The last of the reasons cited is a good working definition of a proprietary advantage; in 1980 it was the last reason that companies looked to universities.

The Bayh-Dole Act of 1980 offered universities the opportunity to gain income from licensing intellectual property rights, making receipt of federal grant funds conditional on universities making an effort to put research results to use. Universities responded by changing their patent rules to assume ownership rights to this research. University offices and administrative procedures were established to patent and market research results. As leading universities went into the intellectual property business, others followed. In a relatively short time, virtually all universities with a significant research capacity developed the capability to identify and market intellectual property. Bayh-Dole dramatically changed the landscape of university technology transfer. The most important contribution of the Act was that, once a secure rule was in place, it enabled a nationwide infrastructure for university technology transfer to be constructed. The law standardized and gave legal sanction to administrative practices in federal agencies authorizing university patenting of federally funded research.

In addition to rationalizing and legitimizing university patenting and licensing, the law induced a psychological change in attitudes toward technology transfer as well as an organizational change in encouraging the creation of offices for this purpose. Previously, only a very few research universities had the interest and capabilities to patent and license technology invented on campus. Post-1980, virtually all universities with significant research funding took on this task. The numbers of universities with technology transfer offices increased from twenty-five in 1980 to two hundred in 1990. The number of

Table 3 Reasons cited for sponsoring academic research in 1980

	%
Gain access to manpower	75
Window on science and technology	52
General support of technical excellence	38
Gain access to university facilities	36
Obtain prestige; enhance company's image	32
Good local citizen; foster community relations	29
Make use of an economical resource	14
Solve problem; get specific information unavailable elsewhere	11

TECHNOLOGY TRANSFER UNIVERSALIZED

patents granted to American universities increased from approximately three hundred in 1980 to almost 2,000 in 1995.

Beyond a simple increase in patent numbers, the Bayh-Dole Act had a broader effect in making research universities an explicit part of the US innovation system by re-structuring the relationship among university, industry and government. The law created an "indirect industrial policy" going from the federal government through the universities to reach firms. Enhancing university technology transfer to industry was not subject to objections of government, attempting to "pick winners" by providing assistance to industry directly. Thus, the law helped create a framework for university–industry–government relations in which each institutional sphere was encouraged to "take the role of the other."

Henceforth, universities would take the role of industry by infusing existing firms with new technology through patent licenses and by using intellectual property rights as the basis to capitalize and grow new firms in incubator facilities on campus. Government would take the role of venture capitalist in extending federal research funding programs to support the next steps in translating research into usable technologies through a Small Business Innovation Research Program (SBIR). SBIR made available a small percentage of federal research funds – initially 0.5 percent, currently 2 percent – to small firms and prospective firm-founders for this purpose. Through relaxation of federal anti-trust laws, industry would take on the role of the university in sharing knowledge among firms though collaboration on so-called pre-competitive R&D projects.

Origins of the law

The potential for university technology transfer was an outcome of the build-up of federal funding for academic research during and after World War II. The expectation was that this research would lead to manifold civilian uses in the post-war era just as it had resulted in innovations in weaponry during the war. The law itself arose from a debate between opponents of patenting who held that research paid for by government should be made freely available to all interested parties and proponents of patenting who argued that potentially interested firms would be unlikely to take up this research unless they could be assured of the limited monopoly protection offered by a patent, and preferably by an exclusive license. The somewhat surprising result was a virtually unanimous vote in favor of the Bayh-Dole Act. This was in part due to a degradation of US industrial competitiveness during the 1970s and the emergence of a feeling, even among many of those who opposed patenting academic research results, that US industry needed all the help it could get so long as it wasn't provided directly by government!

There was a fundamental difference between the role of government in wartime and post-war innovation policy. During the war, a federal agency, the

115

Office of Scientific Research and Development (OSRD) developed a strategy, provided funding and administrative coordination to put research to use. When the OSRD was closed at the war's end, successor military R&D agencies continued to provide all of these functions for their individual services, e.g. Navy, Army, often by funding academic researchers. However, on the civilian side, only funding was provided. Strategy and coordination were expected to occur without government participation and this was typically seen as a virtue. Vannevar Bush, a proponent of government activism in wartime expressed his basic conservatism through the thesis of a "hands off" science policy for the post-war. His classic 1945 statement became the basis of a presumed "contract" between government and university, to provide academic researchers with support, without further intervention.[3] Theorized as a linear model of innovation, research was expected to translate into practical uses merely by the dissemination of the results.

Under both regimes, active and passive, the federal government held patent rights to the research it funded at the universities. During wartime OSRD saw to it that a useful result was put into practice as soon as possible. Without an OSRD equivalent on the civilian side, federally funded research at universities was for the most part not utilized. However, there were a few exceptions in which universities with a tradition of technology transfer, such as MIT, Stanford and Wisconsin, continued the practices they had instituted for patenting and licensing prior to the advent of large-scale government support of research, outside of traditional areas such as agriculture. Prior to the war, patenting and licensing had largely been based on foundation, industry, and self-funded research. During the war, patent rights began to be generated on a large scale from expanded federal research funding.

Management of intellectual property generated under federal funding

As director of the wartime OSRD, Vannevar Bush arranged for the patenting of government-sponsored research. He was aware from his earlier experience at MIT that an expansion of research would generate intellectual property and that patents would have to be managed if conflicts were to be avoided. Even during war there was a view toward peace when, with the lifting of wartime constraints, arguments would likely ensue over property rights in research if precautions were not taken. The basic principle was that no company should have the exclusive right to exploit patents that had been publicly funded by the taxpayer. Thus, licenses were to be made available to all interested parties on the premise that profits from publicly funded research should not accrue to a single company. It was also expected that by licensing more than one company to practice a given invention, competitive forces would keep prices "reasonable."

The Department of Commerce's National Technical and Information Service (NTIS) centrally managed licensing in the early post-war period.

TECHNOLOGY TRANSFER UNIVERSALIZED

Academic technology is typically embryonic, requiring the active involvement of the inventor for its further development. With the inventor located in the university, but NTIS controlling the licensing rights, there was a gap between university, government and industry. Nevertheless, even though NTIS was physically distant from the source of discoveries, the arrangement worked reasonably well when companies learned about relevant research and approached the government for licenses in fields such as mechanical devices, electronics and chemical processes, where development costs and product development times, and consequently risks, were low.

However, by the late 1960s there was increasing evidence of industry failing to take advantage of many of these results, paradoxically, because they were "freely available to all." The approach completely broke down in areas with long development time frames and high costs, such as the pharmaceutical industry. In 1968, the Johnson administration conducted a study that found that no pharmaceutical to which the government owned the patent had ever been developed for commercial use. Companies were unwilling to make the investment required to develop a drug, a cost that could run into many millions of dollars (even then, before the passage of the Food, Drug and Cosmetic Act of 1973 raised the cost of obtaining marketing approval for a new drug substantially), without the guarantee that they would be able to recoup their investment through exclusive marketing rights.

Government was divided internally during the 1970s, with various agencies holding different positions on the best course to follow with respect to the intellectual property they had helped to create. For example, the Atomic Energy Commission wished to keep title within government to inventions in its domain. Other agencies, such as NIH and NSF, were more willing to assign inventions to their sources outside of government in order to facilitate development. Government authorized Institutional Patent Management Agreements (IPAs) in response to the Johnson administration's study. The Department of Health, Education and Welfare (HEW) initially implemented IPAs, followed by the National Science Foundation.

Norman Latker, NIH patent counsel, invented a bureaucratic process for universities to certify that they were taking appropriate measures to manage technology transfer. He invented forms for university administrators to fill out so that a record could be created of their compliance, ideally by establishing professional in-house offices for patenting and licensing.[4] For universities not wishing to make such an extensive commitment, procedures were created for individual patenting. Since the process could take as long as three years a school might find that the potential licensee's interest had lapsed by the time the agreement was in place. Moreover, there were restrictions on the period of exclusivity under IPAs, limited to ten years.

Nevertheless, some government officials, both in the legislative and executive branches, strongly felt that these rights were public property and should not be turned over to the universities to be licensed to industry. There was significant

117

opposition in Congress, for example, from Senator Long of Louisiana, who believed that patenting government-funded research was illegitimate privatization of what should be a free public good. For as long as the few interested universities were able to work out ways of accessing rights to the inventions that they were interested in commercializing, this issue did not come to a head. When Joseph Califano, Secretary of Health, Education and Welfare called a halt to the transfer of NIH patent rights to universities in the late 1970s and ordered its patent counsel, Norman Latker, to be fired, the issue of what to do with the federal government's growing patent portfolio was broached.[5]

Legitimizing academic technology transfer: the Bayh-Dole Act

Frustrated by diverse and shifting regulations that could be changed by administrative fiat, proponents of patenting inside and outside the government sought a secure environment for technology transfer. Officials from a few academic institutions, typically with a "land grant" tradition and/or extensive capabilities in bio-medical research with commercial implications, took the lead in pressing for legislation to establish a stable intellectual property framework. Companies frustrated about difficulty gaining access to patent rights from federally funded academic research also helped build pressure for change. Another impetus for legislation was the industrial downturn of the 1970s and increased international competition, which led to proposals for greater government involvement in innovation. The failure of the Carter administration's "reindustrialization" proposals to assist industry directly to improve its competitiveness created a receptive atmosphere for ideas to assist firms with the results of government-supported research.

Sometimes the idea for a law originates with the lawmaker or one of their staff or, perhaps, from outside of the government with individual citizens, organizations and lobbyists who bring an idea, or even a draft of a bill, to the attention of a Senator or congressperson. Other times the source can be found in the executive branch of government. Laws are always named after their congressional sponsors and, if they are significant innovations, like Bayh-Dole, come to be taken as shorthand for an institutional complex that has grown up around the law. In such cases, sponsors are recruited for bipartisan balance as part of the endgame in policy-making that may have originated deep in the federal bureaucracy. The true authors of such laws are often persons behind the scenes who translate innovations into statutes with the assistance of congressional staff persons. Such was the provenance of the Bayh-Dole Act.

In 1978, Purdue University wanted to negotiate an IPA in order to commercialize promising medical device technology, but was told that HEW had stopped granting such Agreements.[6] They approached their Senator, Birch Bayh, to protest what appeared to be an arbitrary decision, and elicited interest. Bayh found that the Department of Commerce was starting to have concerns about the USA's international competitiveness and felt that the barriers that

TECHNOLOGY TRANSFER UNIVERSALIZED

had developed between academic and industrial R&D were contributing to the problem. In turn, Purdue found support for a change in the current system from other leading universities such as Wisconsin, whose discovery of vitamin D and warfarin had put them at the forefront of developing the academic technology transfer paradigm, starting in the early 1930s, Stanford and MIT.

Bayh, a Democrat, found a bipartisan co-sponsor in Republican Robert Dole, and in 1979 serious consideration started of the Bayh-Dole Bill. The bill came under the jurisdiction of the Senate Judiciary Committee, chaired at the time by Senator Edward (Ted) Kennedy of Massachusetts. The enormous importance of higher education to the economy of Massachusetts ensured a sympathetic hearing for the bill. The Senate Judiciary Committee found that in 1978, the government owned title to over 28,000 patents, and had licensed fewer than 4 percent of them, glaring evidence of the lack of success of the then current approach.

Making a law

A coalition emerged between the universities and small business, with Washington representation groups of both interests consulted on provisions of the draft act. For example, the language of the bill and the administrative regulations worked out after its passage had to be adjusted to allow sufficient time to report inventions without interfering with professors' publication plans. Similarly, small business was concerned with keeping access open to so-called "background inventions," exemplified soon after the act's passage by the Cohn-Boyer genetic engineering patent, licensed non-exclusively by Stanford University.

Lasken, who informally drafted the bill, said that "It is probably the most important thing I have done in my thirty years in government."[7] Universities strongly supported its passage by lobbying their Congresspersons and Senators. The University of Wisconsin, for example, turned initial opposition from Senator Nelson of their state into support and even co-sponsorship. One reason for the success of the bill was that it covered universities and small business but left big business out, allaying concerns, such as those held by Senator Nelson, that patents could contribute to monopolization. Neils Reimers, then Director of Technology Transfer at Stanford, recalls a celebration over coffee, with some of his colleagues who were lobbying Congress, when the law passed.[8]

Although the bill became a law relatively quickly, within one and a half years of its inception, support was not unanimous. In the Judiciary committee, where responsibility for patenting rested in the Senate, MIT's representatives failed to persuade Senator Ted Kennedy to sponsor the bill. The next person on the committee was Senator Birch Bayh of Indiana, whom Purdue University was successful in recruiting. Bayh had special concerns about the effects of the proposed bill on labor, so a special section was drafted with language favoring development in the USA. An intern on Robert Dole's staff, Barry Leshowitz, an academic on leave from the University of Arizona, interested the Senator from Kansas, a minority member of Judiciary, in becoming the co-sponsor, thus making it a bi-partisan bill.

The provisions of the act

The Bayh-Dole Act, PL 96–517, formally known as the Patent And Trademark Amendments Act, applied to not-for-profit institutions and small businesses (defined as those with fewer than 500 employees). It contained six important provisions:

1 Universities could elect to retain title to the results of federally funded research.
2 Universities were required to share proceeds with inventors. This was a most important aspect of the act. The concept of patenting was foreign to most academics. Their academic reputations, under conditions then current, would not be enhanced by adding patents and licenses to their curriculum vitaes. In contrast to corporate R&D scientists who typically are required to sign away their patent rights as a condition of employment, academic scientists and engineers were given a tangible incentive to expand their purview to include the commercialization of research. US academics joined German workers as beneficiaries by law in the fruits of their creativity.
3 Restrictions on licensing terms were removed. Licenses to small businesses could be for the lifetime of the patent. Licenses to large businesses were still limited to ten years.
4 US manufacture was required for products to be sold in the USA. This requirement was to ensure that a reasonable share of the benefits flowed into the US economy. Waivers can be obtained if the licensor can show the agency that funded the research that the licensee cannot economically develop the product if this requirement is enforced.
5 Small business preference. This was one of the most debated aspects of the act. There remained considerable concern in the Senate about handing monopoly power that had been created with government funding to large corporations. It was felt that small companies would be less able to exploit that monopoly power at the expense of the public than would large companies, so a preference for small companies was incorporated into the act. The meaning of the requirement has never been seriously tested. If an institution received equal offers to license a technology from a large and a small company, then clearly it would have to accept the small company offer. However, this is never the case. Licensing proposals always differ, so the overall economic attractiveness of the competing offers must be compared and weighed.
6 The government retained a non-exclusive license to use the technology and march-in rights. The government's license is for its own use only. This

therefore primarily impacts technologies for which the government is the primary consumer and has not been a major factor. The march-in rights give the government the right to take back title if it believes that an important technology is not being properly exploited. This rarely happens and has not been an important factor in technology commercialization.

Another of the issues that was intensively debated at the time was whether the government should receive a share of the results of licensing the technology it had funded. The Senate Judiciary Committee decided that the government's return would come not directly from a share in the proceeds, but rather from the increased taxation that would result from the increased economic activity that would be a consequence of the act's successful implementation.

The purpose of the new federal legislation was to speed the transfer of technology from university to private industrial firms by eliminating governmental restrictions on the private use of the results of government-supported research. According to NSF Counsel Jesse Lasken, the Bayh-Dole act:

> eliminated the problem of who_owns what. The university would then have a right if there was an issue coming out of university work that they are going to be able to give assurances that they could work out some reasonable arrangement. It was a useful law that actually accomplished something. It made it simple. A university could tell a company that was interested in working with them that just because we made this invention on our NSF work doesn't mean we won't have the right to give you a license, because we do have the right.[9]

It was left to academic institutions to make a deal.

Technology transfer as a university mission

Universities that were previously little involved in the transfer of technology quickly established administrative offices in the wake of the federal decision. Universities with some experience either on their own or through arrangements with the Research Corporation soon expanded their efforts to take out patents on the commercializable research of their academic staff. By the late 1980s virtually all research universities had established a technology transfer office. Following on from the growth of these offices, a membership organization, the Association of University Technology Managers (AUTM), was established to represent the emerging profession. AUTM membership has since risen to more than 1,300 regular and more than 1,000 affiliate members and the organization runs its own training programs. AUTM has doubled in size since 1995.[10]

All major, and many minor, academic institutions, as well as an increasing number of government laboratories in the USA, now have technology transfer offices. Some, such as the National Institutes of Health, Stanford, MIT and the

University of California, have offices of 30–50 people. A smaller, less research-oriented medical school, New York Medical College, has a staff consisting of a single person. Awaiting a build-up of research with commercial potential, the Westchester-based medical school is at the stage of developing its policy documents and seeking partners in the pharmaceutical industry to enable it to become a site for clinical trials.

There are two essential elements to academic technology transfer:

- the ability to license established technologies for which patents have been applied; and
- the ability to collaborate with the inventor of the technology to further develop it.

While the first of these two steps in fact constitutes the actual transfer of the technology, because of the very early stage of academic technology, it is not worthwhile unless the second option is also available and the cooperation of the inventor also achieved. Academic scientists in the USA are entrepreneurs. Under the peer review system, they must raise the funding for their research activities themselves. A large research division at a university or teaching hospital can therefore be regarded as a quasi-business with $1–10 million in annual revenues.

Some universities extended their efforts from the taking out and licensing of patents to put income for the university into a portfolio of measures designed to establish new firms and thereby promote regional economic development. All of these efforts depended upon research staff and students bringing their commercializable ideas to the attention of a university technology transfer office. In part because the taking out of patents was expensive, patents were often only sought when a prospective licensee could be identified. Universities had the reputation of being conservative patent-takers. There was either an immediate sale or a long-term prospect of significant gain, with little middle ground. Niels Reimers at Stanford originated the shift from a legal to a marketing approach. Occasionally, a faculty member at a university new to technology transfer manages to go around the office and deal directly with the university's patent attorneys, running up a legal bill for an invention without an assessment of its potential having been made first.

Issues

The Bayh-Dole Act provided a stable ground for university technology transfer and a framework for resolving some issues; other issues remained, however. The potentially contentious issue of division of proceeds appears to have been settled within the context of the Bayh-Dole Act, which guarantees the inventor a share through a more-or-less equal three-way division of proceeds among the university administration on behalf of the institution as a whole, the faculty members' department and the individual themselves. Student-generated rights were traditionally left entirely with the individual, perhaps on the grounds that they paid tuition and did not have employee status. However, since most graduate students in the sciences are on fellowships, often from a government or university source, graduate students have increasingly been defined as "officers of the university" subject to the same intellectual property rules as faculty.

Nevertheless, whatever the administrative definition, student status is quite different in reality. Student work is typically conducted under the control of faculty members' and it can become a matter of faculty discretion whether to include students in disclosure statements unless a university has clear rules and procedures. A below-the-surface issue that rarely comes to light given faculty members' near feudal power over their students in assessing progress toward the PhD and in granting degrees is claims made by faculty members to credit, both intellectual and pecuniary, from graduate student research. The academic system has virtually accepted a system of authorship by status in which provision of resources to conduct research caries with in an entitlement to credit of all kinds. As intellectual property rights become increasingly salient it can be expected that relations among teachers, students and the university will have to become more clearly defined.

Access of academic researchers to patented discoveries has also become an issue. In a previous era when there was a clear distinction between basic and applied research this was not a great problem, since patenting largely took place away from the research frontier. However, at the present time, when basic discoveries in molecular biology produce practical results simultaneously with research advances, the issue of access has come to the fore. The Bayh-Dole Act places control over this problem into the hands of the universities. Universities can protect access of academic researchers by including provisions in licensing agreements authorizing access. What happens when a university licenses to a firm in which it has an equity interest and therefore a potential pecuniary interest in excluding others? Moreover, what happens, or should happen, when the academic requesting access is also a principal in a competing company? Nevertheless, it should be kept in mind that the very act of patenting involves a release of information since that is a basic patent requirement in exchange for a temporary economic monopoly.

Effects on universities

The university's own economic base also begins to be transformed as it generates some of its income from the sale of inventions. In 1992, Columbia University earned $24 million from its intellectual property rights, the equivalent of the income on almost half a billion dollars of endowment. This income rose to $100 million by the end of the decade, most of it derived from a single patent on the transgenic mouse that would soon expire. In recognition of this eventuality, the university is expanding its efforts into additional areas such as software. Academic institutions have also begun to use funds earned from technology transfer to support the operation of the university. Columbia University recently announced a $2 million program to support new research initiatives drawing upon monies earned from patents licensed to companies.

Even at a less intensive level, academic technology transfer efforts have been found to be economically successful. Many observers were quite skeptical a decade ago, and some still are, that universities could even make enough money from their technology transfer efforts to cover costs. In the early 1980s most universities merely hoped to earn enough to pay for the running of a technology transfer office, so that they could satisfy the new government requirements of playing a role in support of industry in exchange for receiving government research funds. That level of income was achieved relatively quickly at many universities, almost to their own surprise. US universities earned a total of $1 billion, mostly in royalty income, in 2000. However, a few large returns came from infringement proceedings, in which a company was found to be utilizing patented research without authorization, and from sale of equity in a firm founded with university intellectual property.

Measuring the economic impact of technology transfer

The economic impact of technology transfer from universities and government laboratories has evolved since the passage of Bayh-Dole and related laws to a point where it can be considered to be playing a recognizable and increasingly significant role in aiding the growth of the US economy. The establishment of technology transfer offices and the array of mechanisms, including incubator facilities and science parks, gives hope (some say, false hope) to regions that have not yet seen a glimmer of a high-tech valley, coast or corridor. In the face of continuing opposition to the protection and marketing of intellectual property, both on principled arguments of free dissemination and economic grounds that it simply doesn't pay for itself, AUTM has attempted to evaluate the contribution of university-originated technologies to the US economy and, by implication, to justify the utility of the technology transfer profession. Its yearly questionnaire to its members provides data on royalty income that can be used to provide a very crude estimate of the economic impact of technology transfer activity from universities and government laboratories.[11]

Based upon the rate paid to the universities and government laboratories of $344.4 million in royalties at a 2 percent average royalty, the total sales of the licensed products can be estimated to be $17.2 billion. Product sales can also be used to estimate the employment generated by technology transfer, giving a figure of 137,800 jobs created.

The figures in Table 4 justify the expense that universities have undertaken in subsidizing technology transfer offices, patiently waiting out the seven lean years that are not expected to pay for themselves as the process gets underway.

TECHNOLOGY TRANSFER UNIVERSALIZED

The drafters of the Bayh-Dole Act also realized their legislative intent to attain public benefit from university technology transfer through contribution to tax revenues. The economic activity arising from technology transfer shows a return to federal and state governments of approximately $3.9 billion in 1993. It is also worth noting that these estimates are undoubtedly low, for two reasons:

Table 4 Estimated economic impact of university and government lab technologies (US$ million)

	1980	1986	1990	1993	1999
Product Sales (US$ million)	365	1,905	6,825	17,220	35,800
Employment (jobs generated)	2,920	15,240	54,600	137,760	270,900

Note: For a discussion of the Association of University Technology Managers (AUTM) Survey and other sources on which this table is based, see Etzkowitz, Henry and Ashley J. Stevens. 1995. "Inching toward industrial policy: the university's role in government initiatives to assist small, innovative companies in the U.S.," *Science Studies* 8(2): 13–31.

1 Once patents expire, royalties cease, but the products remain in the market. For instance, in the mid-1960s, MIT had licensed two very important technologies – synthetic penicillin and computer core memory. Both patents have now expired, but were the foundation of major markets.
2 This methodology doesn't capture the induced investment effect, when technologies are in development and are employing people but not yet generating revenues. Thus, the above figures are conservative estimates of the economic impact of indirect industrial policy.

Inching toward industrial policy

The reorientation of the universities toward a commercial role was not intervention in the sense of specific government measures requiring targeting of particular areas of R&D for support, as in Japan, or requiring enterprises and research institutes to make research contracts with each other, as in the Eastern European socialist model. Instead, incentives were built into the research-funding system to move the universities closer to industry, in their motivation and structure. This occurred in a context in which government was unable to take more direct measures itself.

The Bayh-Dole Act altered the regulatory infrastructure which determined how the results of research which would have been funded anyway could be utilized. No funds were appropriated for its implementation or administration. By changing the rules of the game, placing responsibility for technology transfer in the university where it was being conducted rather than with government, the funder, potentially useful research was moved closer to users. In the context of federal research budgets that were not growing at a fast enough rate to meet

TECHNOLOGY TRANSFER UNIVERSALIZED

academic researchers' needs, universities were given the opportunity to earn monies from the royalties and equity that they could generate from federally sponsored research on their campuses.

The Morill Act of 1861 donated federal land to support the development of higher education for the improvement of agricultural and industrial practice. The Bayh-Dole Act of 1980 turned over intangible property of scientific and technological knowledge to the universities with similar intentions. This legislation encouraged individual academics to include commercial activities in their roles and universities to experiment with a variety of arrangements such as research parks, "incubator" facilities and offices for the transfer of technology to develop fruitful relations with industry. The next chapter focuses on the engagement of individual scientists in entrepreneurial activities.

11

THE MAKING OF
ENTREPRENEURIAL SCIENTISTS

Faculty members and graduate students are learning to assess the commercial as well as the intellectual potential of their research. An increasing number of academic scientists are turning their discoveries into marketable products, broadening their interests from a single-minded concern with publication and peer recognition. Some are going beyond traditional modes of technology transfer, in which the tasks of commercialization were left to others, by participating directly in the creation of entrepreneurial ventures. Academic scientists who are leaders in their field have formed some of these firms. Nobel Prize winner Arthur Kornberg, for example, became intrigued by and increasingly involved in entrepreneurial ventures in biotechnology, much to his bemused surprise.[1] As they seek intellectual property from their findings as well as publishable articles and an enhanced scientific reputation, academic scientists become inventors, developers and entrepreneurs.

Some academic scientists were concerned that entrepreneurial ventures threatened the integrity of academic science and charged that their colleagues who were involved in such ventures had conflicts of interest and obligation. Some of these critics viewed academic scientists' involvement in firm formation as a temporary phenomenon and suggested that these firm founders would return to their traditional tasks. In one sense this prediction has proved true. Relatively few academic entrepreneurs have left the academy. Most have pursued their commercial interests in tandem with their academic work, sometimes taking leave of their professorships to temporarily devote full-time effort to their firm. Use of academic leave provisions has allayed concerns about conflict of obligation, an inability to fully perform regular academic tasks given the time-consuming nature of the early stages of firm formation. Nevertheless, firm formation from academic research has not disappeared, even, though charges of conflicts of obligation have abated.

There are proximate and long-term causes of these developments. The creation of new firms has become a permanent part of the academic scene, with support structures such as incubator facilities created to assist the process. In addition to extending the organizational process forward into the industrial scene outside of the university, the academic world has long been involved in a

THE MAKING OF ENTREPRENEURIAL SCIENTISTS

relatively hidden process of organizational development leading up to firm formation through the expansion of group research. Science and entrepreneurship became ever more closely associated as a consequence of scientists' need to find support for their research, before opportunities to commercialize their research became available.

The research group as quasi-firm

Although the scientist's role as synthesizer of knowledge and the entrepreneur's as economic risk-taker may appear too incompatible to be fulfilled by one individual, their inner logic has much in common.[2] Both roles underscore the importance of individual ingenuity in creating new constructs, whether conceptual or organizational, to bring order to an uncertain environment. Enter the university research group leader. As, increasingly, faculty scientists are managing teams of researchers rather than working one-on-one with individual graduate students, academic research is becoming an entrepreneurial venture similar to a start-up firm.

A university science department typically consists of separately organized groups made up of professors, graduate students, post-doctoral fellows, technical staff and sometimes a research administrator or secretary. The series of photographs depicting these collectives, hung at the entrance to many departments, signifies that the research group really is the basic unit of the contemporary science department. It is headed by a "principal investigator" assisted by a team of colleagues, many of whom are still students or in the early stages of their scientific careers. An assistant professor may be responsible for three or four people, an associate professor for perhaps seven, and a full professor for up to fifteen or twenty, or, in some fields, even more.

These groups exhibit many of the characteristics of private business firms. Their formation and maintenance require large sums of money, and they need to seek funds almost continuously. The transformation of individual investigations into collective enterprises typically funded by outside agencies has required professors (although they are still called "individual investigators") to become enmeshed in the multiplicity of external organizational and economic factors that affect their research, and to undertake collaborations that have led to the contemporary phenomenon of firms founded by faculty members who treat their scientific discoveries as marketable goods.

When visited in their laboratories, these scientists are typically not at the research bench but in an office off to the side, when in residence at all. Many identify their role as that of running a small business, and acknowledge that it has been years since they actually performed an experiment. Instead, they spend their time going to scientific meetings to publicize the research, doing the paperwork to organize the students engaged in it, and dealing with administrative, personnel and other problems more native to commerce. Having many of the characteristics of a small business, some of these research groups are only a

THE MAKING OF ENTREPRENEURIAL SCIENTISTS

short step away from being an actual firm when the opportunity to really become one arises.

The impetus to entrepreneurial science

The introduction of economic values into science follows from scientists' successful quest for the capital and logistical resources to achieve their objective: the extension of certified knowledge. As scientists succeed in their quests for credit through paper production, they accumulate resources (funds, laboratory space and assistants) that enable them to increase their productivity. Indeed, they are able to maintain or to increase their access to resources and hence their rates of production only insofar as they are able to sustain or increase their credibility-based credit.[3] Scientists whose credit rating drops too low lose access to resources because their work no longer qualifies for support grants, and they may have to give up their research or at least research assistance.

A science faculty member's ability to organize and obtain support for a group has become a tacit requirement for appointment to permanent tenure. At some universities this requirement, and its extension into the commercialization of research, is being included in the official criteria for the granting of permanent appointments. The process of translating recognition into grants, equipment, data and articles has been called the cycle of credibility. Successful scientists have as their objective the speeding up of these credibility cycles because such acceleration equates to organizational and structural growth, as additional recognition is used to gain more laboratory space, equipment and assistants.

Combining advanced training with original investigation, the academic research group is a distinctive feature of American academic science. A relatively modest-sized group operates at the level of between the low hundreds and several hundred thousands of research dollars. A group in the biological sciences may have a main grant from a single agency such as the National Institutes of Health, and perhaps a secondary grant from an additional agency such as the National Science Foundation. When the size of the group increases to seven or eight members, professors who were at the bench conducting experiments are forced to remove themselves to devote themselves virtually full-time to organizational and public relations tasks, including:

- fundraising and proposal writing;
- attending conferences to make new contacts and to announce results achieved by the group;
- recruiting new group members and handling the personnel problems of old ones;
- writing and reviewing articles;
- serving on review panels; and
- managing the intellectual direction of the research.

THE MAKING OF ENTREPRENEURIAL SCIENTISTS

Having attained organizational momentum, it is extremely difficult for professors to function again as individual researchers. Occasionally, however, in the nooks and crannies of the experimental science departments of a major research university, sometimes literally in an attic, an individual can be found who *is* working alone, typically in an unfashionable specialty. But this circumstance is now very unusual even though the notion of the individual investigator is still deeply embedded in the ideology of academic science.

As noted above, so-called individual investigators most often operate as the heads of research groups that they must sustain in order for their scientific efforts to survive. They typically expand their teams by appointing sequences of post-doctoral fellows and technicians. As older students graduate and new students carry on the research, the group becomes an activity with a life of its own. The students carrying out research activities establish working relationships among themselves, as well as with their professor, that become important to the success of the group. Groups usually decline in size as a professor nears retirement, or they may disappear altogether at earlier stages as a result of loss of support from patrons, governmental or private. The cycle is renewed when the department appoints as professors former graduates and post-doctoral fellows, either from its own ranks or, more often, from other universities, and they start their own research groups.

The effect of funding pressures

In US academic research, where each principal investigator is responsible for the financing of his or her group, what happens when funding gets tight? Proposals to supporting agencies must, of course, receive higher scores to merit a grant, and the increased competitive pressure forces investigators to seek alternative sources of funding. Under these conditions, some research groups will diminish in size or even close down. Others, however, will increase their size by finding a wider variety of support sources to draw from, with the attendant result of broadening the universe of potential donors supporting academic research.

To keep the level of research going at a pace of quality and quantity that will attract continued funding, an investigator's productivity must go up as the competition increases. One strategy to improve productivity is to expand the size of the research group. The investigator with three or four assistants feels compelled to expand to five or six. If seven or eight is the norm, then the investigator has to break through the scale barrier, leave the bench, and go to nine or ten or even fifteen or twenty. As a research group becomes larger, the lead investigator spends less time on the floor of the laboratory.

As the laboratory becomes larger and more productive, he or she has to spend more time writing papers and proposals and seeking additional grants. Instead of operating with the support of one or two funding sources, the group leader must start cultivating additional agencies. If the relevant federal agencies have been exhausted, then a foundation must be solicited. Then, beyond the foundation and non-profit sector, other donors and new streams of funding must often be sought. State and local governments, for example, are sometimes willing to provide research funds to improve the competitiveness of regional industry. The investigator might also engage in collaborations with colleagues from other disciplines and universities to seek NSF funds under its new programs for creating interdisciplinary research centers related to industry.

From quasi-firms to firm formation

The inner entrepreneurial dynamic of US academic science helps explain why the university–industry divide is often less than what it is reputed to be. Research groups operate as quasi-firms according to the model of classical capitalism in which small entities compete with each other for resources. Firm formation, then, is merely a further step in the process by which scientists manage research groups, not a radical departure from professional practice in academic science. Located in research institutes and universities, these scientific quasi-firms, if they are to survive, require their entrepreneur organizers to continuously search for support. The formation of firms reduces or at least changes the form of this pressure because the entrepreneur can, through the firm's sale of its knowledge or its products or both, provide a continuous source of funds to sustain research activities.

It is usually not the intention of the professor who founds or helps initiate a science-based firm to leave the university and become a full-time entrepreneur. Typically the goal of most academic entrepreneurs, once the firm is underway, is to participate in research as a consultant to the firm and play a role in policy-making as a member of the board of directors. Some academics also wish to provide a site for their graduate students and post-doctorates to be consultants to earn extra monies. They believe that this opportunity will help their research group to be financially competitive with other universities in its ability to attract graduate students and post-doctorates, or expect that their assistants will find consulting opportunities in a colleague's firm to avoid the appearance of a conflict of interest.

The hope is that the firm will produce a successful product and that its stock will become valuable. In this event it is expected that there will be a return of funds from the firm to support the professor's research group. That is typically what academic scientists say is their long-term goal when they get involved in the founding of a firm. Of course they are interested in making money personally, but also express their motivation in terms of a desire to find a stable source of support for their research. The founding of companies by academic scientists, formerly a phenomenon associated with a relatively few universities, has become more widespread in recent years. Sometimes the entrepreneurial culture in which firm formation has been encouraged is spread by scientists who have left universities where this culture had long taken root; other times it is an

THE MAKING OF ENTREPRENEURIAL SCIENTISTS

example gleaned from afar, through the media and informal conversations in departmental corridors and at scientific meetings.

Even those scientific colleagues, who have no desire to become entrepreneurs themselves, rarely look upon their colleagues who do with disdain. The paucity of "definition of deviance" can be explained by examining the position in the scientific world of many of the entrepreneurial scientists. Entrepreneurial activities have been undertaken by leading scientists, who are looked upon as role models. For example, a molecular biologist interviewed at Columbia University viewed his colleagues at Harvard, who had formed firms, with admiration and wished to emulate them. Willingness of a few "low status" scientists to use findings for pecuniary advantage would likely have been taken as evidence of "deviance." If such normative infractions were negatively sanctioned they would even have served to strengthen the old normative pattern. However, for many scientists, formation of a firm has now come to be positively defined as a new badge of scientific achievement.

Professors not inclined toward business, such as the founder of the Genetics Institute, Mark Ptashne, have participated in the formation of firms and, at times, like his colleague Walter Gilbert, taken a leading organizational role. Professor Ptashne of the Harvard University Department of Biological Sciences is a good example of a scientist who is acting on opportunities to commercialize his research, while also remaining committed to the academic mode of basic research. Ptashne was originally apprised of the potential commercial value of his research by a university administrator responsible for securing patent rights for campus-based research at Harvard. Although initially he expressed a lack of interest in pursuing such possibilities, Ptashne soon became intrigued with the notion of establishing a company to recreate his previous academic lab groups by inviting their members to work in the firm.

Ptashne initially invited the university to take the lead in founding the firm and share in its ownership. However, when other Harvard faculty objected to the idea, he took on the entrepreneurial role himself and negotiated successfully for financing a firm independently of the university. Ptashne's colleague at Harvard, Walter Gilbert, took on administrative as well as entrepreneurial responsibilities in his firm, Biogen, serving as Chief Executive Officer for a time. He eventually returned to his position at Harvard after he was replaced by the board of directors. They felt that the firm had to focus more sharply on commercial goals and brought in professional management, a not unusual occurrence in the life-cycle of a technical firm originating in academia.

When he was negotiating to form Genetics Institute in the mid-1980s, Professor Ptashne said that, at this point, "to have no commercial relationship whatsoever is almost ... it's mind boggling. I'm courted every day. Yesterday, some guy offered me literally millions of dollars to go direct a research outfit on the west coast. ... He said any price. Any price."[4] Ptashne chose to remain in Cambridge. He wanted to bring together again, within a company, his "extended family" from the university lab. Ptashne's first thought was to form a

132

firm in partnership with his university, hoping thus to keep the line of communication open. He gave up this effort in the face of opposition from university faculty who opposed, in principle, the direct involvement of the university in commercial ventures.

Moreover, his colleague Walter Gilbert, who was organizing an independent firm, did not like the idea of competing against a university-affiliated firm. A convoluted series of negotiations ensued involving a venture capital firm in which Harvard University had a financial interest as well as other firms. When the negotiations stalled, Ptashne took the advice of the late William Paley, former Chairman of the Board of CBS, and a potential investor, to take charge himself. Professor Ptashne found himself fascinated with the process of organizing a company, comparing it to "a puzzle with five thousand loose pieces. It's night and day, up and down, this guy's out, that guy's in. The money's in, the money's out. The buildings here. ... It's all quite extraordinary."[5] When Genetics Institute was formed, Ptashne retained his professorship and operated two research programs simultaneously. He held that he kept the two entirely separate, applied research at the company and more basic research concerning genes, and the mechanisms by which they are conditioned, in his university lab. In 1992, Ptashne celebrated the sale of a portion of his personal share of the company's stock at a party in Cambridge. He used some of the proceeds to expand his activities as an art collector; he had continued his participation in Harvard's musical activities during his commercial involvement.

The faculty's changing role in technology transfer

The increase in conflict of interest charges against academics involved in the commercialization of research is an indicator of a broader change in the university's purpose and mission: its contribution to economic development. As this change takes place, attitudes are modified and what was once seen as a conflict should come to be regarded as a new confluence of interest. This is not to say that conflicts of interest disappear, but rather that they are managed.

When research was introduced as an academic mission during the late nineteenth century – some said at the expense of teaching (some still say so!) – similar charges of conflict of interest were made. These concerns dissipated as confluence was also found, but they never entirely disappeared. We can discern a similar evolution with respect to technology transfer. The universities, and an increasing number of their faculty members, are learning how to pursue basic research in tandem with the capitalization of knowledge.

The issue of investigator initiation

Although serious controversy has erupted at relatively few universities, a significant division of opinion persists over faculty involvement with industry. At one extreme, private funding is still regarded by a few department chairs as "tainted

THE MAKING OF ENTREPRENEURIAL SCIENTISTS

money," and they tend to abjure support from any sources other than non-profits or government agencies such as the National Institutes of Health (NIH). On the whole, however, there has been a change of attitude among many faculty members in the sciences toward industrial funding, a shift away from the old view of industrial money as unacceptable.

A study of a public university that developed technology transfer mechanisms during the past decade found that departmental support for faculty involvement in technology transfer varies widely, from active encouragement to active discouragement. In between, some departments view technology transfer as simply another bureaucratic requirement of academic life, in this case preparing a disclosure and sending it on to the designated administrator.

On the whole, however, there are indications that the academic atmosphere has become more pragmatic because of the growing recognition that it is one of the functions of a public university to help the economy and that technology transfer is the way to do it.

Faculty technology transfer styles Several attitudes toward technology transfer, reflecting increasing degrees of willingness to participate in commercialization activities, are apparent among faculty researchers:

- residual resistance to industrial involvement – these researchers are often equated to the federal agency that is their primary source of support and referred to, for example, as "NIH persons";
- indifference, opting to leave the matter entirely to the transfer office;
- willingness to play a significant role in arranging transfer of their research to industry because they have business acumen and are aware of its potential commercial value;
- full commitment to industrial development through the seamless integration of their campus research group with an industrial research program.

The approach of leaving it up to the technology transfer office to find a developer and marketer for a discovery has for some time now precisely met the needs of many faculty members who strictly delimit their role in putting their technology into use. This group sees the division of labor in technology transfer weighted toward technology transfer officers, whose expertise and advice they rely on. Although such academics are keenly interested in seeing whether their research could be brought into the market and typically express a strong belief in its worth – some are even convinced it could have a beneficial impact on people's lives – they are likely to add the disclaimer: "I'm not looking to become a business person." This attitude does not necessarily preclude a start-up firm, but it does exclude the possibility that such a faculty member will be the entrepreneur.

A stance of moderate involvement – becoming knowledgeable and comfortable operating in a business milieu while retaining primary interest and identity

THE MAKING OF ENTREPRENEURIAL SCIENTISTS

as an academic scientist – is increasing. One researcher who is taking this approach describes it as a matter of adjusting to changed priorities and timing for "details": In business,

> You have to be very careful about what you say with regard to details because that is what business is about: keeping your arms around your details so that you can sell them to somebody else; otherwise there is no point. ... [T]he details are usually done later. ... [I]n science, you share ideas; there tends to be a very open and very detailed exchange.[6]

Consistent with that insight, faculty are learning to calibrate their interaction to both scientific and business needs, giving out enough information to interest business persons in their research but not so much that a business transaction becomes superfluous. Significantly, even among these more business-oriented researchers, it appears that their primary objective is still scientific; business objectives are strictly secondary.

Financial drivers The pressure to seek alternative sources of support in order to maintain viability as a researcher is surely increasing the numbers of faculty interested in obtaining industrial funds. Financial constrictions in academia, both real and perceived, have motivated faculty to seek new ways to work with industry, particularly as government money has become tighter. Departments typically sanction these quests, on the condition that required disclosures are made and salary arrangements modified. During an era of tightening federal research budgets, soliciting support from private industry is increasingly becoming the thing to do. Researchers point especially to the drying up of NIH funding as causing them to go elsewhere for money. Even given the present expansion of the NIH, competition for research funds remains acute because the number of faculty members and universities competing for their support funds continuously expands.

The university–industrial penumbra: confluence visible

Perhaps the most significant change in faculty–industry relations lies in their intensification, the impetus for a penumbra of companies now surrounding the university. Many businesses, both large established firms and start-ups, want a closer, more involved relationship with the academic scientists with whom they work, and geographical proximity makes a difference in encouraging appropriate interaction. The changed situation has been described this way: "More and more the company's attitude is, 'We want you with your unique expertise to contribute, not to the development of an as yet uninvented product, but to the definition of this product which we as a company may need.'" In this scheme, professors will not merely hand over a technology developed as a by-product of

THE MAKING OF ENTREPRENEURIAL SCIENTISTS

academic research that happens to coincide with a corporate need; they will help to set the company's strategic research direction. Such intensified collaborations make the old model of licensing intellectual property just an initial step in setting the ground rules as to how the relationship should be structured and any profits divided because once the contract is signed, a much more complex level of participation by both parties will occur than a simple relationship between licensee and inventor.

The penumbra of companies surrounding the university has given rise to an industrial pull that augurs an ongoing relationship beyond current projects. Such intensive interaction sheds new light on the question of industrial influence on faculty research direction and whether this is good, bad or irrelevant. The issue of investigator initiation is moot because the investigator brings the university-initiated technology to a company-initiated product in a fairly even intellectual property exchange, effecting a confluence of interest. To the extent that this partnership contributes measurably to regional economic development, moreover, "confluence" may replace "conflict" of interest in public perceptions of university–industry relations.

Previous conflicts attributable to the assumption that a dividing line exists between the academic and industrial sides of a relationship are superseded as divisions disappear. A more integrated model of academic–industry partnerships is emerging along with a diversified network of transfer institutions. Indeed, the very notion of technology transfer, or at least transfer at a distance, is superseded as universities develop their own industrial sector.

Science and entrepreneurship

Scientists have thus come to treat the uses of their research in distinctly different ways. In an editorial in *Communications of the* ACM, Peter Denning, President of the Association of Computing Machinery (ACM), the leading association of computer scientists and engineers, said that:

> I see how these different ways of thinking [extension and capitalization of knowledge], have appeared in my own professional life which began with extensive training in the American research paradigm–federally funded basic research. I see that many of the ideas that I rushed into the public domain through my publications might have been the bases of innovations in computer systems. For example, a working set detector for memory management, a working set loading controlling scheduler or a circulating ring queue for scheduling parallel tasks. My only concern was writing the paper and getting it into the literature. None of the following actions occurred to me: patenting these devices, building prototypes, consulting, forming business alliances with those having a manufacturing capability or starting my own business.[7]

THE MAKING OF ENTREPRENEURIAL SCIENTISTS

Virtually all of the repertoire of technology transfer mechanisms are laid out here. Denning continued: "Indeed, had I engaged in such actions I would have had less time for publication and teaching which would have put my prospects for academic advancement at risk. My actions were consistent with feeding the pipeline."[8] But Denning is writing this editorial not to defend the traditional academic system of which he is a part and whose values he obviously shares. Rather it is to suggest as a possible role model a different scientist than himself, namely Lofti Zadeh of the computer science department at the University of California, Berkeley. He says: "Zadeh's career was in a different direction."[9] Zadeh was the originator of "fuzzy logic", which opened up a new area of computer science and has also led to large numbers of practical uses, most of those having been found not in the USA but in Japan. From controlling banks of elevators to improving techniques in artificial intelligence research – both the practical applications and most of the follow-up research from Zadeh's original ideas have taken place in Japan.

I happen to have interviewed Professor Zadeh, not in the context of a study of academic–industry relations, but as part of a study of the development of computer science as an academic discipline.[10] Zadeh's office is the quintessential academic office. It is logically organized with rows of plastic bins piled in stacks upon one another, each containing a stack of reprints of an article. So Zadeh cannot be taken as an example of an academic who becomes intrigued by industry, leaves an academic career and pursues a different direction. Zadeh has pursued an academic career at the highest level and received due recognition from his peers. But at the same time as he was pursuing traditional academic goals he was also involved in consulting and taking out patents: all of the activities that Denning listed as not having undertaken himself.

Opportunities for commercial utilization of scientific research were often available to scientists, whose norms did not permit them to violate the boundary between science and business. What is new in the present situation is that many academic scientists no longer believe in the necessity of an isolated "ivory tower" for the working out of the logic of scientific discovery. Previously, in the long hiatus between scientific discovery and application, industry was expected to have its industrial scientists pursue research and development, an activity presumed to be too mundane for university scientists. Now, academic scientists are often eager and willing to direct, or participate in, developmental research programs leading to commercial application.

The conduct of science as an organized activity changes the nature of the scientific role and the social, if not cognitive, norms of science. The entrepreneurial scientist seeks financial gain as well as advancement of knowledge and recognition from their peers. Attention to the economic value of academic research has meant that research results have been defined as "intellectual property" and that property in knowledge is contested not only for its symbolic but also for its monetary value. The placement of economic motivation on a comparable status with advancement of knowledge in science has significant consequences for the definition of the scientific role, the social organization of science and the mission of the university.

12

INNOVATION
The endless transition

We are moving from the era of the Endless Frontier, based on an assumption that research automatically translates into use, to the era of the Endless Transition. Three fields of transition in science and technology policy can be identified in innovation, technology and institutions. The first transition is in the relationship between basic research, applied research and product development. The three previously relatively distinct phases are moving together. There will no longer be such strict boundaries between different types of research. Instead, they will blend into each other and move back and forth, without strict separation among them.

The second "endless", transition is between different technological areas. They had been thought of as being connected to different disciplines and different industries but they are now cross-fertilizing each other. Previously there were strong boundaries between individual disciplines. More recently interdisciplinary collaboration has expanded and new disciplines have been created at the intersections between old ones. Biochemistry is an early example. Moreover, new interdisciplinary synthetic disciplines have been created such as bio-informatics, whose components came out of the previous syntheses that created computer science and molecular biology. Now these two have themselves been brought together to form a new field in a continuing process of combination and re-combination that has created other new fields such as behavioral economics.

The third transition is toward the "triple helix" of university, industry and government relations as the framework for innovation systems at the national, regional and multi-national levels. As these three institutional sectors (public, private and academic) interact, a spiral pattern of linkages emerges at various stages of the innovation process. Start-up firms are a common outgrowth of the three sectors: arising from academic research groups, national laboratories and the laboratories of large corporations.

The triple helix

Society is more complex than biology. A "double helix" was sufficient to model DNA. A "triple helix" is required to model university–industry–government interactions. The triple helix comprises universities and other knowledge-producing institutions; industry, including high-tech start-ups as well as multinational corporations; and government at various levels – local, regional, national and transnational.

From various starting points in different parts of the world, there is a movement toward a new global model for the management of knowledge and technology, the triple helix. Four stages can be identified in its development:

1. Internal transformation in each of the helices Universities and other knowledge-producing institutions play a new role in society, not only in training students and conducting research, but also in making efforts to put knowledge to use effectively. Expressed through technology transfer offices and the requirements of government grant programs for the support of research, the entrepreneurial university elides the traditional boundaries between academia and industry. Strategic alliances for R&D among companies and governments taking the role of venture capitalist are parallel, intersecting developments.

2. Influence of one helix upon another The US federal government established a stable framework for academic technology transfer through the Bayh-Dole Act of 1980. This amendment to the Patent and Trademark Law instituted an indirect industrial policy through which government encouraged universities to assist industrial innovation. Secure rules of the game for the disposition of intellectual property, arising from government-sponsored research, encouraged the spread of technology transfer to a broader range of universities and expanded the academic technology transfer profession. Since universities and their representatives were involved in lobbying for the law, the direction of influence went both ways.

3. Creation of a new overlay of trilateral networks and organizations from the interaction among the three helices Such groups typically form to fill gaps in an innovation system by "brainstorming" new ideas. Joint Venture Silicon Valley, established during the economic downturn in the early 1990s, the Knowledge Circle of Amsterdam, organized during the past decade, and the New England Council, founded in the 1920s, included participants from small and large companies, local government and academia. The New England Council played a key role in inventing the venture capital firm, crucial to the growth of Route 128 and Silicon Valley.

4. A recursive effect of these triple helix networks, both on the spirals from which they emerged and the larger society One effect is on science itself. The capitalization of knowledge has displaced disinterestedness, the expectation that scientific knowledge would be freely distributed, with researchers taking their rewards solely in recognition from their peers.[1] This new norm has arisen from the practices of industrial science, an internal entrepreneurial dynamic within academia, and from government policies. The capitalization of knowledge transforms both the way that academic scientists view the results of their research and the role of the university in relation to industry and government. The knowledge base and its role in innovation can be explained in terms of changing relationships between university, industry, and government.

Innovation is increasingly likely to come from outside the individual firm or even from another institutional sphere such as the university where the focus of attention is on original path-breaking developments, whether in science or technology. It was not an accident that US universities were favored over government and industrial laboratories as the site for path-breaking military R&D during the Second World War. Moreover, it can be expected that discontinuous innovations, which originate in one company, are more likely to be utilized in a different environment where the blinders of current taken-for-granted practices or commitment to existing technologies and products are less likely to have effect.

The triple helix model of innovation, with converging institutional spheres of academia, industry and government each taking the role of the other, has been read in different ways in various parts of the world. In countries where the interface is well underway, whether occurring from the bottom up, through the interactions of individuals and organizations from different institutional spheres, or top down, encouraged by policy measures, the triple helix can be recognized as an empirical phenomenon. the USA has been seen to exemplify the former and Europe the latter mode of triple helix development.[2]

Both types of triple helix development may actually be underway in the USA and Europe albeit at different rates and with varying emphases. Top down processes can be identified in the USA, even though they are often hidden behind "bottom up" formats. Thus, Advanced Technology Program (ATP) program managers at the National Institute for Standards and Technology have been known to seek out technical leaders in industry to encourage them to initiate an "industry led" focus program. Nevertheless, as industry takes on the project as its own and draws academics as well, or vice versa, who can say where top down ends and bottom up begins? It may be more accurate to recognize both processes going on simultaneously and in tandem. Indeed, such a dual track for innovation promotion may be more productive than any single path.

Similarly, in Sweden when young computer and business consultants join together to form an e-commerce firm, a new development is at hand in a society whose industry was led by a definable group of large firms for several decades. Certainly government-supported entrepreneurship programs and incubator facilities are available to support these initiatives. Once again bottom up meets top down in a creative fashion, creating a broader context for innovation than would likely arise from either approach in isolation.

In other parts of the world (Latin America, for example) where industry and university have traditionally existed apart from each other, with academia as part of the governmental sphere, the triple helix is sometimes taken as a

INNOVATION

normative model. Some view it as a goal to strive for in bringing about change to enhance the prospects for innovation. Other observers see the coming of the triple helix as representing the downfall of the existing system of innovation, represented by government-owned corporations sponsoring laboratories adjacent to university campuses.

Privatization of companies, it is believed, will reduce the resources available for R&D, including collaborations between the state-owned company laboratory and university researchers. On the other hand, many of these collaborations were not sufficiently market driven and resulted in innovations that lacked a context to be put to use, having been based upon a negotiation between two public laboratories, neither of which was closely enough tied to production and use.[3]

This gap is not only a peculiarity of Latin American public research but has been noted in the large corporate laboratories in the USA that had been separated from production facilities and were operating as isolated entities until quite recently. In the latter case the reintegration of the laboratory into the firm and directing it more closely toward company goals has been occurring at IBM and GM in recent years. Typically, as corporate R&D facilities are moved closer to product development, longer-term R&D is conducted in collaboration with other firms, university research groups and government laboratories.

Beyond "the power elite"

The triple helix model of simultaneously competing and cooperating institutional spheres supersedes C. Wright Mills' societal model in which the military formed the third element of an institutional triad with large industry and the executive branch of the US federal government. Mills argued that the interlocking "power elite," sharing a common educational and social background, ran the major institutions in the United States. He further held that this coalition of institutional leaders transcended mere electoral politics and guided decision making on important policy issues. The end of the Cold War vitiated Mills' analysis, however, especially since the major instance of decision making that he sought to analyze was the nation's ability to initiate World War III.[4]

As geopolitical and military issues were gradually displaced during the 1970s and 1980s by issues of economic competitiveness, decision making became more diffuse, involved other actors, and often devolved from the national to the regional level. Science and technology policy issues, which had been understood as spin-offs of Cold War military and political exigencies – and therefore seen as taking place according to a linear model – required a framework that could account for the increasing importance of the science base and the decreasing relevance of the military. The triple helix model has enabled analysis of the dynamics of innovation in terms of historical trends, new structural arrangements and emerging moments of change.

INNOVATION

Innovation in innovation

Academic research now increasingly intersects with industrial progress and government economic development policy. The growth of industrial "conurbations" around universities, supported by government research funding, has become the hallmark of the new development model, exemplified by Silicon Valley; the profile of knowledge-based economic development was further raised by the founding of Genentech and other biotechnology companies based on academic research in the 1980s. The triple helix thesis is expressed in seven propositions:

1. Arrangements and networks among the Triple Helix institutional spheres provide the source of innovation rather than any single driver New initiatives arising from these networks become the source of innovation policies at national, sub-national, and supra-national levels. Government thus becomes a partner in the policy-making process as policies become an outcome of the interactions among the triple helix agencies.

2. Invention of new social arrangements becomes as important as the creation of physical devices New organizational mechanisms such as incubators, science parks and networks among them become a source of economic activity, community formation, and international exchange. New modes of interdisciplinary knowledge production, involving triple helix partners, translate into firm formation at the Internet and business incubation in various settings.

3. New channels for interaction link the various institutional spheres and speed the pace of innovation The linear model of transfer of knowledge generated in academia is supplemented with the transfer of technology both as intellectual property and through the formation of firms by alumni and staff. The reverse linear model starting from industrial and social problems provides starting points for new research programs and discipline formation. The interaction between these two dynamics results in the emergence of an interactive mode of innovation.

4. Capital-formation takes on new aspects even as new forms of capital are created The transformation of capital cannot be fully understood from the perspective of either the individual firm or the operation of markets. New forms of capital are created based upon social interaction ("who you know") and intellectual activities ("what you know"). Forms of capital are interchangeable. Thus, raising financial capital is based on accumulating intellectual as well as social capital. Human, social, and intellectual capital needs are redefined as firms relate to universities and government.

5. Globalization becomes decentralized and takes place through networks among universities as well as through multi-national corporations and international

143

INNOVATION

organizations As organizational innovations for technology transfer diffuse from one part of the world to another, interaction across regions and nations reinforces globalization. As universities develop links, they can combine discrete pieces of intellectual property and jointly exploit them. These new configurations become the basis of a continuous process of firm formation, diversification and collaborations among competitors.

6. *Developing countries and regions have the possibility of making rapid progress insofar as knowledge sources can be absorbed into the political economy* Political and social arrangements based upon principles of equity and transparency lay the groundwork for rapid development in a stable environment. "Leapfrogging," to skip some stages of development, is thus more likely. Universities and networked incubators can be utilized both to adapt advanced technologies to solve local problems as well as to transfer local innovations abroad.

7. *Reorganizations across institutional spheres, industrial sectors and nation-states are induced by opportunities in new technologies* Technological innovation reshapes the landscape in terms of the development of niches and clusters, relations among firms of different sizes and types and the creation of both public and private sources of venture capital. Enterprises are constructed out of elements from all the relevant institutional spheres, not just from industry itself. Social developments take unexpected turns as new technologies reinforce the dynamics of firm formation and vice versa.

Science has always been "mode 2"

During the first academic revolution, the theoretical and specialized outlook of the graduate schools was conveyed throughout the academic institutional order.[5] In the course of the second academic revolution, the valorization of research has been integrated with scientific discovery, returning science to its original seventeenth-century format prior to the appearance of an ideology of basic research in the mid-nineteenth century.[6]

The so-called "mode 2" of interdisciplinary research, with both theoretical and practical implications, is not new; it is the original format of science from its institutionalization in the seventeenth century. The real question to be answered is why mode 1, meaning disciplinary research isolated from the context of application, has arisen after mode 2, the original organizational and institutional basis of science which consists of collaborations, networks and invisible colleges.[7] Mersenne, before denoting an Internet site, was a person who by visits and letters knitted the early European scientific community together. The Academies of Science played a similar role in local and national contexts from the sixteenth century.

Modern science has always been organized through networks and has pursued practical as well as theoretical interests. Robert K. Merton reported that

144

INNOVATION

somewhere between 40 and 60 percent of discoveries in the seventeenth century could be identified as having their impetus in trying to solve practical problems in navigation, mining, etc.[8] Trying to solve practical problems through scientific means is neither new nor is it a modest part of science. It has been an important impetus to science from its inception. The two have always gone together.

Mode 2 represents the material base of science – how it actually operates. Mode 1 is an ideological construct upon that base intended to justify autonomy for science, especially in an era when it was still a very fragile institution and needed all the help it could get. This ideology appeared in association with the funding of universities by holders of large industrial fortunes and may have served to protect them from interference. There were grave concerns that the industrialists making these gifts would try to directly influence the direction of research at the universities, including the hiring and firing of professors as well as what topics were acceptable to be studied.[9] When universities were a weak institutional sphere, it can be argued that an ivory tower model, emphasizing isolation and de-emphasizing practical concerns, served to protect academic freedom. The President of the American Association for the Advancement of Science, Henry Rowland, posited a sphere of science that would be beyond the control of any one with economic interests. The notion was put forth that if anyone with external interests tried to intervene it would harm the conduct of science. The ideology of basic research carved out a protected space for science.

At the same time there was also the growth of the land grant universities and the founding of MIT as a part of that mode. The two modes have existed, of course, in parallel. The ideology of basic research was then strengthened by Robert K. Merton's positing of the normative structure of science during World War II. This arose from the need to defend science from external attack by the Nazi ideas of how science should be used, as well as from Lysenko in the Soviet Union. Again this formulation of a set of norms was to protect the free space of science.

The third element in establishing this ideology of science was, of course, the 1945 report *Science: The Endless Frontier*.[10] The huge success of science in supplying practical results during World War II in one sense provided its own legitimation. But with the end of the war and the desire to keep science funded, and without awareness in advance of what the Cold War and Sputnik would do, a rationale was needed in 1944 when Vannevar Bush got President Roosevelt to write a letter commissioning the report.

The authors of the report developed an implicit concept of science as a self-regulating mechanism, operating according to a linear progression: put in the money at one end and the results will flow out at the other in 50 years' time. This can be seen in the organizational framework for ensuring that funds for research would be distributed under the control of scientists. In the first draft of his report, Bush proposed to follow the then current British method of funding science at universities. It would be distributed on a per capita basis according to

145

the number of students. In the then current British system of a small number of universities, the funds automatically went to an elite. However, if that model had been applied in the USA, even in the early post-war era, with large land grant universities, the funding would not have flowed only to an elite but would have been much more broadly distributed across the academic spectrum.

In the time between the draft and the final report, the mechanism for the distribution of government funds to academic research was revised and peer review was put in. One could be sure that the peers, the leading elite scientists who would most surely be on these committees, would distribute the funds primarily to their fellow scientists at elite universities. So it was guaranteed through the peer review system that funds would be distributed to a scientific elite, reinforcing a status system of US universities that had been in place since the 1920s.

And in fact this linear model has worked, but not on its own. As we have seen, the USA established a series of programs and a regulatory environment to facilitate technology transfer in order to reap the benefits of munificent research funding. Other countries, such as Sweden, with high rates of R&D spending and relatively low rates of economic return, are currently undertaking parallel steps. The two modes have often existed in parallel. Although the "endless frontier" provided a justification for the establishment of the National Science Foundation, at the same time much greater amounts of funds were devoted to science through the military for practical results in computer science and also for health through the National Institutes of Health.

Nevertheless, why, at this point in time are we seeing the decline of mode 1 and the end of the endless frontier? Why has peer review been disregarded through the very practical method of distributing funds by direct appropriation, often labeled pork barrel? Because these funds are also directed toward serious scientific research and instrumentation projects. In fact, the leading universities, like Columbia when it needed to renew the infrastructure of its chemistry and could identify no other route to fund its projects, went to the same lobbying firm in Washington as universities that wished to break into the funded research mode. Columbia relabeled the chemistry department "The Center for Excellence in Chemistry" and, in time, an appropriation was made and the buildings were renovated. The university did not want to wait to go through the slower process of peer review, and likely receive smaller amounts of funding.

The fundamental reason why the endless frontier model is at an end and we are moving now into an endless transition model, not only in the USA and Western Europe but also in Latin America, the former Soviet Union and the developing world, is that it is now clear that the development of science is the basis for future industrial development. These connections, of course, have always been there. They showed clearly in the mid-nineteenth century in chemistry. This can be traced back to seventeenth-century pharmaceutical science and the development of a pharmaceutical industry in Germany. Marx could find one example, Perkins' research on dyestuffs in the UK, leading to the development of an industry in Germany that he translated into a thesis of the growth of science-based industry on the basis of a single empirical example.

The endless transition

The endless transition means that science and funds for research must now be distributed to all areas of the country. It is no longer acceptable for funds to go primarily to the east and west coasts and a few places in-between in the Midwest. All regions want a share of research funding because they are now aware that it is the basis of future economic growth. That is why the peer system breaks down. It is also why funding decisions are now made on other bases.

The future legitimation of science

The old cultural legitimation still holds, and to some extent the military and health, of course, remain as a strong stimulus to research funding. The future legitimation for scientific research that will keep funding at a high level is that it is the basis of economic development. This often occurs through these newly created disciplines. These disciplines are created not purely out of science the way Ben-David analyzed the splitting-off of new disciplines from old ones in the nineteenth century.[11] New disciplines, more recently, have been created through synthesis of practical and theoretical interests; of elements of older disciplines such as electrical engineering, a bit of psychology and philosophy and a machine, made into computer science. Similar processes operate to create material science bio-informatics and the other sciences that are on everyone's critical technology list.

The triple helix era

The triple helix denotes not only the relationship of university, industry and government, which constitutes these new scientific disciplines and the basis for scientific funding, but also the internal transformation within each of these spheres. The transformation of the university from a teaching institution into one which combines teaching with research is still ongoing, not only in the USA, but also in many other countries. There is a tension between the two activities but nevertheless they co-exist in a more or less compatible relationship with each other because it has been found to be both more productive and more cost effective to combine the two functions.

As the idea of transforming science into economically useful goods is introduced, a process of normative change gets underway. Scientists who adhered to the ideology of pure research, as well as those from the land grant tradition, also become involved in identifying practical results from their research and putting them to use. They find when they become engaged in these practical ventures that they are doing things that are not so different from their work in US universities. Research in the USA grew up in an entrepreneurial mode. The professor was not a civil servant as he or she often is in Europe. To be a researcher you had to be an entrepreneur to get the funds, first from your own university, next from foundations and then from government agencies or from industry. Universities operated as a series of quasi-firms that later became actual firms.

This is why academic scientists that I interviewed often said there is not such a great difference between what they were doing in the university in negotiating for funds and dealing with personnel problems in their research group, and what they were doing helping to organize a new firm. The two are made compatible with each other because the people who are doing this find that they can now have in mind the goals of mode 1 as well as those of mode 2, and they can place them in a compatible relationship to each other. They do not find a contradiction between identifying the economically useful goods of their research and the advancement of theory. Theory can advance practical uses as we know from biotechnology and from computer science, where speech recognition has been developed from artificial intelligence research.

We have similar transformations in industry where there is a shift from the hierarchical model of large firms to small firms, and especially small firms emanating from universities that operate fairly close to an academic model. This can be seen in biotechnology firms that advertise for post-doctoral fellows. Similar processes are at work in transforming government from working in different directions to pursuing a common goal. In countries such as the USA that adhered to a *laissez-faire* ideology, government is playing a more interventionist role in innovation. Conversely, in countries where government was a totalizing force, it has reduced its level of intervention to allow more autonomy to the industrial and academic spheres.

Breaking boundaries and building bridges

Each of these spheres is also taking the role of the other. Universities are taking the role of industry in forming companies. A penumbra of firms generated from the university and/or attracted to the university surround campuses. Governments, especially at the regional and local levels, are playing a new role in industrial development to encourage the growth of science and technology research as a basis for firm formation in regions that formerly lacked these capabilities. Industry is acting a little more like a university in sharing knowledge not only with the universities but also with fellow firms, collaborating with each other through strategic alliances in a quasi-academic mode.

The USA was formerly characterized by relationships among universities, industry and government in a *laisez-faire* triple helix model of separate spheres with strong borders and boundary lines. There was transfer across these borders through technology transfer offices and industrial liaison people, to keep the spheres separate and yet move technology across. The USA is currently moving

INNOVATION

into a mode of integration in which the spheres move more closely together and start to overlap as in a Venn diagram.

It is becoming commonplace to have negotiated arrangements in which universities own intellectual property and assign it to a firm, often started by a professor in the university, with the university retaining part-ownership of the company instead of seeking royalty payments as it typically would from a large firm. Thus when these two interests (academic and industrial) are joined together, it is not necessary to construct a "Great Wall of China" between the firm and the university. Instead data and ideas may go back and forth between the academic and firm laboratories.

If the disjuncture between theory and invention is accepted, the appearance of entrepreneurial scientists is an anomaly.[12] Their research is typically at the frontiers of science and leads to theoretical and methodological advances as well as the invention of devices. These activities involve sectors of the university, such as basic science departments, that have previously, in principle, limited their involvement with industry. Thus, the phenomenon of academic scientists commercializing their research requires a new explanation. It must be one that goes beyond the availability of investment funds since earlier generations of scientists, such as Pasteur and the Curies, seldom took advantage of commercial opportunities.[13] The emergence of this new role calls for the construction of a framework that can account for a pluralistic universe of science and a differentiated normative structure among scientists. Such a model should account for the emergent role of the entrepreneurial scientist in the university as well as industrial scientists who do not necessarily experience role strain in their research setting.

Resource dependency theory suggests that entrepreneurial academic behavior can be explained by the fact that universities follow their interests and seek funds wherever they become available: from government, as in the early post-war period, or from industry, as in the present time.[14] The premise of this framework is that the seeker is subordinate to the funding source. A theoretical analogue, principal–agent theory, has also been applied to understand the so-called contract between government and academia in the early post-war era.[15] However, if entrepreneurial scientists and entrepreneurial universities are now active and equal partners in their relations with industry and government, able to negotiate on an equal basis and maintain fundamental institutional interests such as the ability to publish, then the above explanations are partial, at best.

The first phase of entrepreneurial science is the internal development of academic research groups into "quasi-firms." The second phase refers to academic participation in the externalization and capitalization of knowledge in tangible products and distance-learning courseware. As universities spin-off for-profit entities from their research and educational activities, and fund some of their own research, they shift their institutional focus from eleemosynary to self-generation. The ability to balance multiple sources of support, including

149

industry, state and local government and self-funding can be expected to increase the independence of the university. This transition to decreased dependence upon the federal government is partially hidden by increases of research funding in selected areas such as health.[16]

As the production of scientific knowledge has been transformed into an economic enterprise, the economy has also been transformed, since it increasingly operates on an epistemological base.[17] Intellectual property is becoming as important as financial capital as the basis of future economic growth, indicated by the inadequacy of traditional models of valuing firms primarily in terms of their tangible assets. Although the contemporary research university has not become a fully fledged commercial enterprise, it has taken on some of the entrepreneurial characteristics of a "Silicon Valley" or "Route 128" high technology firm, even as such firms were adopting some of the collegial forms and campus architecture of the university. The university's emergence as a participant in economic development has not only changed the nature of the relationship between industry and the university but has also made the national university a significant regional actor.[18]

An entrepreneurial academic ethos that combines an interest in fundamental discovery with application is emerging as new and old academic missions persist in tension. Rather than being suborned to either industry or government, the university is emerging as an influential actor and equal partner in an innovation promotion and industrial policy regime, the "triple helix" of university–industry–government relations. The institutional spheres of science and the economy, which were hitherto relatively separate and distinct, have become inextricably intertwined.

The university's unique status as a teaching, research and economic development enterprise, whose traditional and new roles reinforce each other, places it in a central position in the new economy. The broader underlying process here is the movement of universities away from being eleemosynary or charitable institutions that gain their support from other sectors of society. It is expected that the generation of their own support from their research activities can rise to a much higher level on the assumption that only a very small proportion of the academic capacities for translating knowledge into the economy are currently being utilized. As the universities' involvement in the capitalization of knowledge increases, their position in society is transformed from a secondary to a primary institution.

Even as the university retains its traditional functions of conservation and production of knowledge, socialization of youth and dissemination of research, it becomes a founder of firms in incubator facilities, playing a new role in forming organizations. These practices represent a potentially fundamental modification of the traditional view of universities as institutions supported by governmental, ecclesiastical and lay patronage. The new arrangements open the possibility that universities will become, at least in part, financially self-supporting institutions, entities obtaining revenues through licensing agree-

INNOVATION

ments and other financial arrangements for the industrial use of new knowledge discovered at the universities. At present, this possibility is little more than that but it certainly represents a novel idea in the history of universities.

NOTES

INTRODUCTION

1 Geiger, Roger. 1986. *To Advance Knowledge: The Growth of American Research Universities, 1900–1940*. New York: Oxford University Press.
2 Bush, Vannevar. 1970. *Pieces of the Action*. New York: Morrow, p. 159.
3 Ibid., p. 168.
4 Veysey, Laurence. 1965. *The Emergence of the American University*. Chicago: University of Chicago Press.
5 Genuth, Joel. 1987. "Groping toward science policy in the United States in the 1930s," *Minerva* 25(3): 238–68.
6 Zusman, Ami. 1999. "Issues facing higher education in the twenty-first century," in Philip Altbach, Robert Berdahl and Patricia Gumport (eds), *American Higher Education in the Twenty-first Century*. Baltimore: Johns Hopkins University Press, pp. 109–50.

1 THE SECOND ACADEMIC REVOLUTION

1 Director of Technology Transfer, Columbia University, Interview with Henry Etzkowitz, 1982.
2 Eugene Schuler, Director, CESTM, State University of New York at Albany, formerly Director, Long Island High Technology Incubator, SUNY, Stony Brook, Interview with Henry Etzkowitz, April 1995.
3 Blakeslee, Sandra. 1996. "A protein tells eaters to stop," *New York Times* 4 January, A1, B10.
4 Jencks, Christopher and David Riesman. 1968. *The Academic Revolution*. New York: Doubleday, p. 12.
5 Oleson, Alexandra and John Voss. 1979. *The Organization of Knowledge in Modern America*. Baltimore: Johns Hopkins University Press.
6 Kerr, Clark. 1963. *The Uses of the University*. Cambridge: Harvard University Press.
7 Apple, Rima. 1989. "Patenting university research: Harry Steenbock and the Wisconsin Alumni Research Foundation," *ISIS* 30 (September): 375–94.
8 Wise, George. 1980. "A new role for professional scientists in industry: industrial research at General Electric, 1900–1916," *Technology and Culture*, pp. 408–29.
9 Noble, David. 1976. *America By Design: Science, Technology and the Rise of Corporate Capitalism*. New York: Knopf. See especially Chapter 7.
10 Faulkner, Wendy and Jacqueline Senker. 1995. *Knowledge Frontiers: Public Sector Research and Industrial Innovation in Biotechnology, Engineering Ceramics, and Parallel Computing*. Oxford: Oxford University Press.

NOTES

11 See Bok, Derek. 1982. *Beyond the Ivory Tower: Social Responsibilities of the Modern University*. Cambridge: Harvard University Press.

12 "Harvard University, in policy reversal, will raise money for investments aimed at bringing faculty members' research to marketplace and making profit for school," *New York Times*, 16 September 1988, I, 14: 1.

13 Kolata, Gina. 1997. "Scientist reports first cloning ever of adult mammal," *New York Times*, 13 February, 1: 1.

14 Aitken, Hugh. 1976. *Syntony and Spark: The Origins of Radio*. New York: Wiley, p. 209.

15 Office of Technology Assessment. 1984. *Commercial Biotechnology: An International Analysis*. Washington, DC: Office of Technology Assessment.

16 Aitken, op. cit.

17 See Etzkowitz, Henry. 1983. "Entrepreneurial scientists and entrepreneurial universities in American academic science," *Minerva* 21: 198–233.

18 Aborn, Timothy. 1996. "The Business of Induction: Industry and Genius in the Language of British Scientific Reform," *History of Science* 31(103): 91–121.

19 Schumpeter, J.A. (1951) [1949]. "Economic theory and entrepreneurial history," in *Change and the Entrepreneur: Postulates and Patterns for Entrepreneurial History*. Cambridge: Harvard University Press, p. 256.

20 Eisinger, Peter. 1988. *The Rise of the Entrepreneurial State: State and Local Economic Development Policy in the United States*. Madison: University of Wisconsin Press.

2 MIT: THE FOUNDING OF AN ENTREPRENEURIAL UNIVERSITY

1 Rogers, William. 1954 [1846]. "A plan for a polytechnic school in Boston," in S. Prescott, *When MIT was Boston Tech*. Cambridge: MIT Press.

2 Ibid.

3 Ibid.

4 Pearson, Henry. 1937. *Richard Cockburn Maclaurin*. New York: Macmillan.

5 See Wolf, Steven and David Zilberman (eds). 2001. *Knowledge Generation and Institutional Innovation in Agriculture*. Dordrecht: Kluwer.

6 Sinclair, Bruce. 1974. *Philadelphia's Mechanics: A History of the Franklin Institute, 1824–1865*. Baltimore: Johns Hopkins University Press, p. 261.

7 Pierson, George. 1952. *Yale College: An Educational History, 1871–1921*. New Haven: Yale University Press.

8 Storr, Richard. 1966. *Harper's University: The Beginnings; A History of the University of Chicago*. Chicago: University of Chicago Press.

9 Wise, George. 1985. *Willis Whitney, General Electric and the Origins of U.S. Industrial Research*. New York: Columbia University Press.

10 Carty, J.J. 1917. "The relation of pure science to industrial research," in *Smithsonian Institution Annual Report – 1916*. Washington, DC: Government Printing Office, p. 525.

11 Ibid., p. 92

12 Servos, John. 1970. "The knowledge corporation: A.A. Noyes and chemistry at Cal-Tech, 1915–1930," *Ambix* November.

3 CONTROVERSY OVER CONSULTATION

1 Wildes, Karl and Nilo Lindgren. 1985. *A Century of Electrical Engineering and Computer Science at MIT*. Cambridge: MIT Press, pp. 47–8.

2 Ibid., p. 49.

NOTES

3 Stankiewicz, Rikard. 1986. *Academics and Entrepreneurs*. London: Frances Pinter, p. 46.
4 Greene, John C. 1979. "Protestantism, science and the American enterprise: Benjamin Silliman's moral universe," in Leonard G. Wilson (ed.), *Benjamin Silliman and his Circle*. New York: Science History Publications.
5 "F.G. Keyes Memorandum Regarding Outside Work: Chemistry Department," 21 January 1931, MIT Archives, Collection AC 4, Box 217, Folder 30.
6 Ibid.
7 "Letter from Watson Vredenburg, President of the National Engineering Inspection Association, to President Compton," 9 January 1932, MIT Archives, Collection AC 4, Box 217, Folder 3.
8 "Executive Memorandum from C.L. Norton To Dr K.T. Compton," 13 February 1931, MIT Archives, Collection AC 4, Box 217, Folder 3.
9 See Kahn, Ely. 1986. *The Problem Solvers: A History of Arthur D. Little Inc.*, Boston: Little, Brown.
10 "F.G. Keyes Memorandum Regarding Outside Work: Chemistry Department," 21 January 1931, MIT Archives, Collection AC 4, Box 217, Folder 3.
11 Servos, John. 1980. "The industrial relations of science: chemical engineering at MIT. 1900–1939," *ISIS* LXXI (December): 531–49.

4 THE TRAFFIC AMONG MIT, INDUSTRY AND THE MILITARY

1 Walker, William. 1920. "Co-ordinating scientific and industrial effort," *Chemical and Metallurgical Engineering*. 22(10): 433.
2 *Technology Review*, 1904: 198.
3 Walker, William. 1920. "The technology plan," *Chemical and Metallurgical Engineering* 22(10).
4 Pearson, Henry. 1937. *Richard Cockburn Maclaurin*. New York: Macmillan, pp. 266–7.
5 Walker, William. 1920. "The technology plan," *Chemical and Metallurgical Engineering* 22(10): 463.
6 Ibid.
7 Servos, John. 1980. "The industrial relations of science: chemical engineering at MIT. 1900–1939," *ISIS* LXXI (December).
8 Morrison, Philip. 1977. *In at the Beginnings*. Cambridge, MA: MIT Press.
9 Guerlac, Henry. 1946. "History of the Radiation Laboratory", B-II 81 MDRC Minutes, 25 October 1940, MIT Archives.
10 Meigs, Montgomery. 1982. "Managing uncertainty: Vannevar Bush, James B. Conant and the development of the atomic bomb, 1940–1945," PhD dissertation, University of Wisconsin.
11 Ibid.
12 MIT (Commission on MIT Education). 1949. "Report of the Committee on Educational Survey to the Faculty of the Massachusetts Institute of Technology," MIT Archives, Collection AC 124.
13 Foster, Leroy. 1984. "Sponsored Research at MIT," unpublished manuscript, MIT Archives, p. 45.
14 Burchard, J. 1948. *MIT in World War II*. New York: Tech Press/Wiley, p. 126.
15 Foster, 1984 op. cit., p. 25.
16 Ibid., p. 28.
17 Ibid.
18 Compton quoted in Burchard, J. 1948. *MIT in World War II*. New York: Tech Press/Wiley, p. vii.
19 Clark, R. 1965. *Tizard*. London: Methuen.

NOTES

20 Guerlac, op. cit: 24.
21 Ibid.: I 75.
22 Ibid.: D-IV 1.
23 Ibid.: D-IV 2.
24 Ibid.: D-IV 2.

5 KNOWLEDGE AS PROPERTY: THE DEBATE OVER PATENTING ACADEMIC SCIENCE

1 See Long, Pamela. 1991. "Invention, authorship 'intellectual property,' and the origin of patents: notes toward a conceptual history," *Technology and Culture*, 32(4): 846–84; see also Macleod, Christine. 1988. *Inventing the Industrial Revolution*. Cambridge: Cambridge University Press, 1988.
2 Article I, Section 8, Clause 8.
3 Mowery, David and Bhaven Sampat. 2001. "Patenting and licensing university inventions: lessons from the history of the Research Corporation," *Industrial and Corporate Change* 10(2): 317–55.
4 Etzkowitz, Henry. 2001. "The Second Academic Revolution and the Rise of Entrepreneurial Science," *IEEE Technology and Society Magazine*, Summer.
5 Potter, A.A. 1940. "Research and invention in engineering colleges," *Science* 91(2349): 6.
6 Association of University Technology Managers (AUTM). 1999. *Licensing Survey*. www.autm.net
7 *Technology Access Report* 1993 6(12): 18.
8 Association of University Technology Managers (AUTM). 1999. *Licensing Survey*. www.autm.net, Executive Summary.
9 Weiner, Charles. 1982. "Relations of science, government and industry: the case of recombinant DNA," in Albert Teich and Ray Thornton (eds), *Science, Technology and the Issues of the Eighties: Policy Outlook*. Boulder: Westview.
10 "Statement Concerning Patent Policy for the 1936 Annual Meeting of the Corporation," 14 October 1936, MIT Archives, Collection AC 4, Box 2, Folder 3.
11 "Institute Policy Regarding Patents," 15 April 1932, MIT Archives, Collection AC 64, Box 2, Folder 3.
12 Lecuyer, Christopher. 1992. "The making of a science-based technological university: Karl Compton, James Killian and the reform of MIT, 1930–1957," *History of the Physical and Biological Sciences* 23(1): 153–80.
13 "Memorandum from Professor John Bunker to President Karl Compton," 17 October 1931. Quoted in "Letter from Professor John Bunker to Vannevar Bush," 19 May 1936, MIT Archives, Collection AC 64, Box 1.
14 "Letter from Professor John Bunker to Vannevar Bush," 19 May 1936, MIT Archives, Collection AC 64, Box 1.
15 Ibid.
16 Ibid.
17 Gray, G.W. 1936. "Science and profits," *Harpers Magazine* 172 (April): 539.
18 "Memorandum on Patent Policy and its Effects," John Bunker to Vannevar Bush, 23 April 1936, MIT Archives, Collection AC 64, Box 1.
19 "Massachusetts Institute of Technology," Speech by Karl T. Compton, 25 October 1935. MIT Archives AC 64, Box 2, Folder 1.
20 "Minutes of Meeting of Institute Patent Committee," 6 November 1936, MIT Archives, Collection AC 64, Box 1.

155

NOTES

21 National Research Council. 1992. "Global dimensions of intellectual property rights in science and technology," Conference, Washington, DC.

6 THE REGULATION OF ACADEMIC PATENTING

1 Etzkowitz, Henry and Andrew Webster. 1994. "Science as intellectual property," in James Peterson, Gerald Markle, Sheila Jasanoff and Trevor Pinch (eds), *Handbook of Science, Technology and Society*. Beverly Hills: Sage.

2 Bliss, Michael. 1982. *The Discovery of Insulin*. Chicago: University of Chicago Press.

3 The award was given jointly to Banting and Professor J.J.R. Macleod, the academic sponsor of the research; Banting split his prize money with Best and Macleod split his with J.B. Collip, the biochemist on the project. The appropriate allocation of credit became part of the issue of ownership when it was realized that it was necessary to insure a valid patent.

4 "Statement of Patent Policy," 15 April 1932, MIT Archives, Collection AC 64, Box 2, Folder 3.

5 "Minutes of Meeting of Institute Patent Committee," 6 November 1936, MIT Archives, Collection AC 64, Box 1.

6 "Statement of Patent Policy," 15 April 1932, MIT Archives, Collection AC 64, Box 2, Folder 3.

7 Foster, Leroy. 1968. "Sponsored research at MIT," unpublished manuscript, MIT Archives, Volume 1, p. 104.

8 Anonymous, "For the Information of MIT Patent Committees," 1945, MIT Archives, Collection AC 64, Box 2, Folder 3.

9 "Minutes of Meeting of Institute Patent Committee," 7 April 1938, MIT Archives, Collection AC 64, Box 1.

10 "Letter from Vannevar Bush to members of the Patent Committee," 21 May 1936, MIT Archives, Collection AC 64, Box 1.

11 Professor Harold Edgerton, Interview with Henry Etzkowitz, July 1986.

12 "Minutes of Meeting of Institute Patent Committee," 5 November 1935, MIT Archives, Collection AC 64, Box 1.

13 "Letter from Vannevar Bush to members of the Patent Committee," 21 May 1936, MIT Archives, Collection AC 64, Box 1.

14 Ibid.

15 Ibid.

16 Ibid.

17 Ibid.

18 Ibid.

19 "Statement Concerning Patent Policy for the 1936 Annual Meeting of the Corporation," 14 October 1936, MIT Archives, Collection AC 4, Box 2, Folder 3.

20 "Memorandum on Patent Policy and its Effects," John Bunker to Vannevar Bush, 23 April 1936, MIT Archives, Collection AC 64, Box 1.

21 "Minutes of the Patent Committee," 11 February 1936, MIT Archives, Collection AC 64, Box 1.

22 The Institute Gazette, "Patenting of Institute inventions", Technology Review, XXXIX (June 1937) pp. 348–50.

23 McKusick, Vincent. 1948. "A study of patent policies," *Journal of the Franklin Institute* March: 194–225.

24 The arrangement lasted until the early 1960s, when MIT and the Research Corporation parted ways over differences about how to license the core memory patent to IBM. The Research Corporation wished to obtain maximum income. However, when IBM objected to the terms, MIT was willing to reduce its rate, aware that its relationship to IBM covered a broader field of topics than a single patent.

156

NOTES

When the Research Corporation refused to relent, MIT severed its relationship with the Corporation and assumed direct responsibility for managing its patents.

25 Anonymous, "Statement of Patent Policy," 15 April 1932, MIT Archives, Collection AC 64, Box 2, Folder 3.
26 "For the Information of MIT Patent Committees," 1945, MIT Archives, Collection AC 64, Box 2, Folder 3.
27 "Minutes of Patent Management Committee," 11 January 1945, MIT Archives, Collection AC 64, Box 2, Folder 1.
28 Ibid.
29 "Letter from Karl Compton to Ralph Flanders, President, The American Research and Development Corporation," 19 December 1946, MIT Archives, Collection AC 64, Box 2, Folder 3.
30 Anonymous, "Industrial Office," n.d., MIT Archives, Collection AC 64, Box 2, Folder 3.
31 "Letter from Karl Compton to Ralph Flanders, President, The American Research and Development Corporation," 10 December 1946, MIT Archives, Collection AC 64, Box 2, Folder 3.
32 Ibid.
33 Memo for File Re: Forrester Patent Meeting in MIT President's Office, 7 September 1962, MIT Archives, Collection AC 35, Box 2.
34 "Letter from President Stratton to J. William Hinkley, President, Research Corporation," 28 August 1962, MIT Archives, Collection AC 35, Box 2.
35 "Letter from R.J. Horn, Institute attorney to Julius Stratton, President of Massachusetts Institute of Technology," 5 September 1962, MIT Archives, Collection AC 35, Box 2.
36 "Letter from Institute Counsel R.J. Horn to President Stratton," 19 November 1962, MIT Archives, Collection AC 35, Box 2.
37 "Memo for File Re: Forrester Patent Meeting in MIT President's office," 7 September 1962, MIT Archives, Collection AC 35, Box 2.

7 ENTERPRISES FROM SCIENCE: THE ORIGINS OF SCIENCE-BASED ECONOMIC DEVELOPMENT

1 Bush, Vannevar. 1970. *Pieces of the Action.* New York: Morrow.
2 See Israel, Paul. 1998. *Edison, a Life of Invention.* New York: John Wiley; and Josephson, Matthew. 1954. *Edison: A Biography.* New York: McGraw-Hill.
3 See Wade, Richard. 1964. *The Urban Frontier.* Chicago: University of Chicago Press.
4 Jones, Lawrence. 1960. "Legislative Activities of the Greater Boston Chamber of Commerce," PhD Dissertation, Harvard University Graduate School of Business Administration.
5 The New England Council, Inc. "60 Years of Leadership." circa 1985.
6 Leman, Albert N. 1940. "Research for small business," *Forbes,* 1 February: 17.
7 "Proposal of the Massachusetts Institute of Technology to the New England Council for the establishment of an Institute of Industrial Cooperation and Research," MIT Archives, Collection AC 4, Box 216, Folder 13.
8 Ibid.
9 "Letter from Karl Compton to Mr Ray M. Hudson, Technical Advisor, The New England Council," 12 December 1930, MIT Archives, Collection AC AC4, Box 217, Folder 2.
10 "Letter to Dr Karl Compton, President of the Massachussetts Institute of Technology from Mr Ray M. Hudson, Technical Advisor, The New England Council," 18 December 1930, MIT Archives, Collection AC 4, Box 217, Folder 2.

157

NOTES

11 "Letter from C.F. Weed, President, New England Council to Paul Cloke, Director, Maine Experiment Station, Orono, Maine," September 1939, MIT Archives, Collection AC 4, Box 235, Folder 3.

12 Karl Compton. "Industrial Development in New England," an address prepared for delivery before the 75th anniversary of the University of New Hampshire in the Joint meeting of the New England Council and the American Association for the Advancement of Science at Durham, New Hampshire, 24 June 1941, MIT Archives, Collection AC 4, Box 235, Folder 11.

13 Ibid.

14 Ibid.

15 "Memorandum to Dr Karl T. Compton from Richard B. Cross, 'Agenda for November 3rd Meeting of New Products Committee,'" 24 October 1939, MIT Archives, Collection AC 4, Box 235, Folder 3.

16 Ibid.

17 "Letter from A.F. Kingsbury to Richard B. Cross," 21 March 1940, MIT Archives, Collection AC 4, Box 235, Folder 5.

18 Ibid.

19 "Letter from Richard B. Cross to A.F. Kingsbury," 27 March 1940, MIT Archives, Collection AC 4, Box 235, Folder 5.

20 Ibid.

21 Ibid.

22 "Memorandum: New Products for New England," n.d., MIT Archives, Collection AC 4, Box 235, Folder 2.

23 "Memorandum from Richard Cross to Karl Compton, 'Appointment of Subcommittee Members,'" 29 November 1939, MIT Archives, Collection AC 4, Box 235, Folder 4.

24 "Memorandum to Dr Karl T. Compton from Richard B. Cross," 3 October, 1939, MIT Archives, Collection AC 4, Box 235, Folder 3.

25 "New England Industries, Inc.," unpublished manuscript, 29 December 1940; MIT Archives, Collection AC 4, Box 235, Folder 5.

26 Ibid.

27 Ibid.

28 "Memorandum to Ralph Flanders from Richard Cross," 16 October 1940, MIT Archives, Collection AC 4, Box 235, Folder 6.

29 "New England Industrial Research Foundation, Inc.," MIT Archives, Collection AC 4, Box 235, Folder 11.

30 "Letter from Richard B. Cross to David Prince, Vice President, General Electric Company," 12 January 1942, MIT Archives, Collection AC 4, Box 235, Folder 14.

31 Ibid.

32 "Letter from Karl T. Compton to L.C. Bird, President, Phipps Bird Inc.," 10 March 1943, MIT Archives, Collection AC 4, Box 235, Folder 15.

33 "Letter from Earl Stevenson, President, Arthur D. Little Co. to Karl T. Compton," 26 September 1942; MIT Archives, Collection AC 4, Box 235, Folder 12.

34 "Letter to Mr Norman Klivens from Karl T. Compton," 23 April, 1941; MIT Archives, Collection AC 4, Box 14, Folder 14.

8 THE INVENTION OF THE VENTURE CAPITAL FIRM: AMERICAN RESEARCH AND DEVELOPMENT (ARD)

1 "New England Industries, Inc.," unpublished manuscript, 29 December 1940; MIT Archives, Collection AC 4, Box 235, Folder 5.

2 Karl Compton. "Industrial Development in New England," an address prepared for delivery before the 75th anniversary of the University of New Hampshire in the

158

NOTES

Joint meeting of the New England Council and the American Association for the Advancement of Science at Durham, New Hampshire, 24 June 1941, MIT Archives, Collection AC 4, Box 235, Folder 11.

3 Letter from President Karl T. Compton to Richard B. Cross, 19 October, 1939, MIT Archives, Collection AC 4, Box 235, Folder 3.

4 Grow, Natalie. 1977. "The 'Boston Type' open end fund: development of a national financial instrument," PhD Dissertation, Harvard Business School, pp. 284–5.

5 Aguren, W. 1965. "Large nonfinancial corporations as venture capital sources," SM thesis, Massachussetts Institute of Technology, Sloan School of Management, p. 10.

6 "The Prudent Boston Gamble," *Fortune* November, 1952

7 *The Saturday Evening Post,* 31 July 1954.

8 "Aims of the the American Research and Development Corporation," unpublished manuscript, 1 January 1947.

9 William Congleton, Interview with Henry Etzkowitz, July 1986.

10 "Something ventured," *Time Magazine,* 19 August 1946.

11 "A plan for the formation of a company to encourage and facilitate the development of new inventions , products, processes and industries," n.d., Dubridge papers 121.8, California Institute of Technology Archives.

12 Interview with Longstreet Hinton, Retired Director, Morgan Guaranty Trust Department, April, 1989.

13 Hinton, Longstreet, John Meyer and Thomas Rodd. 1979. *Some Comments About the Morgan Bank.* New York: Morgan Guaranty Trust Company. The head of the Trust department at Morgan had earlier served with Doriot on the board of directors of a corporation and his personal confidence in Doriot's abilities carried over to the new venture.

14 "Letter to Georges Doriot from Robert Lehman, Lehman Bros," 11 October 1965; "Letter to Georges Doriot from Joseph Ripley, Harriman, Ripley," 21 March 1967, Box 4, Doriot Papers, Manuscript Division, Library of Congress.

15 "Letter from Karl Compton to Horace Ford," 22 March 1946, MIT Archives, Collection AC 4, Box 46, Folder 9.

16 Charles Coulter, President of American Research and Development, Interview with Henry Etzkowitz, June 1986.

17 King, Frank. 1946. "Investment Banking Accepts a Challenge," *Investment Dealers Digest,* 26 August.

18 Georges F. Doriot. 1947. "American Research and Development Corporation," founding statement, 1 January.

19 Ibid.

20 William Congleton, American Research and Development Technical Director, quoted in "Boston and the 'Science' Industry," *Investor's Reader,* 6 February 1957, 28(3): 5.

21 "Confidential Memorandum of Conference of certain Members of the Board of Directors of Tracerlab Inc.," 8 December 1952, Leahy Business Archives, American Research and Development File 294.

22 "Letter from Georges Doriot, American Research and Development to Charles Cotting, Lee Higginson Corporation," 12 December 1952, Leahy Business Archives, American Research and Development File 294.

23 "Personal and Confidential Letter from Georges Doriot to Denis Robinson," 28 April 1950, Leahy Business Archives, American Research and Development File 287.

24 Bylinsky, Gene. 1967. "General Doriot's dream factory," *Fortune* August: 132.

25 William Congleton, retired American Research and Development staff member, Interview with Henry Etzkowitz, July 1986.

26 Ibid.

NOTES

27 Ibid.

28 Robert J. Van de Graaff, MIT Archives, AC 4, Box 274, Folder 1.

29 "Memorandum: Van de Graaff Patent: Non-Development," n.d., MIT Archives AC 4, Box 241, Folder 18.

30 Redmond, Kent and Thomas Smith. 1980. *Project Whirlwind*. Maynard, MA: Digital Equipment Press.

31 William Congleton, Interview with Henry Etzkowitz, July 1986.

32 Aguren, W. 1965. "Large Nonfinancial Corporations as Venture Capital Sources," SM thesis, Massachussetts Institute of Technology, Sloan School of Management, p. 10.

33 Ibid., p. 33.

34 Anonymous, 1969. "In on the ground floor," *Newsweek* February.

35 Anonymous, 1970. "There's lots more fun in venturing," *Financial Times* 24 December.

36 National Venture Capital Association. 1980. *The Guide To Venture Capital Sources*. Arlington, VA: National Venture Capital Association.

37 Armitage, W. 1979. "The role of the venture capitalist in new ventures," SM thesis, Massachussetts Institute of Technology, Sloan School of Management.

38 Charles Coulter, President of American Research and Development, Interview with Henry Etzkowitz, February 1989.

39 Kloess, Michael. 2001. "Chad Brownstein, Cofounder, Managing Partner, ITU Ventures," *Technology Access Report* 14(2): 15–16.

9 STANFORD AND SILICON VALLEY: ENHANCEMENT OF THE MIT MODEL

1 Norberg, Arthur. 1976. "The origins of the electronics industry on the Pacific Coast," *Proceedings of the IEEE* 64(9).

2 Braun, Ernest and Stuart Macdonald. 1983. *Revolution in Miniature*. Cambridge: Cambridge University Press, p. 126.

3 Ginzton, Edward L. 1975. "The $100 idea," *IEEE Spectrum*, February 30–39.

4 Israel, Paul. 1998. *Edison: A Life of Invention*. New York: John Wiley.

5 "Letter to Paul Davis, General Secretary, Stanford University," 29 December 1943, Terman Papers, Stanford University Archives.

6 Ibid.

7 Ibid.

8 Ibid.

9 Ibid.

10 "Memorandum to Dean Hilgard from E.L. Ginzton, Microwave Lab," 9 April 1953, Terman Papers, Stanford University Archives, p. 7.

11 "To: File From FET Re Shopping Center #SC – 160 III 32–10 1/20/65," Terman Papers, Stanford University Archives.

12 "Letter from Terman to J.E. Wallace Sterling," 9 November 1951, Terman Papers, Stanford University Archives.

13 Saxenian, Annalee. 1994. *Regional Advantage: Culture and Competition in Silicon Valley and Route 128*. Cambridge: Harvard University Press.

14 Kidder, Tracy. 1981. *The Soul of a New Machine*. Boston: Little, Brown.

15 Hamel, Gary. 1999. "Bringing Silicon Valley inside," *Harvard Business Review* September–October: 71–84.

NOTES

10 TECHNOLOGY TRANSFER UNIVERSALIZED: THE BAYH-DOLE REGIME

1 Some of the materials for this chapter are drawn from Etzkowitz, Henry and Ashley J. Stevens. 1995. "Inching toward industrial policy: the university's role in government initiatives to assist small, innovative companies in the U.S.," *Science Studies* 8(2): 13–31.
2 See Peters, Lois and Herbert Fusfeld. 1982. "Current U.S. University–Industry Research Connections," in National Science Board, *University–Industry Research Relationships: Selected Studies*. Washington, DC: US Government Printing Office.
3 Pursell, Carroll. 1979. "Science agencies in World War II: the OSRD and its challengers," in Nathan Reingold (ed.), *The Sciences in the American Context: New Perspectives*. Washington, DC: The Smithsonian Institution.
4 Norman Latker, Former Patent Counsel, National Institutes of Health, Interview with Henry Etzkowitz, 1998.
5 Approximately a year later, Latker was restored to his position at NIH through an appeal process. Since he had earned more from private legal practice than his government salary during this period, he was not entitled to back salary.
6 Personal communication from Howard Bremer, Wisconsin Alumni Research Foundation to Ashley Stevens.
7 Norman Latker, Former Patent Counsel, National Institutes of Health, Interview with Henry Etzkowitz, 1998.
8 Niels Reimers, Interview with Henry Etzkowitz, August 2001.
9 Jesse Lasken, Assistant General Counsel, National Science Foundation, Interview with Henry Etzkowitz, 1998.
10 Fraser, John. 2001. "Membership needs task-force results," *Association of University Technology Managers Inc. Newsletter* August: 1.
11 Government laboratories were placed under a licensing regime similar to Bayh-Dole through the Stevenson-Wydler Act of 1986.

11 THE MAKING OF ENTREPRENEURIAL SCIENTISTS

1 Kornberg, Arthur. 1996. *The Golden Helix: Inside Biotech Ventures*. Sausalito, CA: University Science Books.
2 See Aborn, Timothy. 1996. "The business of induction: industry and genius in the language of British scientific reform", *History of Science* 31(103): 91–121.
3 See Latour, Bruno and Steve Woolgar. 1979. *Laboratory Life*. Beverly Hills: Sage.
4 Mark Ptashne, Interview with Henry Etzkowitz, Cambridge, MA, 1986.
5 Ibid.
6 Denning, Peter J. 1990. "Patent or perish," *Communications of the ACM* 33(9): 15–16.
7 Ibid.
8 Ibid., p. 16.
9 Ibid., p. 16.
10 Lofti Zadeh, Interview with Henry Etzkowitz, Berkeley, CA, 1989.

12 INNOVATION: THE ENDLESS TRANSITION

1 Agres, Ted. 2001. "Cloning capsized?" *The Scientist* 15(16).
2 Stolberg, Sheryl. 2001. "Patent laws may determine shape of stem cell research," *New York Times*, 17 August, pp. A1, 15.
3 Quoted in Stolberg, op. cit.

NOTES

4 When WARF was founded in the 1930s, academic research as the basis of industrial development was a nascent phenomenon. WARF was established to commercialize discoveries at arm's length from the University of Wisconsin's academic activities. Proceeds from Vitamin B-12 and other discoveries enabled the University of Wisconsin to become a research powerhouse in the biological sciences during the depths of the Depression. See Apple, Rima. 1989. "Patenting university research: Harry Steenbock and the Wisconsin Alumni Research Foundation," *ISIS* 30 (September): 375–94.

5 WARF was central to an earlier controversy over the commercialization of research. Decades earlier, margarine producers had charged WARF with using its control of patent rights to protect Wisconsin dairy farmers from competition.

6 Merton, Robert K. 1973 [1942]. "The normative structure of science," in Norman Storer (ed.), *The Sociology of Science*. Chicago: University of Chicago Press.

7 See Mills, C. Wright. 1957. *The Power Elite*. New York: Oxford; and 1958, *The Causes of World War III*. New York: Ballantine.

8 See Storr, Richard J. 1953. *The Beginnings of Graduate Education in America*. Chicago: University of Chicago Press; Geiger, Roger. 1986. *To Advance Knowledge: The Growth of American Research Universities, 1900–1940*. Oxford: Oxford University Press; and Altbach, Philip, Robnert Berdahl and Patricia Gumport (eds). 1999. *American Higher Education in the Twenty-first Century*. Baltimore: Johns Hopkins University Press.

9 Kevles, Daniel. 1978. *The Physicists: The History of a Scientific Community in Modern America*. New York: Knopf.

10 Gibbons, Michael, Camille Limoges, Helga Nowotny, Simon Schwartzman, Peter Scott and Martin Trow. 1994. *The New Production of Knowledge*. Beverly Hills: Sage.

11 Merton, Robert K. 1970 [1938]. *Science, Technology and Society in Seventeenth-Century England*. New York: Harper & Row.

12 Storr, Richard J. 1968. *Harper's University*. Chicago: University of Chicago Press.

13 US Office of Scientific Research and Development. 1945. *Science: The Endless Frontier, A Report to the President on a Program for Post-war Scientific Research*. Washington, DC: US Government Printing Office.

14 Ben-David, Joseph. 1980. "The ethos of science: the last half-century," in *Silver Jubilee Symposium*, Volume I. Canberra: Australian Academy of Sciences.

15 Aitken, Hugh. 1976. *Syntony and Spark: The Origins of Radio*. New York: Wiley.

16 Etzkowitz, Henry. 1983. "Entrepreneurial scientists and entrepreneurial Universities in American academic science," *Minerva* 21 (Autumn): 198–233.

17 Slaughter, Sheila and Larry Leslie. 1997. *Academic Capitalism*. Baltimore: Johns Hopkins University Press.

18 Guston, David. 1999. *Between Politics and Science: Assuring the Productivity and Integrity of Research*. Cambridge: Cambridge University Press.

INDEX

academia: conflicts of interest 39; decision-making process 38; nineteenth-century US scientific institutions 20; post-war symbolic contract with government 53–4, 116; recent trends in intellectual property 58; relationship with industry 2, 33, 33–5, 102, 103–4, 112, 113, 141; role and influence of MIT 1, 21; transformation of role in World War II 46–7

academic consultation *see* consultation

academic formats: amalgamated in nineteenth-century USA 23–4; synthesized in entrepreneurial university 18–19, 20

academic scientists: commercialization of research 127–8, 137, 149; as entrepreneurs 28, 122; expertise needed by firms 135–6; and firm formation 127–8, 131–3; liaison with military during World War I 42, 46; opportunities to apply discoveries 17; peer review system 146, 147; polytechnic movement 26; problems with patenting 56–7, 63; research teams and groups 50–1, 129–30, 131; Rogers' vision of training 23; traditional view of role 60, 137; in triple helix era 147–8, 149; war-related projects during World War II 12, 27, 46–7, 53–4; *see also* entrepreneurial science

academic technology transfer *see* technology transfer

Academies of Science 144

ADL *see* Arthur D. Little Company

agriculture: innovation system created in USA 18, 23; nineteenth-century researchers 11; *see also* farmers; land grant system

Air Force: and Whirlwind project 97

American Association for the Advancement of Science (AAAS) 11, 28, 145

American Research and Development Corporation (ARD): Compton and role of MIT 74–5, 89, 90–1, 93–6, 94, 100, 101; and firm formation 96–8, 111; foundation and early years 4, 74, 90–2, 99, 100, 101

Amgen 9

Amrad 2

Anderson, Harlan 98

ARD *see* American Research and Development Corporation

armed forces *see* the military

Arthur D. Little Company (ADL) 3, 30, 36–7, 86, 94–5

artificial intelligence: research 6, 148

Association of Computing Machinery (ACM) 136–7

Association of University Technology Managers (AUTM) 121, 124

At&T Corporation 47

Atomic Energy Commission 70, 117

atomic science: research facilities at Chicago 52; Stanford research in 1939 104

Axel, Richard 9

Babcock, Stephen 66–7

Banting, Frederick 66

Bayh, Birch 118–19, 119

Bayh-Dole Act (1980) 8, 16, 57, 112, 113, 115; as framework for technology

INDEX

transfer 4–5, 114–15, 118–21, 122, 124, 125, 125–6, 140
Beadle, George 25
Ben-David, Joseph 147
Berkeley University (California) 12, 47, 50, 106, 137
Best, Charles 66
Bible: quoted at 1904 MIT alumni reunion 43
biochemistry 139
bio-informatics 139, 147
biology: molecular 139; Wisconsin as research center 13
biotechnology 127, 148; firms 16, 32, 110, 143, 148; and patent rights 9, 55; SUNY creation of industry 105
Bok, Derek 15
Boston: Bush's connections 3, 107; business and industry in nineteenth-century 2, 22, 80; and Edison 79; financial community's involvement in ARD 4, 90, 91, 93, 101; post-war technology corridor 78, 103, 110; ring road 111; and Rogers' vision for MIT 2, 21–2, 23; significance of MIT 6, 26, 52, 72, 103
Britain: post-war funding of academic science 145–6; scientists' work with the military 50–1
Bunker, John 62–4, 67, 97
Bush, Vannevar: Compton's tribute 64–5; consulting and entrepreneurial activities 3, 37, 38, 78, 104, 107; "Endless Frontier" report (1945) 2, 87, 145–6; initiatives for working with the military 42, 46, 47–8, 48–9, 116; and origination of university-based high-tech firm 2–3, 110; position on patenting 62, 64, 71–2, 78; work on inventions 50, 70

Cal Tech 14
California: informality of style 111; Institute of Technology 20, 30; and Stanford's initiatives 102, 103–4, 108; technology push model of innovation 107; University see University of California at Los Angeles; see also Berkeley University
Cambridge (Mass.): biotechnology firms 32, 110; Ptashne's entrepreneurship 132, 133

capital: formation and transformation 143
capitalism: classical model 131
Carnegie, Andrew 43
Carnegie Institute of Washington 29, 46, 47
Center for Integrated Systems 112
Chandler, George Frederick 11, 27, 34, 35
chemical engineering: MIT 30, 40
chemical industry: links with engineering schools 13
chemistry: emergence of research at MIT 29, 30; and Liebig's development of artificial fertilizer 10; organic 11
Chicago University 11, 24, 28, 47, 48, 52, 109
Clark University 28
classical learning: eighteenth-century teaching colleges 27; and emergence of research 10–11
classical teaching colleges: academic format 18, 20, 21; expansion of into universities 24, 27–8
Cohen-Boyer patents 9, 119
Cold War 54, 142, 145
Colorado University 9
Columbia University 12, 27, 34, 35, 47, 132, 146; early initiatives and expansion 11, 24; patents and intellectual property rights 9, 123–4; "seed" venture capital fund 100
communications: Edison's solution for New York 102, 107
companies see corporations; firm formation; firms; small firms
Compton, Karl: early work for New England revival 2, 4, 79, 80, 82–3, 86, 87, 87–8, 101; and formulation of patents policy 61, 74; MIT and ARD 42, 49, 70, 89, 90, 91, 94, 96, 97, 98, 111; tribute to Bush 64–5
computer science 137, 139, 147, 148
computers: ARD's focus on 97–8; Bush and Wiener's research 50; early firms 5; magnetic core memory 76–7, 125; Silicon Valley 112
Conant, James 42, 46, 47
conflict of interest 39, 136; scientists' entrepreneurial ventures 127–8, 133–5
Congleton, William 98
Connecticut: agricultural experiment station 24–5; changing of securities laws 90

164

INDEX

consultation 7, 14, 21, 30, 33–5, 34–5, 131; Bush's approach 3, 37; controversy and resolution at MIT 31, 32–3, 35–7, 38, 39, 40, 67

Cornell University 28

corporations: attracting branch plants in New England 85–6; debate about patenting 58; Harvard Business School's links with 92; multi-national 143–4; research labs 29, 81; sponsoring of labs in Latin America 142; and start-up firms 139; *see also* firms

Cottrell, Frederick G. 73

Cross, Richard 83, 85

Curie, Marie and Pierre 149

Data General 111

David, Donald 91

defense: MIT research projects 49; Stanford University research 110

Delaware: Bush's idea for patents office 71–2

Denning, Peter: *Communications of the ACM* 136–7

depression: academics' refusal of federal funding 48; effects on university–industry relationships 13, 36–7; New England's economic problems 78, 112; Stanford's academic–industrial development 102, 104

developing countries: transfer of innovations 144

Digital Equipment Corporation 96, 97–8, 99, 111

disciplines: recent trend towards collaboration 139, 147

DNA 17, 139

Dole, Robert 119

Doriot, Georges 4, 86, 92, 94–5

Duncan, Louis 33

Dupont Corporation 43, 47

Eastern Europe: socialist model of research contracts 125

Eastman, George 43, 45

Eckert-Mauchly 97

e-commerce: late 1990s ventures 100

economic development: increasing role of universities 1, 8, 12, 15, 18, 19, 39, 77, 133, 134, 150; and research and education 5–8, 133; role of patents 56, 59; science-based 17, 79, 82, 89, 101, 107–8, 110–11, 143, 147; *see also* regional economic development

economy: impact of technology transfer 124–5, 134; increasing importance of intellectual property 150; and science 1, 9, 129–30, 137, 147, 150; *see also* regional economic development

Edgerton, Grier and Germeshausen (EGG) 70

Edgerton, Harold 69–70

Edinburgh: research leading to cloned sheep 16

Edison, Thomas Alva 79, 102, 107

electrical engineering: Edgerton's research 69–70; MIT teachers from industry 40; at Stanford 104, 108–9

electrical industry: development in San Francisco 103; and early engineering schools 13; emergence in New England 79

electromagnetics: Maxwell's theory 17

electronics: early firms 5, 70; research build-up during World War II 47, 108; Stanford and emerging industry 103, 104, 106, 108, 109, 110; *see also* Raytheon Corporation; Research Laboratory for Electronics (RLE)

electrostatics: Cottrell's device 73; Van de Graaff's generators 59, 96–7, 111

Eli Lilly Company 66

Ely, Richard 28

employment: generated by technology transfer 124; recruiting of graduates from institutes 45, 53

engineering: Rogers' vision of training 23; scientists in war-related projects 12, 54; at Stanford 102, 103–4, 108–9, 110, *see also* polytechnic engineering schools

engineers: consulting practices at MIT 30, 33, 36, 38; role according to polytechnic movement 26; Silicon Valley 103; traditional view of role 60

entrepreneurial science: academic participation in 127–8, 137; causes 16–18; dynamics 5–8, 140–1, 149–50; and firm formation 127, 131–3; impetus to 129–30; MIT as model 2, 21, 113; precursors 10, 17; Silicon Valley 103, 150

entrepreneurial university 16, 18–19, 149; and firm formation 131–3; importance

165

INDEX

of relations with industry 9, 140, 141; introduction of model into Stanford 7, 21, 102; MIT as model 1, 2, 4, 7, 18–19, 21, 40, 62, 102; and research 8, 148

ethics: rules on patents 66; university–industry interface 15

Europe: ARD as inspiration for venturers 99; informal university–industry relationships 41; move towards endless transition model 146; origins of patents in early Renaissance 56; ownership of intellectual property 59; technical schools 6, 24; triple helix development 141; *see also* Britain; Germany; Portugal; Sweden

farmers: scientific experiments in nineteenth-century USA 24–5, 34; *see also* agriculture

fertilizer: Liebig's development of 10; New England firm's attempt to specialize in 84–5

financial industry: recent revival of New York model 107

firm formation: assisted by ARD 91, 92, 97; involvement of academic scientists 92, 127–8, 131–3; role of universities 5, 9, 77, 102, 110, 143, 144, 148; strategy for New England 78, 86–8; and venture capital 4, 100, 112

firms: issue of exclusive licenses 74–5; MIT's development of close links with 4, 21, 36–7, 43, 67; and patent rights from discoveries 56–7, 76, 118; professors' consulting links with 3, 14, 21, 40, 43–4; survey on sponsoring academic research (1980) 114; universities' similarities with 148; *see also* corporations; firm formation; industry small firms; venture capital firm

Flanders, Ralph 86, 92

Ford, Horace 3–4, 98

Forrester, Jay 76, 98

Genentech 143

General Electric Company 29, 47, 75

General Motors (GM) 142

genetic engineering 9, 17, 119

Genetics Institute 132–3

Georgia Tech 26

Germany: development of pharmaceutical industry 146–7; model of chemical research laboratory 11; precursors of entrepreneurial science 10, 17

Giessen University 11, 34

Gilbert, Walter 132, 133

Gilliland, Edwin Richard 94

globalization 143–4

government: early use of academic consulting 34; effect of Bayh-Dole Act 115, 120–1, 124–5; new role in industrial development 149; post-war funding for research 7, 13–14, 48–9, 50, 53, 77, 113, 115, 116–18; post-war small business development programs 99; relations with universities 7, 8, 15, 41, 42, 48, 53–4, 113; wartime contracts dealt with by MIT 41, 42, 45, 48, 49; World War II model for relations with universities 47–9, 141; *see also* triple helix

Griswold, Merrill 91, 92

Hansen, W.W. 106

Harper, William Rainey 28

Harvard Business School 4, 7, 43, 86, 90–1, 92, 93, 101, 110

Harvard teaching college 24, 28, 80

Harvard University 1, 42, 108; controversies over relations to industry 15; Corporation 9, 15; emergence of technology firms 3, 4, 132; initiation of research 11; Lowell Scientific School 27; and Mark Ptashne 132–3; MIT's rejection of affiliation offer 24, 27, 43, 64

Health, Education and Welfare (HEW) 117, 118

health-related sciences: current research funding 147, 150; post-war government funding 53

Hewlett, William 104

Hewlett-Packard 4, 111

High Voltage Engineering Corporation 75, 96–7, 111

high-tech industry 140; Bush's origination of university base for 2–3; Compton's initiatives 61, 87; Doriot's interest 92; in New England today 80; New York model and Silicon Alley 107; regional policies 111–12, 124; Stanford's generation of 7, 102, 103–4; studies

INDEX

111; venture capital firms 100

human resources: New England's advantage 83, 86; as tool in venture capital firm 93

Hunsaker, Jerome Clarke 94

Hutchins, Robert 52

IBM (International Business Machines) 74, 76–7, 142

incubator facilities 10, 14, 124, 126, 141, 143

industrial scientists: role during World War II 47

industry: and academic research prior to Bayh-Dole 114, 117; administration of technology transfer 10; breaking down of separation with science 9, 149, 150; Bush's experience 3; controversy over universities' relations to 14–16, 133–4, 136; emergence of closer relationship with research 17, 102, 109; emergence of relationship with academia and universities 2, 6–7, 13–14, 30, 33–5, 39, 40–1, 78–9, 102, 103–4, 105–6, 112, 125–6, 135–6; MIT's close links with 1, 9, 21, 26, 30, 33, 35, 36–7, 40, 41, 53, 54, 62, 103, 113; New England's decline and efforts to revive 79–80, 81–2, 83–5, 89; primacy of Boston 22; recent trend towards collaboration 139, 148; traffic with university and the military 42, 52; translation from agriculture to 23; *see also* corporations; firms; small firms; triple helix

information: firms' need for availability of 15, 16; release of required for innovation 57, 123

innovation: interactive model 112, 143; "market pull" model 102, 106–7, 112; "science or technology push" model 102, 107, 107–8, 112; triple helix dynamic 140, 141, 142, 143–4, 148; *see also* technical innovations

institutions: academic elite 1, 146; triple helix model 139–40, 143

intellectual property: Bush's capturing of 78, 116; controversy 7–8; debates and considerations at MIT 59, 60, 68, 69, 70–2; differences in different countries 59–60; economic value 14, 137–8, 150; effect of Bayh-Dole Act 4–5, 8, 16, 112, 113, 114, 123–4; generated under

federal funding 59–60, 77, 116–18; and patenting 16, 55, 57, 58, 106, 116, 123–4; receipts from licensing 5, 58–9, 60, 123–4; university–industry collaboration 136, 143, 144, 149; *see also* knowledge

Internet 55, 107, 112, 143, 144

inventions: Bush's experience and activities 2, 3, 64–5, 70, 71; intellectual property and patenting 55, 56, 57, 59, 60, 66–7, 68, 113, 117, 120, 123–4, 127; MIT's policies and controversies 67, 68, 72; proposals to ARD 93; and Research Corporation 72–3; Rogers' vision of training 22; Stanford graduates in 1930s 103, 106; and technology transfer 122–3; from universities 6

investment: in ARD 92, 93, 93–4, 94; and "seed" venture capital funds 100–1; and venture capital 91, 100–1

Jackson, Dugald 33

Japan 41, 59, 125, 137

Jefferson, Thomas 25

Jewett, Frank 47

Johns Hopkins University 11, 16, 24, 28, 47, 48, 109

Joint Venture Silicon Valley 81, 140

Jones and Lamson Machine Tool Company 86, 91

Kerr, Clark 12

Keyes, F.G. 35

Kidder, Tracy: study of high-tech 111

Klystron tube: invention 106

knowledge: capitalization of 1, 55, 60, 133, 140–1, 149, 150; debates about patenting 56–7, 59; and development of research 10–11; triple helix model for management of 140–1, 143; and universities' new entrepreneurial role 1, 5, 9, 10, 40; and venture capital firm 93; *see also* intellectual property

Knowledge Circle of Amsterdam 81, 140

Kornberg, Arthur 127

laboratories: collaboration with production in corporations 142; and start-up firms 139; *see also* Radiation Laboratory (Rad Lab); research laboratories

167

INDEX

Land, Edwin 4
land grant system: equivalent in Bayh-Dole Act 16, 126; origins 24–6, 126; and status of MIT 23, 26, 53, 64, 145; tradition of economic development 1, 5, 118
land grant universities 25–6, 118, 146; academic model 18, 19, 20, 24, 25, 145
Lasken, Jesse 119, 121
Latin America 141–1, 146
Latker, Norman 117, 118
Lawrence, Ernesto Orlando 47, 50
laws: legitimization of venture capital concept 93; origination of ideas for 118
Leshowitz, Barry 119–20
Lewis Report (1949) 49
liberal arts 20, 26, 27, 43
Liebig, Justus 10, 34
Little, Arthur D. *see* Arthur D. Little Company
Litton, Charles: and patent for high frequency oscillations 106
Lodge, Oliver 72–3
London University 15
Los Angeles *see* University of California at Los Angeles
Lowell: manufacturing industries 22, 81
Lowell Institute 23

manufacturing: Harvard Business School 92; industries of New England 22, 80–1, 83, 86; Rad Lab 51
Marconi, Guglielmo: patent application 17
Marx, Karl 146–7
Massachusetts 9, 22, 23, 71–2, 119; *see also* Boston
Massachusetts Institute of Technology *see* MIT
Massachusetts Investment Trust 90, 91
Maxwell, James Clerk: theory of electromagnetic field 17
media industries: recent revival in New York 107, 111
medical device technology: Purdue University 118–19
Mellon Institute 82
Mersenne, Marin 144
Merton, Robert K. 144–5, 145
metalworking industry: decline of firms in New England 5, 22, 79
military, the: British work with 50–1; and

electronics devices developed at Stanford 108; Mills' societal model 142; post-war support of research 7, 116, 146, 147; science's role in wartime 42, 46, 47, 51–2; and universities during wartime 45, 46–7, 53
Mills, C. Wright 142
MIT (Massachusetts Institute of Technology): Bush's work and influence 2–5, 107, 110, 116; close relationship with industry 9, 21, 26, 30, 33, 35, 40, 41, 53, 54; commercialization of research 59–60; Compton's achievements 79, 96, 111; controversy over consultation 31, 32–3, 35–7, 38, 39, 40, 67; as development model for Stanford 103, 107–8, 109, 110; development of research 29–30, 32–3, 40; development of technological base 20, 21, 30; dynamics of this study 5–8; effect of depression 36–7; as entrepreneurial university 1, 2, 4, 7, 18–19, 40, 62, 102, 113; financial crisis after World War I 42, 43–5; founding of 21–3, 80, 110, 145; involvement in ARD 74–5, 90–1, 94, 95–6, 98, 100, 101; as land grant academic model 23, 26, 53, 64, 145; military research and liaison 42, 53; and New England's industry 28, 78, 79, 81–2, 86; patenting controversies and management 55, 59, 60–5, 67–77, 97, 125; rejection of Harvard's affiliation offer 24, 27, 43, 64; research teams 50–1, 63; Rogers' vision 20, 110; role in invention of venture capital firm 89, 90–1, 93, 95–6, 101; synthesis of academic formats 24; Technology Plan 44–5; technology transfer initiatives 98, 113, 119, 121–2; and Van de Graaff 59, 75, 96–7, 111; World War II government contracts 41, 42, 45, 48, 49, 50, 74, 97; World War II's impact 51–2, 73–4; *see also* Radiation Laboratory (Rad Lab)
molecular biology: research 6
Monsanto Corporation 32
Monticello: Jefferson's estate 25
Morill Act (1864) 23, 25, 126

National Institute for Standards and Technology 141

168

INDEX

National Institutes of Health (NIH) 52, 117, 118, 121–2, 129, 134, 135, 146
National Research Council 96
National Science Foundation (NSF) 16, 52, 117, 121, 129, 131, 146
National Technical and Information Service (NTIS) 116–17
networks 143–4, 144–5
New England 28; economic decline 79–80, 81, 83, 84–5, 112; economic growth strategy 7, 78–9, 82–8, 89, 101; *see also* Boston; Connecticut; Massachusetts
New England Council 78, 80–2, 86, 140; New Products committee 83–5, 86–7, 92
New Enterprises 90
New London: submarine research center 46
New Scientist 15
New York: Edison's communications solutions 102, 107; legitimation of ARD 92; missing links for high-tech projects 112; recent revival of business and industries 106; *see also* Research Corporation of New York; Silicon Alley; State University of New York at Stony Brook
New York Medical College 122
New York Times 15, 16
New York University 28, 100
North Carolina State University 105
Northwestern University 100
Noyes, A.A. 29, 30
nuclear physics: research build-up during World War II 47; Stanford research in 1939 104; use of electrostatic generators for research 97

Office of Naval Research 52, 110
Ohio State University 105
Olsen, Kenneth 98
OSRD (Office of Scientific Research and Development) 47, 48, 49–50, 50, 97, 116
Oxford University: Van de Graaff 96

Packard, David 104
Pasteur, Louis 149
Patent and Trademark Act: amended by Bayh-Dole Act 4–5, 8, 120, 140
patents and patenting 55, 123; and

biotechnology firms 9, 55; Bush's experience and position 2, 3, 62, 78, 116; controversies 7, 59–60, 66–7, 74–5, 117–18; increase in awards from 1980s 5, 115; issue of exclusive licenses 74–5; legislative debate and tensions 56–7; MIT's policies and controversies 40, 55, 59, 60–5, 67–77, 97, 125; origins 56; prior to World War II 116; and publication 16, 55, 57, 60; released for use by Stanford 106; role in economic development 56, 59; royalties 124, 125; and universities 12–13, 54, 57–9, 66, 122, 123–4; Van de Graaff generators 59, 75, 97, 111; Zadeh's involvement 137; *see also* Bayh-Dole Act
Pennsylvania University: technical school 26
Perkins, William Henry: research on dyestuffs 146–7
pharmaceutical industry: early development of in Germany 146–7; government-owned patents 117; licensing of product to firm 66
Philadelphia: initiative for technical school 26
physics: development of research at Stanford 104, 106; *see also* nuclear physics
Pittsburgh *see* Mellon Institute
Polaroid Corporation 4
polytechnic engineering schools 18, 20, 21, 26, 113
polytechnic movement 24, 26–7, 43
Portugal: controversy over consulting 39
Princeton University 59, 96, 111
production: New England's focus on natural resources 85–6; Rogers' vision 22; scientists' rates of 129; universities as factors of 78
products: development 139; and links between firms and academic scientists 135–6; marketing of scientific discoveries 127, 128, 131
professors: assuming of multiple roles 31; consultation practices at MIT 7, 30, 31, 32–3, 37, 38; consulting links with firms 14, 21, 37, 43–4; as entrepreneurs 131, 148; industrial engineers at MIT 6–7; nineteenth-century initiation of research 11; organizational and PR

169

INDEX

tasks 129–30; position in intellectual property regime 60; post-war expansion of research 53, 109; Terman's expansion of Stanford 109, 110
Ptashne, Mark 132–3
publication: and patents 16, 55, 57, 60
Purdue University 118, 119

radar: electronics inventions at Stanford 106, 108; MIT's wartime laboratory 42, 50; projects during World War II 12
Radar Counter-Measures Lab (Harvard) 107–8
Radiation Laboratory (Rad Lab): as model for Stanford 106, 108, 109; wartime work at MIT 48, 50–1, 52, 74, 97
radio astronomy 12
Radio Corporation of America 76–7
radio technology: Bush's venture 2–3; Marconi's patent 17; Terman's plans for Stanford 108
Raytheon Corporation 3, 107
regional economic development: Compton's work 2, 4, 79, 80, 82–3, 87, 87–8, 101; land grant movement 1, 25–6; MIT's goal 75–6; New England's dilemma and strategy 79–80, 81, 83; policies for high-tech 111–12, 124; Rogers' vision 2; Stanford's assistance for 102
religious knowledge: classical teaching colleges 27, 80
Renaissance: origins of patents in Europe 56
Rensselaer Polytechnic Institute 21
research: applied and basic 1, 17, 27, 145; Bush's approach 3, 37, 107; combined with teaching 1, 19, 147; commercialization of 9, 12–13, 55, 59–60, 67, 96–7, 122, 127–8, 132–3, 137, 149; conflict between "pure" and practical 27, 29, 30, 35; conflict with teaching 1, 14, 32–3, 39, 133; controversies over relations to industry 14–16, 29, 30, 62–3; Denning's view of 136–7; development of at MIT 29–30, 32–3, 40; development of firms from 89, 102, 105–6, 110; during World War I 46; during World War II 47–8, 51–2, 116; early US agricultural universities 25; and economic development 5–8, 133; effect of Bayh-Dole Act 4–5, 16,

113, 114–15, 123, 125–6; "endless frontier" thesis 1, 2, 87, 139; "endless transition" era 139, 146, 147; entrepreneurial dynamic 8, 18, 131, 148; and firm formation 4, 78; first academic revolution 10–12, 28; funding pressures 130–1, 133–4, 135; and industry prior to Bayh-Dole 114, 117; interdisciplinary 54, 139, 144; New England initiatives 81–2, 83–4, 88, 101; in nineteenth-century 23; post-war federal funding 42, 48, 50, 52–3, 54, 113, 115, 116, 116–18, 145–6; Rowland's "pure" research model 11, 28, 35, 145; Terman's ideas 105, 107; triple helix dynamic 143; and universities' new self-generating role 149–51
research and development (R&D): before and after Bayh-Dole 115, 119, 120; experience during World War II 47, 89, 141; MIT's Technology Plan 44; post-war federal funding 42, 116; Sweden 146; targeting of by government 125; triple helix dynamic 140, 142
research centers 10, 12; Stanford University 108, 109–10; World War II 47, 52
Research Construction Corporation (RCC) 50
Research Corporation of New York 51, 55, 58, 67, 71, 72–3, 96, 121; patents dispute with IBM 74, 76–7
research groups and teams: growth of 50–1, 63, 109–10, 128, 139; as quasi-firms 128–9, 131, 149
research institutes 53, 125, 131
research laboratories: in chemistry 11, 29–30; development of 29–30, 56; early industrial 13; funding pressures 130–1; MIT's proposals in 1930 82; wartime 42, 48, 50, 52; see also Radiation Lab (Rad Lab)
Research Laboratory for Electronics (RLE) 52
research universities: academic format 18, 19, 20, 23–4, 24; early relations with industry 13; evolution 28–9; "ivory tower" model 102, 137, 145; new entrepreneurial characteristics 150; Stanford as model 102; and technology transfer 114–15, 121; transformation of

170

INDEX

relations with government 54
Research-Cottrell 73
Rice Institute (Houston) 92, 100
Riemers, Neils 119, 122
risk management: research 6
Robinson, Dennis 95, 97
Rockefeller, John D. 28
Rockefeller University 9
Rogers, Henry 21–2
Rogers, William Barton: vision and founding of MIT 2, 5, 20, 21–3, 26, 110, 113
Roosevelt, Franklin D. 145
Route 128 4, 7, 78, 107, 111, 140, 150
Rowland, Henry: "pure" research model 11, 28, 35, 145

St Louis University 9
San Francisco: biotech firms 110; *see also* Silicon Valley
Saxenian, Annalee: study of high-tech 111
Say, Jean Baptiste 18
science: breaking down of separation with industry 9, 135; change in role and social norms 137–8; and economic development 17, 79, 82, 89, 101, 107–8, 110–11, 143, 147; as economic endeavor 1, 9, 129–30, 137, 147, 150; "endless frontier" thesis 2, 54, 145–6; interrelation with technology 21, 26; "modes 1 and 2" 144–7, 145, 148; nineteenth-century farmers' experiments 24–5; original seventeenth-century format 144–5; post-war government funding 13–14, 53; pure 12, 21, 55; Rogers' vision for application of 22–3; Terman's strategy for Stanford 104, 108–9, 110; triple helix dynamic 140–1; typical university departments 128; *see also* entrepreneurial science
science parks 111, 112, 114, 124, 126, 143
scientific discoveries: access through publication 55; change from "ivory tower" view 137; integration with research 144; as marketable products 127, 128; patenting and intellectual property rights 56–7, 67, 71, 73, 113, 117; practical impetus in seventeenth century 145

scientists *see* academic scientists; industrial scientists
Securities and Exchange Commission 90
semi-conductor industry 106, 112
seminar: origin of 11
shoe industry: New England 79–80, 81
Silicon Alley 107, 111
Silicon Graphics 5
Silicon Valley 7, 107, 110, 111, 143, 150; common origin with Route 128 107, 140; from early 1990s 112; inter-firm collaboration 105, 112; origins 103–4; university–industry relations 105–6; *see also* Joint Venture Silicon Valley
Sillimans, father and son 12, 27, 34–5
Small Business Innovation Research Program (SBIR) 115
Small Business Investment Corporation 99
small firms: effect of Bayh-Dole Act 115, 119, 120; founded for new genetic technology 17; recent shift towards 148; similarities with academic science departments 128; support of in New England 81–2, 84–5
Smith, Charles E. 26
Smithsonian Institution 29
social sciences: post-war government funding 53
software firms 55, 107
Soviet Union 145; former states of 146
Spencer Thermostat Company 3
Stanford University: Cohen-Boyer patents 9, 119; commercializing of research 9, 122; effect of World War II 108–11; initiatives in technology transfer 116, 119, 121–2; introduction of MIT's development model 7, 21, 101, 102, 107–8, 109, 110; joint venture with Silicon Valley 102, 105–6; origins and academic development 103–5; post-war development of research 109–10; research for study 5; Science Park 111, 112; Terman's creative expansion of 4, 104–5, 106, 107–8, 108–9
State University of New York at Stony Brook 105
students: inventions and rights 6, 69, 123; MIT graduates' employment 37, 45; MIT's industry placement schemes 40; post-war research support for graduates 53, 54
SUN 5

171

INDEX

Sweden 141, 146

teaching: combined with research 1, 19, 147; conflict with research 1, 14, 32–3, 39, 133; and economic development 6; interactive approach of Bush 3, 37; *see also* classical teaching colleges

technical innovations: base created by Stanford 103–4; and need for business advice 93; and patenting 55, 57, 59; problems of New England small firms 85, 101; *see also* innovation

technology: cross-fertilization between different areas 139; and industry in development of MIT 4, 20, 21, 26, 30, 113; New England in early nineteenth century 81; in new model of higher education 26–7; new triple helix model for 140–1; and origins of patent law 56; selling of by universities 10; Stanford and university–industry relations 105–6, 110; *see also* high-tech industry

technology development: firms and academic scientists 135–6; and issue of patenting research 66, 113; post-war military funding 54

technology firms: building from university-originated ideas 100; development from research at Stanford 102; North Carolina State University initiative 105; San Francisco 103; Silicon Alley 107

Technology Plan (MIT) 44–5, 49, 82

technology transfer: attitudes towards 134–5; and Bayh-Dole Act 4–5, 112, 114–15, 118–21, 122, 124, 125, 125–6, 140; Denning's view of research 136–7; economic impact 124–5, 134; expansion of universities' activities 10, 14, 113, 124–5, 136, 140; and innovation 143, 146; Latker's invention of bureaucratic process 117; MIT's administrative initiative 98, 113, 116; origins of potential for 115–16; university offices 41, 114–15, 121–2, 124–5, 126, 134, 140; and university's mission 66, 121–2, 125–6, 133

Terman, Frederick 2; creative expansion of Stanford 4, 100, 104–5, 106, 107–8, 108–9, 110

Terman, Lewis 105

Texas Instruments 3

textile industry: decline of firms in New England 5, 80, 81; New England 22, 79–80, 86

Time Magazine 91

Toronto University: management of patent on insulin 66, 67

training: MIT's ideals 20; programs for entrepreneurship 10, 141; programs for research 11, 129; Rogers' vision 22; US agricultural research institutions 25

triple helix 8, 139–44, 147–51

Tufts College 2

United States of America (USA): building of university–government relations 41; concerns about competitiveness 118–19; endless transition model of science 146, 147; entrepreneurial mode of research 8, 131, 148; entrepreneurial role of government 18; establishment of patent rights 56; first academic revolution 11–12; influence of MIT on educational development 21; intellectual property rights 59–60; Mills' idea of "power elite" 142; nineteenth-century separation of scientific institutions 20; processes of triple helix development 141, 148–9

United Water Cooler Service Company 70

universities: academic decision-making process 38; and the Bayh-Dole Act 57, 112, 113, 114–15, 119–120, 123–4; controversies over relations to industry 14–16, 62–3, 133–4, 136; as core institution of society 1, 8, 39–40, 52, 140, 150; development of close relations with industry 6–7, 8, 9, 10, 13–14, 39, 40–1, 44, 78–9, 103, 105–6, 125–6, 135–6, 143; equity in firms 5, 9; first academic revolution 10–12; government contracts during World War II 7, 45, 47, 48, 53–4; and intellectual property rights 60, 70–2, 77, 112, 114, 123–4, 137–8; new role in economic development 1, 8, 12, 18, 39, 77, 133, 134, 150; new role as self-generating 149–50, 150–1; old and new roles 5–6, 39, 66; original purpose and development of research 10–11; patenting policies and controversies 55, 57–9, 60, 66–7, 74, 122; post-war

172

INDEX

federal funding for research 42, 48, 50, 52–3, 54, 113, 145–6; relations with government 7, 8, 15, 41, 53, 54, 113; relations with the military during World War I 45, 46, 53; second academic revolution 12–13; "seed" venture capital funds 100–1; similarities with firms 148; and technology transfer 41, 114–15, 117–18, 121–2, 124–5, 125–6, 133, 136, 140; Terman's view of administration 109; typical organization of science 128; World War II model for relations with government 42, 47–9, 53, 141; *see also* entrepreneurial university; land grant universities; research universities; triple helix

University of California at Los Angeles 48, 100, 122

Van de Graaff, Robert J.: and research on high voltage 59, 75, 96–7, 111
Varian, brothers 106
Venetian state: origins of patent law 56
venture capital: creating role for 93–6; creation of sources by technological innovation 144; government's role in extending research funding 115; pioneering role of Compton and MIT colleagues 2, 4, 90, 101; realization of New England's need for 86; recent focus of Research Corporation 58; Silicon Valley 103; trajectory of 99–101; universities' role 9, 100–1
venture capital firm 2, 4, 74, 86, 88, 112; e-commerce 100; invention of by Compton and MIT colleagues 74–5, 89, 91, 98; precursors 90; "seed" funds 100–1; transplantation of mechanism to Stanford 107; *see also* American

Research and Development Corporation (ARD)
Virginia Polytechnic Institute 16
vitamin D: discovery of 119

Walker, William H. 29–30
warfarin: discovery of 119
wars *see* World War I; World War II
Washington University 9
West Point engineering school 21
Westchester: medical school 122
Westinghouse corporation 97
Whewell, William 18
Whitney, Josiah 30
Whitney, Willis 29
Wiener, Norbert 50
Wilson, Caroll L. 71–2
Wisconsin University 16, 55, 60–1, 66–7, 71, 116, 119; Alumni Foundation 12–13, 67
World War I: academic scientists' liaison with the military 42, 46; relationship between universities and the military 45, 46, 53
World War II: academic scientists in war-related projects 12, 27, 46–7, 51–2, 53–4, 145; disruption of New England Foundation plan 87–8; effect on Stanford University 108–11; ideology of basic research 145; impact on MIT 51–2, 73–4; MIT's government contracts 41, 42, 45, 48, 50, 74, 97; role of government in innovation 115–16; Stanford's electronics inventions 106; university–government links 7, 47–9, 53–4, 141

Yale teaching college 28
Yale University 12, 27, 34; Sheffield School of Technology 20, 27

Zadeh, Lofti 137

CPSIA information can be obtained
at www.ICGtesting.com
Printed in the USA
BVOW06s2104270317
479593BV00002B/4/P